J. J. ABRAMS VS. JOSS WHEDON

J. J. ABRAMS VS. JOSS WHEDON

Duel for Media Master of the Universe

Wendy Sterba

ROWMAN & LITTLEFIELD
Lanham • Boulder • New York • London

Published by Rowman & Littlefield
A wholly owned subsidiary of The Rowman & Littlefield Publishing Group, Inc.
4501 Forbes Boulevard, Suite 200, Lanham, Maryland 20706
www.rowman.com

Unit A, Whitacre Mews, 26-34 Stannary Street, London SE11 4AB

British Library Cataloguing in Publication Information Available

Library of Congress Cataloging-in-Publication Data

Names: Sterba, Wendy.
Title: J. J. Abrams vs. Joss Whedon : duel for media master of the universe / Wendy Sterba.
Description: Lanham : Rowman & Littlefield, 2016. | Includes bibliographical references and index.
Identifiers: LCCN 2016016800 (print) | LCCN 2016024157 (ebook) | ISBN 9781442269903 (hard-
    back : alk. paper) | ISBN 9781442269910 (electronic)
Subjects: LCSH: Abrams, J. J. (Jeffrey Jacob), 1966—-Criticism and interpretation. | Whedon, Joss,
    1964—-Criticism and interpretation.
Classification: LCC PN1998.3.A27 S84 2016 (print) | LCC PN1998.3.A27 (ebook) | DDC 791.4302/
    33092—dc23
LC record available at https://lccn.loc.gov/2016016800

Printed in the United States of America

To my sisters:

Sandy, who, Spock-like,
can always tell me what's logical, and
Mindy, who would survive any zombie apocalypse.
In thankfulness to both for watching all those horror,
science fiction, and Hollywood B classic films
together on TV when we were kids.
Who'd've thunk there's a living in it?
Never give up! Never surrender!

CONTENTS

PREFACE

Conceit. It is such a lovely word and one rarely heard these days and yet this book is based on it. That is not to say that either Joss Whedon or J. J. Abrams is in the least conceited. If anything, as heroes of the Geek Underground, the opposite is true. They are self-abasing, modest souls who are thrilled and surprised by their own popularity and success. No, the conceit is mine. In 1977 George Lucas and Steven Spielberg set the film world ablaze with the release of their space spectacles *Star Wars* and *Close Encounters of the Third Kind*. *Star Wars* and Spielberg's earlier hit *Jaws* turned the motion picture industry on its ear, changing sound, visuals, special effects, and both audience and studio expectations, all at the wave of a helmet or a very large shark tail. As geniuses of the screen, Lucas and Spielberg have dominated a generation of movies, but in our own galaxy—not as long ago nor so far away—it's hard not to think of the future and to wonder, who's next? With their successes and the changes they have made in the media world, Abrams and Whedon seem poised to inherit the empire. Each has revealed ingenuity and virtuosity in television and film production as well as creativity in the use and expansion of new media as art. But who is the new Spielberg? Where is the new Lucas?

Abrams and Whedon are famous for their legions of fans and succession to the throne is an issue that has already erupted into fictional violence when Lethea used the well-known fan, rivalry as fodder for a satiric post, that a "J-Squared" (Abrams) fan gave a Whedon-supporting "Browncoat" a bloody nose.[1] When Abrams locked in the direction of the seventh Star Wars film, the site invented Whedon as reputedly tweeting, "Episode VII: Re-Return of the Jedi, or How Lens Flare Saved the Empire. Good luck, JJ! Congrats, bro. #sarcasm." The Abrams simulacrum then replied sarcastically, thanking "Whedon" for taking time to tweet from his busy schedule writing episodes for the (canceled) series *Dollhouse* and *Firefly*, ending with #LucasChoseMe.[2]

Lethea's tale of war in the Twitterverse is satire, but it nonetheless suggests a question that is on the minds of thousands of fans and is a question that sorely needs an answer: How far have we come since 1977 and who is the Hollywood heir-apparent to Spielberg and Lucas for the next generation? This book revolves around the idea of an imaginary contest to crown the new, undisputed Most Royal Geek Leader of the media universe. This conceit allows for an exploration of all the exceptional things that these producer/writer/director/creators have done and also for an understanding of how the world of media, and particularly the world of media of the fantastic, has changed through their agency. In the end, we know that both are distinctive and brilliant and have different strengths and weaknesses. Each is a winner in his own right. The conceit is a diversion, an amusing pastime, a way to explore changes in the industry, changes in our times, and the genius of these two creators. With that being said, let the games begin!

ACKNOWLEDGMENTS

A book is always the sum of more than its parts and authored indirectly by more than the name honored on the spine. Thanks go to my editors at Rowman and Littlefield, Stephen Ryan and Bowdoin Van Riper, who inspired the topic, encouraged me along the way, and also put up with the many editing challenges, both novel and mundane, that I was able to invent. Bow is particularly worthy of praise and should have been given credit for several ideas mentioned on these pages. I also want to thank my sisters, who turned out to be useful experts on unexpected things like early episodes of *Star Trek* and which giant ant movie had Florida sugar plantations. Many, many kudos to my niece, Dorothy Colp, who guided me through much of the anime and graphic novel material from an insider's perspective. Thanks to Susan Clark, Karen Ritzenhoff, Margret Eifler, Ralf Nicolai, Ottomar Rudolf, Kaspar Locher, and Dieter Paetzold, for holding my feet to the academic fire and always making me answer one more question, be it through streaming tears of confusion or transcendent joy. I would be remiss in not again thanking the library people at College of St. Benedict and St. John's University and the institutions themselves for giving me time and support to work. Thank you, Sarah Pruett and Karen Erickson, for championing my efforts. Annette Atkins, I could never have finished this without your help and the writing workshops, sponsored by our anonymous donor who stipulated we should write simple, clear sentences for real people and leave the esoteric jargon behind. I am hugely indebted also to my eighty-seven-year-old mom, who still reads everything I write. Without you, I would never have thought about why we like Bette Davis better than Joan Crawford. Finally I want to acknowledge my husband, Don, who has put up with disorder (no, chaos!), nerves, frustrations, and funks while I've been writing this book. Thank you for forcing me to watch things that I was sure I would hate, and usually loved, and which almost always ended up finding an important place in what I was writing. Now if you could only train the cat to stay off my computer keyboard!

INTRODUCTION: J. J. VS. JOSS

A Love Story

The secret to the movie business, or any business, is to get a good education in a subject besides film—whether it's history, psychology, economics, or architecture—so you have something to make a movie about. All the skill in the world isn't going to help you unless you have something to say.—George Lucas

We know that Joss Whedon and J. J. Abrams are media geniuses of our times, but . . . who is the best? With their creativity and willingness to try new things, they have brought us back to the movies and back to our TVs by guaranteeing new and interesting takes on old, deep questions. Abrams and Whedon have attracted huge followings of loyal and passionate fans, who defend their honor and champion their works. But who tells it like it is? Who is better at creating that warm, sentimental feeling? Who has the superior imagination? And does Abrams's genuine demonic tongue from *The Exorcist* beat Whedon's *Alien* egg in a contest for the title of "Greatest All-Time Film Geek"? This book seeks to answer these questions once and for all.

This book is for the fans, but it is also for the haters and for those who have just become aware of J. J. or Joss and want to know more about the people who brought them *Felicity*, *Fringe*, *Firefly*, the new *Star Trek*, *The Avengers*, and the new *Star Wars*. You don't have to like these people to find them interesting, but I confess, I do. I like them. I adore J. J. and I adore Joss!

As a film professor, I often have to hear: "Yeah, so I get it. You like [eyes rolling] Joss Whedon and J. J. Abrams, but honestly, who do you think is better? More creative? Who will be remembered? Who is the next Steven Spielberg?" Both were heavily influenced by the master before either was anything but a young Hollywood wannabe. Whedon told *The Guardian*, with characteristic wit, that Spielberg's *Close Encounters of the Third Kind* was a life-altering experience: "That blew the brains out of my head and I wore them on my shoulders as epaulettes. I realised, 'Oh! Other people have gone through this!'"[1] But Abrams one-ups Whedon. With his boyhood friend Matt Reeves, he participated in a youth film festival, and they got mentioned in the newspaper. Spielberg just happened to see it and had his office offer the boys a chance to repair some splices on Spielberg's own teenage films, so Abrams was inspired by the master in person.[2]

We academics pride ourselves on impartiality, but since that quality has clearly gone out the window with my repeated watchings of *Angel*, *Lost*, *Star Trek*, and *The Avengers*, I decided I wanted to look at the work of these great writers, creators, and producers through the eyes of the typical movie and television fan, of someone who watches and enjoys watching lots of video. I wanted to compare the works of J. J. Abrams and Joss Whedon but not their lives, so this is not a biography. It is a book about their works, what some might call their art.

The concept of auteur is important here because many people these days feel that you cannot talk about a film by Steven Spielberg or by Alfred Hitchcock or by James Cameron. They think the business of Hollywood involves too many people to give credit to just one. I want to take a minute to explain why these filmmakers are important and why we should talk about auteurs because the point of this book fails or succeeds on the willingness to believe that a single person can leave an obvious and indelible mark on a movie or TV series.

Film and television productions are the artifacts from a huge, industrialized community. As money-making propositions, these works are overseen by corporate studio bean-counters and shipped from department to department to ensure that the individual parts, like sound effects, costumes, sets, music, and so on, are provided efficiently and economically (at least by film-industry standards). The point is that it would seem nigh impossible for one person to affect all the various creative and technical areas necessary for making a film as it moves from the writers to producers to the director to the set designers, costumers, and props people to electricians and lighting guys to the actors to the cinematographer to the sound recorders (not to mention film editors, Foley artists for sound effects, the music department and sound editors, dialogue loopers, and on and on). Of course, all of this, however, is punctuated by the back and forth between producers and directors and still leaves out a lot of very important people. It makes the idea of herding cockroaches look like a stroll in the park on a sunny afternoon.

The really great, proven directors, however, get to play a role in decisions about most areas of the film that affect the overall vision, style, and themes of what is being produced. They hire and work intimately with people that share and reflect their visions, so that the final work has a consistent aesthetic and thematic center that can be linked back to them. Is everything on the screen a result of decisions by Francis Ford Coppola, Martin Scorsese, or Steven Spielberg? No, of course not. Do their editors, costumers, screenwriters, electricians, cinematographers, and so on deserve personal credit for what they have done? Absolutely! Yet, the works these great directors oversee often share styles, motifs, and artistic concerns, and that means we can give the people at the helm credit for a consistent style and narrative, for making good decisions about details, and for choosing people who can provide the things that serve their visions. That means they can still be considered creative geniuses and hence auteurs.[3] We viewers recognize a film helmed by Steven Spielberg, by Alfred Hitchcock, or by James Cameron, and no one can tell us we do not.

Such is the case with both Joss Whedon and J. J Abrams. It doesn't hurt that both started as writers and then continued on with such success to become idea people, creators, producers, and directors, often playing multiple roles for the series or films that they were bringing into existence. No doubt much of the look, style, and success of these projects is connected to their own very wise personnel choices. When we see a Whedon TV series, it is likely better labeled a Whedon/Greenwalt/Espenson/Fury/Noxon/Minear (plus many others) masterpiece. Yet, Whedon deserves the credit for creating the idea; writing the initial narratives; bringing on board talented people who could continue the writing, directing, and production; and controlling quality with each succeeding season. The same holds true for works of Abrams/Goddard/Lindelof/Kurtzman/Orci and others helmed by J. J. Abrams. Like the little dog Nipper who peers into the RCA gramophone cone, we the audience can hear the "master's voice." Even as the other people who work on the projects with J. J. and Joss change, we can see consistent elements across their oeuvres.

So can the fans. They rave about the work of their beloved favorites and feel responsible for having brought these geniuses to light and for making them the successful people they are. Both auteurs acknowledge this with gratitude. Despite their passion, the fans can be amazingly fair and insightful. Of course, not everyone is awestruck by the dynamic duo. Plenty of people promote alternative opinions.

Several independent websites and blogs specifically pit the one against the other. IMDb's Friday Face Off Live Poll: Whedon vs. Abrams from 2014 gave Whedon the edge 879 to 530.[4] Meanwhile, Sherry Vint wondered, in the *Los Angeles Review of Books*: "Who would win in a fight between Bad Robot and Mutant Enemy?" Despite the violent imagery of her metaphor, she is conciliatory: "While Bad Robot comes out ahead in quantity, Mutant Enemy has the edge in longevity."[5] Doubtless there will be further blogs and articles to come with varying responses.

A cursory search of the Internet before *Star Wars* and the second Avengers films came out for the four expressions "I love Joss Whedon," "I hate Joss Whedon," "I love J. J. Abrams," and "I hate J. J. Abrams," showed that hating came easier than loving. "Hate" posts about Whedon outnumbered "love" ones two to one (37,200 to 19,300), and Abrams was even more seriously despised, with 91 percent weighing in on the hating side (29,000 to 2,760).[6] Some posters professed to love Abrams, but . . . then went on to list the fifteen things he did to ruin *Star Trek*.[7] Since *Star Wars* and *Age of Ultron*, comments have been much nicer. A more recent search now puts Whedon at 54,000 love comments to only 1,880 hate ones and Abrams at 4,570 love hits to 2,960 hates. This suggests that *Star Wars* has won Abrams favor with fans and perhaps that movie fans are nicer but less vocal than television fans. It also accentuates how difficult it is to find a good and consistent means of evaluation.

This book uses seven criteria to compare Whedon's and Abrams's works. It contrasts various works and accomplishments from particular times in the auteurs' lives to see who is better in each category. Creativity is judged in two categories: for written style and strength and for visual acuity and exploration. Other fields of competition are profitability, popularity with the fans and critics, creative innovation, and personal growth (particularly with regard to diverse media). Another category involves being able to work within the industry climate, which can be frustrating and involve a lot of tact and negotiation difficult for the creative individual: in other words, being able to work the system despite the adversity and difficulties involved in film and TV production. An eighth category is a wild card so that exceptional brilliance that might not fit into any of the other generic categories can also be recognized.

Whedon and Abrams have produced (in all senses of the word) prolifically. They have written scripts, literary works, and comic books. They have done political pieces, created Internet musicals, and composed music and theme songs. They have produced plays in their backyards as well as the spectacular blockbusters for which they are best known. They have done all this in the space of about twenty-five years, and yes, they have made money doing so. Their development has been similar, in terms of both activities and themes, so this work examines their careers in parallel, comparing the things they did at around the same point in their lives. By book's end, the reader will have a sense of who is the most deserving of the Spielberg crown, er . . . baseball cap and tennis shoes. The final chapter tallies up the pluses and minuses, all the pros and cons and extenuating circumstances in an attempt to answer the question: J. J. or Joss? It is of course a ridiculous question, for we already know the answer is J. J. *and* Joss, for the world would be a far poorer place without one or the other. This book is, in the end, an homage to both Whedon and Abrams—people who, as Steven Spielberg has said of all filmmakers, "dream for a living."[8]

1

FIRST SCRIPTS

Doctoring, Conceiving, and Giving Birth

You must stay drunk on writing so reality cannot destroy you.—Ray
Bradbury, *Zen of Writing*

When they appeared together at a Comic-Con panel, Joss Whedon and
J. J. Abrams highlighted the importance of education. When asked about
film school, Abrams disclosed his father's (Gerald W. Abrams's) advice:
"'Go learn what to make movies about, not how to make movies.' And it
was sort of the best advice I ever got." Whedon marveled, countering
with his dad's (Tom Whedon's) advice: "Don't be a writer. It's too much
work."[1] Such instructions explain a lot about the ways each man ended
up approaching the industry. Abrams began writing by using what he had
learned in college about what makes a good film or a good piece of art.
Whedon tried to avoid writing for television until he eventually found
himself following in his father's and grandfather's footsteps, writing
spec(ulative) scripts that he hoped would be produced and working too
hard. Both sets of advice, however, let them know that the basis of a good
film is good writing (and that, yes, it is indeed hard work!).

Both young men turned to writing after leaving college, with fair
success. Their early work (as could be expected) is full of youthful exu-
berance and idealism, but the themes and seeds of later work are clearly
visible under the rougher surfaces of those early pieces. Both graduated
from small liberal arts colleges, and although neither went to a special-
ized film school—or even a university with a dedicated film-production

program—both came away full of ideas and eager to work in the industry. When Abrams graduated from Sarah Lawrence College in 1988, he'd already begun writing film scripts with his friend Jill Mazursky, daughter of producer and director Paul Mazursky. The elder Mazursky interested Jeffrey Katzenberg, then head of Disney, in one of their scripts,[2] and Abrams was able to go straight from college to Hollywood with no intermediate way stations.

Katzenberg helped place *Taking Care of Business* (1990) with Hollywood Pictures, Disney's branch for more "mature, adult audiences." Directed by Hollywood icon Arthur Hiller—known for *Love Story* (1970) and collaborative work with authors like Paddy Chaefsky and Neil Simon—*Taking Care of Business* was a silly slapstick comedy about a hopelessly upbeat convict who wants to see the Chicago Cubs win the World Series. (See what I mean by silly?) Whether *Taking Care of Business* really fits Disney's classification of a more "mature, adult film" is up for grabs, but it definitely launched Abrams's career in Hollywood.

Whedon, who is two years older than Abrams by four days, graduated from Wesleyan College in 1987 and left school wanting to direct films. Of course, no one hands you a job as a director at a major studio (or any studio for that matter) just on the strength of your desire and a degree in the liberal arts. Whedon had to travel a more circuitous route than Abrams to realize his dreams. In interviews Whedon repeatedly registers his rejection of being "3G TV"—shorthand for "third-generation television writer," a term coined by a Wesleyan friend who teased him about it being an inescapable fate.[3] Ultimately, the need for an income made Whedon reconsider.

At first the younger Whedon tried other approaches, living with his father while he took on a series of lousy jobs such as working at a video store and writing for the American Film Institute's Lifetime Achievement Award ceremony. Eventually he discovered that resistance was futile and let his father, who he joked was trying to get him to move out, help him into the business. Whedon *fils* wrote five spec television scripts including, in 1989, one for an episode of *Roseanne*.[4] Amy Pascale of *Newsweek* tells of Whedon landing the writing job with *Roseanne*, noting the general rule was:

> that a writer should never send a spec of a series to *that* series, since a show's own writing staff can be particularly picky. . . . But apparently

> Joss's script was good enough to get . . . an offer to work on what Joss felt was one of the most important shows on television. . . . The producer [Jeff Harris] told him to bring in his no. 2 pencil on Monday, so Joss went out and bought a hundred no. 2 pencils.[5]

He likely used them all, and broke a few in frustration too, while he worked for the show.

Although *Roseanne* was one of the best comedy shows in television and Whedon wrote for it during its stellar second year, it was not a heartening situation. Whedon told Emma John,

> Writing for Hollywood is . . . a "brutal, soul-crushing" experience. "I've described it to students as like climbing to the top of the mountain and finding out it's surrounded by more mountains and there's no view at all." Actors mangled his lines; directors and producers rewrote entire scripts. "You have to be Prometheus and have your heart removed every day."[6]

He learned important lessons from his work there, however, such as how to keep his head down and avoid direct criticism, how to work with difficult people, and even how *not* to behave.

The most important thing he discovered was from his first group meeting with the series' eponymous star, Roseanne Barr. At the time she was suffering from negative press and fired a number of the show's writers. She then held a meeting with the new staff in which she ranted about the negative press leaks. Whedon told Ken Plume about a speech she made,

> about how the tabloids were really giving her shit and how they were infiltrating the crew and stuff. . . . "So you fucking writers better keep your mouths shut or I'll have you all fired." I realized, this was the perfect opportunity to make a speech that brought everybody closer together, that said, "It's us against the world, and dammit, we've got good work to do here, let's all get it done"—and instead she used it to attack. It made me realize, at that moment, that every time somebody opens their mouth they have an opportunity to do one of two things—connect or divide.[7]

This lesson was likely a prime factor in Whedon's later success as a producer and director. Those who have worked repeatedly with him insist that he forms a bonded group—a family—with those working on his projects. He tends to hire the same people, and they seem to get along. His ability to connect with both employees and fans is legendary no matter how difficult or ornery they are.

Whedon would move from *Roseanne* to *Parenthood* (1990), and although the show was canceled quickly, it allowed the young writer to move up to co-producing and to experience a mentoring relationship. By the second half of his year at *Roseanne*, Whedon had been working alone and eventually said he was being paid to sit in his office and not work. Creativity functions best as commerce between creative people, and the twenty-four-year-old Whedon had no chance to blossom under the mentorship of older, more experienced writers. With *Parenthood* executive producer David Tyron "Ty" King, Whedon finally got the chance to bounce ideas around with a peer and thus to develop professionally, even though the studio itself was not supportive of the show. In a conversation when he and King were bemoaning the network's treatment of *Parenthood*, biographer Amy Pascale reports that King turned to Whedon and said: "I'm just so angry," then smiled, saying: "This is so much fun," at which point both broke into laughter.[8] Writing is hard, often lonely work, but it usually benefits from the exchange of ideas with other writers. At *Roseanne*, Whedon did not have that support, but the one good thing about his lonely hours there was that he had been able to craft a film script during his empty time "writing" for *Roseanne* and had it "in the can" when *Parenthood* was canceled almost as soon as he was hired.

The early 1990s was a time of broad, often less-sophisticated comedy, and both Whedon and Abrams would find themselves writing scripts for movies that were silly and for the most part unrealistic. Whedon completed a comedy-horror film script, titled *Buffy the Vampire Slayer*, a film that he hoped people would take seriously.[9] Abrams worked on several scripts, including *Taking Care of Business*. The latter was shot in a year when it seemed like the ill-fated team might actually go all the way, but in fine Cubs tradition they lost 4–1 to the San Francisco Giants in the National League play-offs, leaving the film's premise at odds with unfortunate reality. An over-the-top comedy of manners, the film pits Spencer Barnes (Charles Grodin), an uptight businessman who lives by his Filofax calendar, against easy-going convict Jimmy Dworski (Jim Belushi). Up-and-coming comic Jim Belushi, who had finally broken into lead roles a few years after his older brother, John, had died of a drug overdose in 1982, was a casting stroke of genius. No doubt partially due to his Chicago roots and fondness for baseball, he makes the character of convict and number one Cubs fan, Jimmy Dworski, his own and is really the best reason to see this otherwise barely-above-average comedy (unless of course you are a Cubs fan and have a hankering to see them finally win a World Series). The writing is mostly good, but it suffers from an inability to recognize when it has taken things too far—something that, given the subject matter, is particularly easy to do.

The plot of *Taking Care of Business* depends on a mistaken identity mishap. It allows escaped convict, Jimmy, entrée into an upper-class world and mansion that causes him to exclaim, "Wow! I'm on fucking *Dynasty*!" The class criticism is fairly well executed, as Jimmy, pretending to be Barnes, winds up in the mansion of Barnes's well-to-do boss. There he explores the absurd toys and perks of the boss's ostentatious home, with its automated lights and music and a fountain activated by remote control. Johanna Steinmetz's review calls the characters "thinly drawn" writing:

> It's a dubious sign when a comedy invites you to laugh at things rather than at actors. In *Taking Care of Business*, James Belushi and Charles Grodin compete with vibrating chairs, remote-controlled sculptures, a Filofax datebook, a security alarm system and an assortment of snappy cars. This isn't a movie, it's a Sharper Image catalog. [10]

Character aside, for some of us the Sharper Image catalog reminds us of what we'll never have in our modest homes and a Filofax datebook turns out to be a pretty hilarious prop.

Coincidences keep getting ever more preposterous as Jimmy meets clients, takes a Lamborghini out for a drive, and even beds the boss's daughter, all while masquerading as Charles Grodin's more or less happily married Barnes. A BBC reviewer drily highlighted the film's tendency to not know where to draw the line:

> The movie only slightly exaggerates how desperate Cubs fans are to see their team win a championship. [It] had some funny moments, but a large percentage of people who saw this movie did so just to see the Cubs in the World Series. Cub fans also got to see longtime first baseman Mark Grace make his acting debut, hitting a home run in the World Series. Clearly, *Taking Care of Business* is one of the most unrealistic movies of all time. [11]

Belushi reportedly brought the Cubs into the mix because he was such a fan. Responding to reviewer Jim Abbott's reminder that the last Cubs series win was in 1908, "he points his finger and cautions that the film 'is not a fantasy—understand that.'"[12] But this is the same guy who distinguishes White Sox fans from Cubs fans, noting that the former are cynical, but Cubs fans are "delusional."[13] Still, delusional works for the purposes of the film. Despite some inconsistency, when the writing is good, it is laugh-out-loud funny.

Abrams's second screenplay veered away from comedy, although class differences still played a pertinent role. The young writer had the good fortune of having Mike Nichols direct his second script and of seeing it brought to life by the talented acting of Annette Bening, Bill Nunn, and Harrison Ford. *Regarding Henry* (1991) is a sanguine little tale of a viciously ruthless attorney who suffers brain damage and develops a conscience in the course of his recovery. *Taking Care of Business* (1990) showed good control of timing and humor, which got it past the rough patches, but weaknesses in drama are harder to disguise. The implausible cheerfulness of Henry's rehabilitation and the kindliness shown him by all the characters, including his formerly pitiless law firm partners, simply strain all credibility. Henry begins as a man who is just plain mean to his wife, daughter, and courtroom opponents and who, after getting shot in a convenience store hold-up, suddenly becomes simple-minded and kind. The film has poignant moments by a great cast, but the script is weak and poorly paced, and even the great acting by Bening, Nunn, and Ford cannot save the film.

At times in *Regarding Henry*, Abrams tries to cut corners by tossing in humor to close a serious moment. As famed critic Roger Ebert complains, the screenplay "constantly goes for the laugh over the possible reality. It has an annoying trick of teaching Henry a new word and then having him proudly trot it out to wrap up a complicated scene."[14] Having Henry get lost and end up in a porn theater, uncomprehending and confused, is amusing but detracts from what could have been a serious film about the effects of brain damage. A reviewer for *A.V. Club* asserts,

> It's a film . . . about redemption through brain damage. The implications of that are pretty staggering. Forget education, wit, sophisticated thinking, and higher reasoning: What the world needs now is for everyone's brain to be deprived of oxygen just long enough for them to want to go out, eat a hot dog, and buy a puppy, as Ford does.[15]

In the end everyone, including Henry's impossibly supportive wife, understands and forgives him, and he is offered lavish financial support from the same cutthroat law firm that backed his attack on an impoverished, cancer-ridden plaintiff in the opening scene. The script makes a noble effort to work against Hollywood clichés, but the characters feel inconsistent and often unmotivated and the final product never finds a convincing voice. Cloyingly saccharine and sentimental, most of us will be happier not regarding *Henry*.

There are, nonetheless, occasional character moments in the film that look ahead to the better writing and greater success that lay in Abrams's future. Themes that will play major roles in his future work—like the importance of compassion and empathy—appear, perhaps a bit too ferociously. Also notable are poignant moments (both painful and sentimental) that Henry shares with his wife and child, which rival some of the best character work in later series like *Felicity* and *Fringe*. One of the most striking scenes is a Spielberg-like moment revealing the alienation between Henry and his daughter. Henry, sent by his wife to apologize,

A nicer Henry (Harrison Ford) after his accident working with his daughter (Kamian Allen), from *Regarding Henry* (1991). *Paramount Pictures / Photofest © Paramount Pictures*

enters the daughter's room, but rather than ever saying he is sorry, he instead tells her he was angry "with a reason." Quoting a Latin legal phrase, pointing in her face, and not knowing her doll's name are sure indications of his uncompassionate lack of fatherly skills.

Abrams excels at the dialogue and in depicting the driven, self-satisfied Henry. The opening court scene likewise is crushingly brilliant in its irony and in the language Henry uses to destroy a sympathetic client who should have had a guaranteed courtroom win. Still, these are two masterful moments in an overly sanguine story that otherwise lacks nuance—a story that shows Abrams had not yet mastered the more finely toned voice necessary for a serious subject like brain damage.

In the meantime, Whedon had been shopping his *Buffy the Vampire Slayer* film script around. His memory of the experience is that "everyone liked the script and I had lots of encouragement, but no one wanted to pick it up."[16] So to make ends meet, he ended up doing loop lines for movies like *The Getaway* (1994) and *The Quick and the Dead* (1995), and it wasn't until 1991 that Sandollar Productions finally sent his script into preproduction . . . a couple of years after it had been optioned.[17] Sandollar executives Howard Rosenman and Gail Berman showed the script to Fran Rubel Kuzui, who loved it and then sold the idea to 20th Century Fox for immediate film production with her as director.[18]

The movie was not as bad as legend would have it, but it was not really good either. Whedon was horribly disappointed in the results. It was a moderate financial success; budgeted for $9 million, it made $16 million.[19] Janet Maslin justly calls it "a slight, good-humored film that's a lot more painless than might have been expected."[20] The film had a fairly prominent cast, including Luke Perry from the then-popular series *Beverly Hills 90210* (1990–2000), Rutger Hauer, Donald Sutherland, and Paul Reubens of *Pee-Wee's Playhouse* (1986–1990) fame. Reviews, though mixed, were depressing, and there was a great deal of finger-pointing by a variety of people about what went wrong and who was to blame.

At the time of filming, Whedon was deeply disenchanted. The film was nothing like he had envisioned, and a lot of his (probably understandable) youthful rancor fell on veteran actor Donald Sutherland, who did not seem to take it seriously enough. Interviewed for the *Onion*'s "A.V. Club," Whedon describes the actor as "a prick," justifying his opinion this way:

> He would rewrite all his dialogue and the director would let him. He
> can't write—he's not a writer—so the dialogue would not make sense.
> And he had a very bad attitude. He was incredibly rude to the director,
> he was rude to everyone around him, he was just a real pain.[21]

There was clearly a visceral friction there, but the animosity seems a bit
excessive.

Assessing blame in such situations of mutual finger-pointing is no
easy feat. Noted Whedon scholar David Lavery supports the scriptwrit-
er's opinion, underscoring:

> Anyone who thinks Whedon's antipathy for Sutherland is merely sub-
> jective or . . . the result of a veteran's perhaps understandable impa-
> tience with a novice director, would do well to watch Damian Petti-
> grew's documentary about Federico Fellini . . . in which Sutherland
> unashamedly exhibits every attribute Whedon accuses him of . . . and
> insists that working with him was a "torment" and "hell on earth."[22]

No doubt Sutherland can be difficult to work with, but of course the great
Fellini himself was infamous for his nastiness, his abuse of actors, and his
ill-tempered ranting. In an interview done some fifteen years later, a
calmer Whedon admits, "I believe that part of the problem was that the
director was unable to control the big, fat, wannabe movie star."[23] This
statement shows his anger but also a recognition that it was really the
director's fault. More tellingly, he then goes on to say, "They were changing their lines," so we can conclude that it was not just a matter of a single
bothersome actor causing a problem.[24] Lead actress Kristy Swanson,
however, remembers it differently: "Donald was unbelievable. . . . I was
blown away by how supportive and sweet he is."[25] There may be room to
lay blame on both sides. Certainly no writer likes having his lines modified, let alone butchered, but the protests against Sutherland seem more
related to having a weak director, a problem with the film that Whedon
also recognized but was much more tactful about addressing.

Kuzui, as David Lavery stresses, was the reason the film got made at
all, and Whedon was well aware of this fact and showed enormous gratitude to her despite her entirely different vision for the film.[26] Nonetheless, as Whedon explained to Ken Plume, it is the director who is responsible for everything about the final product.

> But, you know, as Jeanine [Basinger, Whedon's film professor at Wes-
> leyan] put it once, or probably more than once, "A director doesn't
> have to create anything, but he is responsible for everything." Same
> thing goes for an executive producer on TV. I don't have to write a line
> of the script—although there's not a script for my shows that I don't
> have a line in, or a scene, or a pitch, or something. I don't sew the
> damn costumes, I don't say the words—but I'm responsible for every
> thing in every frame of every show.[27]

Whedon's feeling that the director is the boss left him feeling that he
could not tell Kuzui about his difference of vision. He articulated gratitude, and frustration, in his interview with Plume:

> So, I didn't agree with the way the movie was going, but I also kept
> my mouth shut because you respect the director. . . . You respect the
> person above you, and you make suggestions and do your best. . . . But
> you don't ever disrupt the chain of command. You have to have faith
> in the person who is running it or things will fall apart.[28]

In the long run, not keeping the proper tone or keeping actors in line are
signs of weak direction. It was painfully evident that Whedon's and Kuzui's visions were as harmonious as singing is to *Angel*'s Pyleans (that is,
not at all). Whedon felt he had written a script that "was a horror-action-
comedy. It had fright, it had camera movement, it had acting. . . . It was
supposed to have a little edge to it . . . rather than a glorified sitcom where
everyone stands in front of the camera, says their joke and exits."[29] Fran
Rubel Kuzui, on the other hand, believed that "it isn't a vampire movie,
but a pop culture comedy about what people think about vampires."[30]
Instead of fear, Kuzui gives us vampires with ears that make them look
like humorously deformed elves. Instead of edge, we get overly dramatic
camp. This is not a match made in heaven!

  It is quite possible therefore that Sutherland had nothing whatsoever to
do with destroying the film. The way Kathleen Tracy sees it:

> According to [the director's husband] Kaz Kuzui, Donald Sutherland
> [who played Buffy's Watcher Merrick] and Rutger Hauer were not
> amused at the tone the film was taking. "They were very difficult. . . .
> They thought the movie was very serious and became insecure. They
> tried to make their roles more complex, more emotional"—in other
> words, the way Joss had originally written the characters.[31]

Movie Buffy (Kristy Swanson) hones her vampire-slaying skills in *Buffy the Vampire Slayer* **(1992). 20th Century Fox Film Corp. / Photofest © 20th Century Fox Film Corp.**

Later, according to Candace Havens, Whedon would have to accept that "the director ruined it."[32] As Neil McDonald concludes in comparing the film to the television show, over which Whedon had far greater control, "The television series demonstrated something the film industry . . . finds very hard to admit: more often than not, writers do know best."[33] Here he did.

Undeniably, the *Buffy* script is good, especially if one can imagine a more respectful and nuanced version of the material under Whedon's own guiding hand. It tells of Buffy before her move to Sunnydale and how she learns from her first Watcher that she is the chosen Slayer. It is scary and humorous and even has a bit of characteristic Whedon political commentary to make the story's serious aspects more salient. A speech by the vampire leader Lothos (Hauer) revealing the evilness of vampires, for example, meshes easily with the materialism of 1990s Los Angeles:

> Are we so strange? So alien to you? I've seen this culture, the wealth, the greed, the waste . . . it's truly heartwarming. The perfect place to spread my empire. Honestly, Eastern Europe was so dead. The Communists just drained the blood out of the place. It's livened up a bit in the past few years, but it's nothing compared to this . . . this Mecca of consumption.[34]

The script also has the evisceratingly witty zingers for which Whedon would later become known. For example, one of Buffy's friends whines, "You're acting like the Thing from Another Tax-Bracket; it's too weird." In another exchange, cut from the film, someone calls the school counselor short. A second student chimes in: "Yes, but what he lacks in height he makes up in shortness." This could just as easily have come from the mouth of TV Buffy's geeky high-school friend Xander and is Whedon in all his glory.

The writer does not really always know everything, however, and Kuzui tightened up a script that takes too long to get to the meat (or rather blood) of the matter, cutting dialogue and scenes that slowed the pace and added little to the narrative. Whedon's version has several dream sequences before there is any hint of Buffy's destiny, and some of the teen dialogue in the original drags on while adding little character depth. The writing also gives us no reason to like Buffy but many reasons to find her annoying. Kristy Swanson plays her as a stereotypical valley girl, sharp-tongued and much more similar to the TV-series character of Cordelia than to Sarah Michelle Gellar's version of Buffy.[35] All the members of her clique are self-absorbed and sardonic and simply not very likable. The kernel of the Buffy character is there, but Whedon does not yet have the verbal finesse to make her sparkle. Thus while the wife and improved Henry of J. J. Abrams's *Regarding Henry* (1991) are just too nice to believe, the teens in *Buffy* (1992) are just too vapid. Both writers, while revealing completely opposite aspects of characters that interest them, still fail to deliver personalities with a balance of frailty and humane strength.

Despite *Regarding Henry*'s hokeyness, Abrams managed to get another heart-warming, sentimental screenplay green-lit: *Forever Young* (1992), a golden-age Hollywood-style star vehicle for the hugely popular Mel Gibson. In the film, World War II pilot Captain Daniel McCormick cannot quite commit to his ladylove, Helen. Due to an accident, she ends up in a coma and Daniel ends up with a guilty conscience, so he allows himself to be cryogenically frozen for an experiment, only to be forgotten about until he accidentally gets thawed out by kids some fifty years later. (You may be detecting a few plot weaknesses here already.) The *New York Times* aptly proclaims:

> *Forever Young* has nothing much to do with anything except the movie conventions of an earlier time when near-fatal accidents, wild coincidences and miraculous resurrections were the way life was lived on the silver screen. Plausibility is not important . . . [and] everything depends on the charm, style and verve with which it's played.[36]

Gibson delivers the charm, which is a strong aspect of Abrams's writing here, but as noted by Vincent Canby above, the film fails miserably in terms of plausibility.

Nor is the film terribly interesting in and of itself, but it contains incipient elements Abrams would include more successfully in much of his later work. *Forever Young*'s use of the science-fiction trope of cryogenics immediately springs to mind, but other themes for which Abrams would later become known are also present and starting to bud. Not only is the movie egregiously sunny, but children play a visible role in the modern-day part of the story. In a Spielberg-like move, two boys and a single mom help Daniel evade authorities and reach his true love, Helen, before the effects of his cryogenic thaw render him decrepit and incapable of redemption. As in *Henry*, redemption, love, and biological family allow the protagonist to conquer all obstacles. One can only wonder if forever young also entails being forever naïve!

Forever Young offers an interesting contrast to Whedon's work from the same time period. While (film) Buffy's parents barely seem to know her name, the closeness of children and parents is a primary issue for Abrams. Henry must learn to interact with his daughter emotionally to make things right, and it is the loving cooperation of the Cooper family that allows Captain McCormick to reunite with his beloved. Whedon's young people in *Buffy* are on their own and unsupported by the adults around them. Buffy's parents think nothing of going out and leaving her unattended, and they certainly do not know her boyfriend's name. The school counselor is authoritarian and ineffectual. Only Merrick, Buffy's Watcher, has something to offer, but it is not emotional support so much as a reminder of duty. Moreover, love solves no problems. Even in the early Whedonverse, we are alone and attachments are a burden. Buffy, for example, must bail her boyfriend, Pike, out of trouble on several occasions. Abrams's and Whedon's outlooks already diverge wildly.

After their movie work in 1992, neither Whedon nor Abrams succeeded in making their work public and thus they honed their skills behind the scenes. Abrams focused on writing and a little producing. Whedon worked on a script for 20th Century Fox called *Nobody Move* that did not go anywhere. Then his mother (Lee Stearns) died unexpectedly of a cerebral aneurysm.[37] As Amy Pascale notes, this gave Whedon a chance to spend time with his father. They wrote scripts on spec and dreamed up a Siskel and Ebert/*Odd Couple* TV series that would contain actual film reviews for the week each episode would air.[38] Mostly, however, the next years found him doing script-doctoring and loop lines. Loop lines or ADR (automated dialogue replacement) are added lines of dialogue placed into the film after a scene has been filmed and edited. Such lines usually are dubbed in by the original actors at a point in the scene when the character's lips are obscured. They are used to clarify a situation, add a little comedy, or spice up a sequence that drags. Whedon, with his facility for short, pithy one-liners, was a natural for the work, but script-doctoring and loop-lining are both thankless tasks, essential for making weak areas stronger and helping questionable projects succeed but usually providing no credit to the writers responsible.

Whedon's most notable work from the period was on *Speed* (1994), *Twister* (1994), and *Waterworld* (1995). Doctoring scripts could be a lucrative profession, and Whedon was bringing in as much as $100,000 a week on some jobs.[39] He told Tanya Robinson: "When I was a script doctor, I was wealthy and miserable. I never had less fun succeeding at a job in my life."[40] Whedon said:

> Aside from rewriting 90 percent of the dialogue on *Speed*, the best work was the stuff that nobody would ever notice: just trying to make the whole thing track logically and emotionally so that all of those insane and over-the-top stunts—one after the other—would make sense.[41]

Work on *Speed* also involved paring things down along with work on "dialogue straight through . . . [and] a couple of plot things just to make connections."[42] In a 2001 interview with Robinson, Whedon summed up his experiences on both *Speed* and *Twister* nicely:

> Most of the dialogue in *Speed* is mine, and a bunch of the characters. . . . Getting arbitrated off the credits was un-fun. But *Speed* has a bunch. And *Twister*, less. In *Twister*, there are things that worked and things that weren't the way I'd intended them. Whereas *Speed* came out closer to what I'd been trying to do. I think of *Speed* as one of the few movies I've made that I actually like.[43]

The bottom line was that even though Whedon was robbed of credit for his work because of arcane Writer's Guild of America rules, he could be happy with what he accomplished.

He was much less satisfied when it came to working on *Waterworld*. Even though he got to go to Hawaii, he spent seven miserable weeks achieving very little.[44] The *Onion* interview again succinctly sums up Whedon's experience, which he compared to being a highly paid stenographer:

> When I was brought in, there was no water in the last 40 pages of the script. It all took place on land, or on a ship, or whatever. I'm like, "Isn't the cool thing about this guy that he has gills?" And no one was listening. I was there basically taking notes from Costner, who was very nice, fine to work with, but he was not a writer. And he had written a bunch of stuff that they wouldn't let their staff touch. So I was supposed to be there for a week, and I was there for seven weeks,

and I accomplished nothing. I wrote a few puns, and a few scenes that
I can't even sit through because they came out so bad. [45]

In another interview, Whedon says, "Waterworld is one of the projects
that proved to me that the higher you climb, the worse the view." [46] These
experiences were important because they drove home repeatedly the importance of having control over one's own material. Luckily Whedon
could wash away the bad taste by remembering that he had also, just
before his trip to Hawaii, come off of what would be one of his greatest
script-doctoring successes: working on *Toy Story* for Pixar.

Whedon had started work at Disney because he had hoped to pen
musicals. [47] Drew Taylor summarizes Whedon's early work for Disney on
two animated projects, early versions of:

> *Atlantis: The Lost Empire* (in the words of Whedon his version was
> *Journey to the Center of the Earth* meets *Man Who Would Be King*)
> and a musical version of "Marco Polo" in the vein of *My Fair Lady*.
> What makes the "Marco Polo" project so tantalizing is that, beyond the
> finished script, Whedon also contributed at least three songs (with
> music by Broadway stalwart Robert Lindsey-Nassif). Let's just restate
> that: a Disney musical, with a script and songs by Joss Whedon, is
> sitting in the Disney vault somewhere, going unmade. [48]

Whedon indicated that he is credited on the *Atlantis* film because he "was
the first writer on it, even though I had not a shred in it." [49] This may not
be precisely true as some of his characters and structures no doubt remained. An astute blogger insists *Atlantis* is another example of a forma-
tive undertaking that is echoed in Whedon's later work:

> Joss Whedon contributed to the story for *Atlantis* and it is so shocking-
> ly obvious to anybody who's seen *Firefly*. Traces of Zoe and a dry run
> of Kaylee are visible in Helga Sinclair and Audrey Ramirez, respec-
> tively. Really, all the female characters seem to have come out of the
> Whedon-verse. I thought *Alien: Resurrection* (Dir. Jean-Pierre Jeunet,
> 1997) was the only explicitly proto-*Firefly* work written by Whedon,
> but I was wrong. [50]

Regardless there is not much other information available about his input
on this work, so the extent of Whedon's contribution must remain a
mystery.

At about the same time, Pixar, a new division of Disney, was having trouble developing their new computer-generated animated feature *Toy Story*, so they called in the script doctor to see what he could do. Whedon recalls that he actually ended up working on it twice:

> I spent about four months on it before we got the green light. When . . . they were putting it together, I walked away, started doing other things, then came back a couple of months later. They had shut the movie down. I went up to Pixar and they actually said [to the crew], "Listen, we're having to shut down for awhile. . . . Many of you are going to be laid off and Joss is here to fix the script."[51]

Seven writers worked on the project altogether, so it is difficult to know what Whedon provided specifically. David A. Price, in a book on Pixar, said: "As for under-recognized people, I'd say one of them is Joss Whedon. Most people don't know he was one of the writers of *Toy Story*. The point when that film really started to come together was when Joss started working on it."[52] He earned the accolades he would receive for the script.

Whedon indicated to interviewers that he introduced the character Rex the dinosaur. He also wanted to bring in a strong female toy, Barbie, at the film's end to save the day, but Mattel refused to grant permission for his "Barbie-as-Sarah-Connor rescue scene."[53] Whedon said what he was most proud of was "getting a little more voice and a little more edge into the jokes and into the bits, and just helping the structure."[54] It seems likely that some of the themes in the film are also his. Certainly a group of misfits banding together to overcome adversity is a recurrent Whedon theme, as is the fear and pain of being alone, which is an integral part of Woody's on-screen persona. Whedon was improving his writing and learning the field. This time around, he got a writer's credit and also an Oscar nomination for writing. The tide was beginning to turn for him just a little, but he was still a long way from being able to hang ten and lie out on the beach.

J. J. Abrams, too, was once again working on movie scripts during this period. He seems to be one of those people who stays close to and likes to work with his good friends because he teamed up once again with Jill Mazursky for the buddy film *Gone Fishin'* (1997). They began filming in 1995 and had several production difficulties, including the death of a stuntwoman in a boat collision in the Everglades. The film itself was yet another silly 1990s romp, this time with two hapless fisher-wannabes and a fishing contest in Florida. Joe Pesci and Danny Glover play childhood friends with not much sense but a lot of heart. Critics' consensus on *Rotten Tomatoes* is that the story is "sloppy, formulaic, and unfunny. *Gone Fishin'* marks a painful low point in the careers of its two talented leads."[55] You know that the movie is not terribly good when the "Big Bad" at the end of the movie is an oversized, mechanized mother alligator.

Aside from a couple of cameo roles in other peoples' films, like *Six Degrees of Separation* (1993), in which Abrams played Doug, and in *Diabolique* (1996), in which he played Video Photographer #2, the budding filmmaker was not really seen for a while. As a follow-up, he quietly threw his hat into the producing ring. He fronted financial support to old friend Matt Reeves (with whom he used to make 8mm movies as a teen) for Reeves's project *The Pallbearer* (1996) and later acted as producer on the *The Suburbans* (1999). Neither film was particularly successful, although Roger Ebert did not hate *The Pallbearer*, labeling it "a goofier, gloomier trek across some of the same ground covered in *The Graduate*."[56] The kinds of twists and turns of the plot used in *The Pallbearer* would resurface in later cooperative work between Abrams and Reeves, such as *Cloverfield* (2008) and *Felicity* (1998–2002). Generally though, production was not yet a good match for Abrams's skills, and his projects did not fare well.

Abrams also did a stint of script-doctoring, being hired by Jerry Bruckheimer to fix up the screenplay of *Armageddon* (1998), and guest-wrote, without credit, for the second season of *Avatar: The Last Airbender* in 2007. Abrams was one of nine writers attached to the script for *Armageddon*, and only five would garner credit after a Writer's Guild of America arbitration decision.[57] With so many writers and a dearth of information about the film's writing process, it is hard to know where Abrams might deserve credit and where not. The film got horrible reviews, implying he might want to distance himself from the project, but it was a huge financial success and popular with viewers, so then again, maybe not. Roger Ebert despised it, calling it the first 150-minute trailer and lamenting, "No matter what they're charging to get in, it's worth more to get out."[58] The film was nominated for a Saturn award for best science-fiction film and best film by MTV but also for a Razzie for worst screenplay.

A script for *Armageddon* written by Abrams and Jonathon Hensleigh exists, and it is quite different from the film at several points, so it may be possible to disentangle some Abrams elements. *This Distracted Globe* reports that

> Bruckheimer . . . brought in a succession of script doctors, parceling out specific incidents. . . . Robert Towne was hired just to develop a mutiny scene. Scott Rosenberg was asked to supply dialogue for the supporting cast, notably Steve Buscemi. Ann Biderman supposedly did the same for Liv Tyler. Tony Gilroy was tasked with writing a new beginning, because no one liked Hensleigh's concept that two kids would spot the asteroid, then be quarantined to prevent the story from leaking out. J.J. Abrams did an overall dialogue polish because Bay was a fan of his snappy repartee.[59]

Hensleigh maintains that Bruckheimer liked to employ him (Hensleigh) to get down the "overall structure" and for "funneling the action towards an explosive conclusion."[60] This seems like a probable scenario. The opening with three children discovering the meteor is in the Abrams/Hensleigh co-written screenplay, so although it could have been purely a Hensleigh contrivance, it fits well with the Abrams aesthetic. The fact that it is not two children but three and includes a girl (as in *Super 8*) is also quite possibly an Abrams touch.

The cooperative screenplay also has a much larger role for the female astronaut, Watts, than the finished film. Most of the on-screen actions she performs in the screenplay are given to a male astronaut in the film, an unfortunate change because Watts is given no chance to display her competence early in the film. The scene in the climax in which she tries and fails to fix an equipment malfunction could have served to heighten the sense of the direness of the situation by showing a formerly competent scientist cracking a bit under pressure. Instead, she simply looks like a ninny when she cannot fix the failing thrusters. In the film version, she is pushed aside by a crazy Russian cosmonaut, who solves the problem by brute force: banging on the failing part. So much for a woman who is described in the original script as "30s and tough as nails."[61]

The film is also more reactionary than the script penned by Hensleigh and Abrams. The crazy Russian cosmonaut, Lev Andropov, has more depth and is much more fond of America in the Abrams-doctored script. He is a huge fan of Hollywood movies and also likes to make bad home videos himself. *Armageddon* does retain oilman Harry Stamper's verbal attacks on the Greenpeace protestors for having an energy-hog boat and using electricity-gobbling hair dryers, but the script also had an unfilmed lyrical moment in which Harry, upon seeing the splendor of Earth from space, has regrets. When asked what he is thinking, he replies: "How beautiful it is. Thinkin' about all that oil I sucked out and spit into the air. Funny how a man can live 46 years and realize he ain't been doing the right thing."[62] These kinds of tranquil, reflective scenes find no place in the actual Bay production.

Abrams may also be responsible for the sweeter, more innocent versions of characters. There is romance in the cooperative script, but unlike in the film, it does not involve masculine exhibitionism. Steve Buscemi's character "Rockhound" is an intelligent geologist and not the flawed, lascivious loser of the film.[63] The script's introduction to the romantic leads—Harry's protégé A. J. and daughter Grace—occurs as the sensitive young man shyly tries to figure out how to propose and not (as in the film) with him hiding her from her suspicious father under the postcoital bed covers.

There is also a gentle humor to the Hansleigh/Abrams script that did not find its way onto the screen. Cosmonaut Lev learns English in order to impress his visitors, practicing lines from his English phrasebook like "Would you like an appetizer or an aperitif?" He later proudly shows the new arrivals a shelf of his homemade films: "'Lev loves cargo.' 'Lev sleeps.' 'Lev prepares for Americans.' 'Lev gets bored so he gets drunk.'" About the latter, he comments, "Funny but . . . too long."[64] There are also several film jokes in the script referencing films like *Star Wars* and *The Dirty Dozen*, which for the most part did not make it into the actual movie.[65]

Regardless of the specifics, a look at Abrams's work on *Armageddon* underscores his ability to thrive in an environment in which he can work with (or more properly on) material created by other people, that he is collaborative, and that he is quite good with dialogue. The Abrams/Hensleigh script enjoys an emphasis on romance, as opposed to sex in the film, and on the importance of family, both in terms of the relationship between the main character, Harry, and his adult daughter and between "street philosopher" Chick and his young son. Amid the fast cuts and explosions, familiar Abrams tropes can still be spotted. Some of these are the importance of faith and of the impossible, and of the poignant and the kindly. There is also the gentle humor of Lev's eccentricities and, in the opening sequence of both the script and the film, a dog that likes to attack dinosaur stuffed animals.

As Abrams began to delve into script-doctoring, Whedon got a chance to get out of that business and write a genuine script for actual credit. Whedon had developed a relationship with an executive vice president at Fox Studios, Jorge Saralegui, when he was working on the *Buffy* film. Saralegui had gotten Whedon the work on *Speed* and then offered him the opportunity to write a script for a continuation of the *Alien* franchise.[66] Since the main character, Ellen Ripley, played by Sigourney Weaver, had been killed off in the third film at Weaver's insistence, Saralegui wanted a script focused on a younger character called Newt, who was introduced in the second film, *Aliens* (1986), as a surrogate daughter for Ripley. Whedon was able to produce a great thirty-four-page treatment that had a lot of people excited.[67] The studio conversely decided they really wanted Weaver back for the project, so Whedon then had to do additional versions that brought Ripley back from the dead. These were so good that they in turn brought Weaver back to the project. Resurrection, as it turns out, became something Whedon would be very good at, whether it involved aliens, vampires, or even their Slayers!

Despite all this good news and getting an edgy, young director suggested by costar Winona Ryder, Whedon counted *Alien: Resurrection* as the most miserable (but educational) moment of his career. In no way did Jean-Pierre Jeunet's vision of the material mesh with his own concept of his screenplay, so Whedon found himself in a replay of the *Buffy* filming experience. The writer insists he delivered brilliant material and feels the direction was weak and incapable of producing the required tonal nuance of his script. Furthermore Jeunet was not careful enough budget-wise, which necessitated rewriting the ending repeatedly in order to save money. Whedon vented to James Kozak:

> Rather than go into all of the reasons why *Alien: Resurrection* is disappointing to me, I will tell you that, yes, I wrote five endings. The first one was in the forest with the flying threshing machine. The second one was in a futuristic junkyard. The third one was in a maternity ward. And the fourth one was in the desert. Now at this point this had become about money . . . but I still wrote them the best ending I could that took place in the desert. And then finally they said, "Y'know, we just don't think we need to go to Earth." So I just gave them dialogue

and stuff, but I don't remember writing, "A withered, granny-lookin' Pumkinhead-kinda-thing makes out with Ripley." Pretty sure that stage direction never existed in any of my drafts.[68]

Although there was general agreement with Whedon's conclusion—Joe Baltake of the *Sacramento Bee* quipped, "This *Alien* should never have been resurrected,"[69]—there were also those who found the film beautiful or funny. The *Washington Post* reviewer noted:

> But the surprise is not how wet it is, it's how funny. The movie never scales the heights of pure skull-in-the-vise horror that Ridley Scott's original managed. And it never develops the cool marines-vs.-bugs carnage of James Cameron's second installment. But it brings a mordant, crackerjack wit to the world of chest-busting, head-ripping creepazoids from beyond.[70]

Others did not appreciate Whedon's wit and blamed him exclusively for the film's failure. Tom Meek of *Filmthreat* insists, "Weaver and Jeunet's efforts are short-changed by the ineptness of Joss Whedon's script, that seems to find a way to make action sequences unexciting. They are simply void of any real suspense."[71] Unfortunately there may be some discrete amount of truth to this pronouncement.

It is easy in retrospect, given the experience with the *Buffy* TV material, to know that what Whedon can pull off with his own writing is amazing and probably beyond the command of a typical director who is not (and cannot be) invested in the material in the same way that he is. As with the *Buffy* movie script, there is no question that some of the sequences are ponderous and a little slow. Could Whedon have pulled off a resurrection of the material if he had directed the film himself? Quite possibly. In retrospect he admits that in directing he has to become a second person and that means looking at the material differently. Eight years after his work on *Alien: Resurrection*, he gave Daniel Roberts Epstein a more mature take on the process.

> After *Alien Resurrection*, I did put my foot down and literally said, "The next person who ruins one of my scripts is going to be me." Then you get into it as a director and you realize, "Oh, I actually missed something that I wrote," . . . like this stage direction or this nuance, or I didn't bring enough energy in this scene and you want to club yourself so you can only imagine what it's like for people who aren't you.[72]

Without a doubt, the film would have been different on-screen if Whedon had had the opportunity to direct it himself, but he would also probably have changed the structure and action to make the material and pace smoother and sleeker.[73]

Whedon's *Alien* script, with its flaws and strengths, looks forward to much of the work he would create in the future. The situation of a bunch of smugglers on a ratty little spacecraft, for instance, undoubtedly presages his science-fiction/Western TV series, *Firefly*, a fact noted by both fans and academics who have written on the series.[74] It turns out even Whedon realized that *Resurrection* was foundational for other projects, such as *Buffy* and *Firefly*. He told S. F. Said that

> the metaphor that I had begun to strike at in *Alien: Resurrection* became the central concept behind *Buffy*, and that's how I sold it. . . . Then we came to *Firefly*, and *Serenity*, where I took away the metaphorical aspect—but science-fiction always opens you up to every element of history that you want, because the future is just the past in a blender. And . . . it was more an idea of, "I can take anything from the human experience that I've read about or felt or seen." . . . The idea behind the show was . . . "nine people look out into the blackness of space and see nine different things."[75]

One can only imagine what the film might have been like if Whedon had been able to direct and play around with his own script while filming.

Even so, *Alien: Resurrection* gives us many themes that resurface in other of the writer's works. Most obviously we see political themes that are dear to Whedon undergird the reasons for all the bad things happening in that particular universe. These themes come, in part, from the original *Alien* movies. Weyland Yutani, also known as "The Corporation," is behind the near extinction of Earth via alien beings in the first two films because corporate greed makes them think science can use the uncontrollable and destructive alien life forms for capitalistic profit. In Whedon's version, Ripley is told not to fret because Weyland failed years before. The character Wren explains: "Our Ripley's former employers Terran Growth conglomerate had some defense contracts under the military. Before your time, Gediman—they went under decades ago, bought out by Walmart. Fortunes of war." Wren understands corporate progress in terms of a martial system. He tells Ripley she need not worry: "This is United Systems military, not some greedy corporation. The potential benefits of this race go way beyond urban pacification. New alloys, new vaccines . . ." The scariness of the physical monster is reinforced by the scariness of the political monster. Raz Greenberg underscores the *Alien* franchise's influence on Whedon:

> *Firefly* is perhaps [his] most direct attempt to expand on and realize elements that did not work well in *Alien Resurrection*. . . . The oppressive authority is represented mostly by armed forces, there are . . . the monstrous experiments conducted by this authority, and, finally, the rebels who do not see themselves subjected to this authority—the crew of the *Betty*—can be seen as a spiritual predecessor of the *Serenity* crew.[76]

In contrast to *Armageddon*, where the military and business (oil production) represent all that is great about America, *Alien: Resurrection* shows them as pure evil. This conflation of corporation and military will recur in Whedon's more mature works such as *Dollhouse*, *Firefly*, and even of course the ever-popular *Avengers* movies as they interrogate the relationship between Stark Industries, S.H.I.E.L.D., and the military in terms of protecting versus threatening the world.[77]

Greenberg, while recognizing the substantial import of the *Resurrection* script to Whedon's development, also confesses that not only does most of his script work for the film get up on the screen (thus discrediting somewhat the blame he placed on the director, casting, and acting), but she also insists that this script "is not one of his better efforts."[78] Greenberg astutely puts her finger on one of the reasons and identifies its recurrence in the sixth season of the *Buffy* TV series. In both cases, a caring main character is resurrected and cannot find emotional connection to the world after being brought back from the dead. "Ripley is apathetic and indifferent," Greenberg notes, "surrounded by other characters that viewers have little or no reason to like or care about."[79] Likewise in *Buffy*, she feels they have little reason to feel "for an apathetic protagonist. Much like Ripley, Buffy is also a victim of her 'unholy' resurrection."[80] This observation, however, also underlines the differences between television and film as media and how important it can be to play to the strengths of a particular medium.

For Whedon, the *Alien* films were probably strong enough in his memory that Ripley's humanitarian side could not be effaced. On the other hand, it had been eleven years since audiences had seen Ripley in the theater and her humanity was most likely no longer fresh in their minds. Thus, although changing a character to one that is disillusioned and apathetic could be a painful moment on the way to a greater recognition of duty and the need to be engaged, Whedon's film script fails to remind us of who this dedicated and caring protagonist was before she became the apathetic, resurrected industrial tool that we meet at the beginning of the film.[81]

In a TV series, it is easier to sustain these kinds of character changes because the viewers watch the episodes over a period of weeks. They get repeated reminders of characters' natures, thus audiences are able to more easily retain the memory of what has gone before. Greenberg points out that the viewers of *Buffy* were unhappy with the changes in their heroine, but perhaps this is Whedon giving his audience what it needs as opposed to what it wants, so that he could bring Buffy around slowly and give viewers the emotional satisfaction that they craved at a later time. In a film, though, (and particularly in an action/horror film), there is limited time to do a psychological double reversal of this kind. It seems Whedon might even have been aware of this problem because he originally included a scene (albeit only one) that could possibly have bridged this emotional gap. The one connection to a loving Ripley gazing at the image of the surrogate daughter in Whedon's script, however, got cut out of the film. Still, it likely would not have been enough screen time to reconnect the viewer with Ripley in preparation for forgiving her newfound apathy. Due to the limited economy of film action, this particular theme was probably lost or deemphasized, and it ultimately undercut the emotional impact of the story.

The most fascinating theme in the film is the mother/daughter connection, but it falls flat in terms of the alien mother and its child and the monster child's relationship to Ripley, who carries some of its alien DNA. It fails because of the directing and visualization but also because of the writing. In *Aliens* (1986) the theme works because we see the monster protecting her young in an all-out battle against Ripley, who is also protecting a child, but in *Resurrection* this same theme misses the mark, failing because the anthropomorphizing of the alien is so poor and because the idea of Ripley's maternal connection to the alien is badly set up through ridiculous exposition. In that scene, the half-dead doctor Gediman is shown captured and cocooned but is still somehow able to mumble out his perception of how the audience should react to the scene.

The human mother/daughter story part of the film—concerning Ripley and one of the smugglers, a female cybernetic being named Annalee Call—works better. As with *Blade Runner* (1982), *Alien: Resurrection* broaches what it means to be human and the bittersweet experience of human love, loss, and compassion. When Ripley discovers that Call is a synthetic being, she delivers the *Blade Runner*-esque line, "You're a robot. I should have known. No human being is that humane." The reaction of the human crew to Call is a series of brutal criticisms. They mock her with comments such as "You're the 'new model' droid" and "Great. She's a toaster oven. Can we leave now?" The sequence is poignant—good solid writing and good film, too.

Both Call, the synthetic being who hates herself for not being human, and Ripley, who is "impure" due to her alien-tainted DNA from her cloning process, struggle with what it means to care. When Ripley asks Call why she cares, we are given the only answer there can be: "Because I'm programmed to." Humans and their progeny care because we have to, no matter what happens to us. That, rather than pure biology, is what makes us human. Ripley and Call end the film as outsiders who at least find each other, despite the impossibility of community with the regular but less humane human beings. In an early version of the ending, Whedon writes them standing supportively side by side. In a somewhat similar but not as moving rendition, the film gives us a final shot of the two of them sitting next to each other before a ruined Earth. This is a very subtle extension of an earlier theme in the *Alien* franchise. Ripley is the biological mother of a daughter she will never see again and later becomes a surrogate mother to the orphaned child Newt. More importantly, *Resurrection* illustrates two of the primary themes in Whedon's later corpus: the difficulty of being an outsider and the importance of choosing one's own family. Perhaps these themes are not handled as well as they might be, but they are noticeable and hint at Whedon's influence on the film. This also suggests that he will need more space to deal adequately with the topics that are important to him. More space, like the kind you find in TV.

Whedon would continue script-doctoring right into the new millennium. Even though the *Buffy* series would follow on the heels of *Resurrection*, Whedon would still do script work on *Titan AE* (2000) and *X-Men* (2000), but he was reaching a place where he realized it was time to

Ripley (Sigourney Weaver) confronts her surrogate daughter Call (Winona Ryder) in _Alien: Resurrection_ (1997). _20th Century Fox / Photofest © 20th Century Fox_

expend his energy on his own creations. Abrams too was at a point where he needed to find a better match for his talents.

It is time to compare Abrams and Whedon at this youthful stage of the game. Both men's early years set them up nicely for what was ahead. Both excelled in writing; Whedon's numerous script-doctored films are probably better known and more popular than Abrams's early pieces, but neither has yet made a name that is recognized by the public so there is no award for popularity. Abrams has more film scripts, but _Toy Story_ and _Speed_ are more memorably written than _Taking Care of Business_ and _Armageddon_. Whedon's writing style is more mature at this stage, and he has a stronger sense of how to use a humorous line. Whedon scores for writing. His script-doctoring and loop lines probably also earned him more money than Abrams, so Whedon is granted the award for profitability. Abrams, on the other hand, has probably shown greater facility for the image with his full scripts and inventive settings for _Forever Young_ and _Gone Fishin'_. So he gets the point for visual creativity and the point for innovation. Both have struggled with the system. Whedon has learned important leadership and collaborative skills as far as getting things produced, but Abrams has numerous films to his credit and the Hollywood connections to help them get made. There is a tie for working the system. Abrams also deserves a personal growth point for using ironic self-delusion and writing against type. The score stands at Abrams 3.5 (innovation, personal growth, visual creativity, and working the business); Whedon at 2.5 (profitability, writing, working the business).

Clearly, both young men had dreams they set about following, and both had mixed success doing so in the world of film. In the next part of their lives, this changed and they pursued their ambitions in the medium of television, a place where their interest in character could be more fully realized.

2

GETTING THE GIRL

Buffy, Felicity, and Sydney

I love to see a young girl go out and grab the world by the lapels.
Life's a bitch. You've got to go out and kick ass.—Maya Angelou

Both Abrams and Whedon cut their teeth on movie scriptwriting, with varied success. For each, the move to the smaller screen was a natural next step. Each had a familial connection to the TV industry. Abrams's father had been a commercial retailer who decided to sell commercials for CBS and became a TV movie producer, and his mother (Carol Ann Abrams) entered the TV production business after her son went to college.[1] As mentioned earlier, Whedon had fought hard not to enter the family business. Both his father and his grandfather had been very successful television writers. His grandfather John had written for *The Donna Reed Show* (1958–1966), *The Andy Griffith Show* (1960–1968), *The Dick Van Dyke Show* (1961–1966), and even *Leave It to Beaver* (1957–1963), while Whedon's father had continued in the comic tradition by making a name for himself on shows like *Captain Kangaroo* (1955–1992*), Alice* (1976–1985), and *The Golden Girls* (1985–1992), as well as writing for Dick Cavett (on *The Dick Cavett Show*, 1968–1974).

Whedon didn't want to be a third-generation television writer: "No, no. TV's not 'ahhhrt.' That's 'art' with three h's," he told Brian Truitt of *USA Today*.[2] For Whedon, however, the force was not with him, and eventually his talents as a writer combined with the need for a job led him to begin writing for *Roseanne* (1988–1997) in its second season. He would even change his mind about television, telling Truitt: "And then I discovered that I was wrong. TV's a lovely thing."[3] I would like to take a second look at Whedon's work on *Roseanne*, this time concentrating not on the influence it had on him as a writer but on the material itself.

Roseanne is recognized as a groundbreaking sitcom and with good reason. As Roseanne Barr herself notes, "The show was about women, gender, politics, the working class. Did I think that it would be successful? . . . I actually did. Because I knew it was filling a void."[4] Given that Marcy Carsey and Tom Werner originated the show, this success was not surprising, since they were responsible for a long line of innovative programs ranging from *Mork and Mindy* (1978–1982) to *The Cosby Show* (1984–1992), *Grace under Fire* (1993–1998), *Cybill* (1995–1998), and *Third Rock from the Sun* (1996–2001). *Roseanne* clearly filled a void, for it hit number one in Nielsen ratings in its second season, the year that Whedon began writing for it at the ripe old age of twenty-four.[5]

Television writers work in a kind of stable to churn out each weekly show, and what ends up being produced and aired is usually a concoction of material by a variety of contributors. As noted by *Splitsider.com*, "Whedon's wry, hyper-articulate voice is so distinct it's practically trademarked," and unsurprisingly in the five episodes for which he garnered a writing credit, his voice shines forth brightly.[6] His snarky humor and cynicism were well matched to the show, but his credited episodes also tend to concentrate strongly on personal and familial relationships, and there is a fullness and delicacy in the portrayal of the teen characters that will also stand out in his later *Buffy* series. "Brain-Dead Poets Society" features realistic and finely tuned exchanges between Roseanne and the daughter she strong-arms into reading a poem at a school event. Believable interactions between sisters Becky and Darlene in "The Little Sister" exhibit both the familial caring and the friction so common between siblings.[7] Whedon credits his picked-on-younger-brother status and his bond with a strong feminist mother with helping him write his female characters. Whedon recalls: "When Roseanne read the first script of mine that got into her hands without being edited by someone else she said, 'How can you write a middle-aged woman this well?' I said, 'If you met my mom you wouldn't ask.'"[8] He identified strongly with the underdog and wanted to make a statement about that kind of unfairness in the world.

As Whedon and Abrams made their moves to television, change was in the air. The networks were struggling to reinvent themselves and show more hipness and political openness. Things that had been taboo in the past were suddenly sought out in the hopes of bringing back audiences who were deserting to cable television.[9] At the time cable offered fewer commercials and more adult subject matter than the networks, which took a more family-oriented approach. The new networks, however, were looking to find a new niche market by attracting a younger, with-it audience. This meant that J. J. Abrams, along with his college buddy Matt Reeves, could sell a show on the relationship issues of early adulthood that related to their common experience as youthful friends and Whedon could do something similar with his experiences of high school. It also meant they would have more freedom to vary from the stereotypes of previous series.

Women had had their own television shows since near the beginning of TV broadcasting. While there were plenty of series like *The Bob Cummings Show* (1955–1959), *Bachelor Father* (1957–1962), and *The Jack Benny Program* (1950–1965) that centered on men, there were also many shows focused on women, such as (to name just a few) *A Date with Judy* (1951–1953), *Our Miss Brooks* (1952–1956), *Honestly Celeste* (1954), *The Annie Oakley Show* (1954–1957), and *The Donna Reed Show* (1958–1966), as well as various variety shows hosted by women. The most successful of the women-centered shows was, of course, *I Love Lucy* (1951–1957). These shows mostly followed genre expectations for women and were thus comedies, variety shows, or family dramas.

Because television was considered a center of the domestic world, women were not infrequently at the focus of popular series, whether involving the crazy antics of America's favorite redhead Lucy, her twenty-one-year-old brunette version in *My Little Margie* (1952–1955), the zany and perennially perplexing witch Samantha from *Bewitched* (1964–1972), or the marriage-desperate, most incompetent genie of all time (except perhaps for her little dog, Djinn Djinn) from *I Dream of Jeannie* (1965–1970). These female characters, even so, had severely restricted roles, playing either domestically oriented or harebrained characters, if not both.

By the late 1980s, the networks' hopes for better ratings made them more courageous and allowed for less narrowly defined and more serious and realistic portrayals of women and others to sneak onto the screen.[10]

Following rapidly on the heels of shows like *Cagney and Lacey* (1981–1988), *Roseanne* (1988–1997), *Cybill* (1995–1998), *Murphy Brown* (1988–1998), and, most importantly, *Moesha* (1996–2001), there was finally space for a series about a teenage girl who had to deal with significant social issues. Because of these groundbreaking shows and the proclamation of 1992 as the "Year of the Woman," Whedon and Abrams were able to pitch young female characters with depth and intelligence, who could be taken seriously (mostly) on the little screen.

So the time and political climate were right for Whedon to avenge the earlier injustices done to his horror/adventure screenplay. As Susanne Daniels, former WB (Warner Brothers Television) president, explained about her pursuit of a televisual form for the less-than-successful Buffy movie in the 1990s: "At the time we were pitching two things, teenage female superheroes, and a contemporary version of *The Nightstalker* . . . so we didn't know enough to say, 'You don't buy a drama series based on a failed movie.'"[11] The network in fact encouraged Whedon to make a half-hour kiddie show revolving around his blond valley girl superhero.

Whedon's *Buffy* was not the first TV series to feature a naïve but magical female teen protagonist.[12] *Sabrina, the Teenage Witch* (1996–2003) came out the year before, but *Buffy* was the first to offer one with teeth: vampire teeth, that is, and a young woman strong enough to fight them. Although *Sabrina* was a sitcom, it featured a peppy and perpetually chipper young teen who suddenly discovered she had inherited magical powers. Buffy was a physically strong but angsty heroine exploring the metaphor of high school as hell (who also, it turned out, had a form of inherited magical power). *Buffy* was funny like *Sabrina*, but it was also scary and had a serious edge.

Whedon indicates that after the frustrating experience of seeing his film turned into what amounted to campy fluff, it had not really occurred to him to revamp (so to speak) the *Buffy* story for TV. The credit for the idea (along perhaps with the conspiracy of the film's director Fran Rubel Kuzui) goes to Gail Berman, who according to Whedon,

> had been saying, "This is a series. This is a series." And everybody said, "Ha Ha Ha. You are a fool!" And then about four years after the movie came out, she got some people interested in developing it. Somebody eventually said, "You are not a fool!" Then, when they came to me, they had been offered to do it like a Power-Ranger type show.[13]

In reworking the material, however, Whedon came to feel that he wanted to do something more serious than a humorous kiddie show, so he re-pitched the project as an hour-long drama, getting an instant okay that made him feel "like somebody came along and kissed Sleeping Beauty."[14] It was, he recalled, as if someone had said, "You can have your dream back now."[15]

J. J. Abrams joined the youth-focused WB television network a year later with his new program about a young woman striving for independence and adulthood as she moved across the country to attend her first year of college.[16] As with Whedon, Abrams wanted to do something serious and personal. The way Matt Reeves, Abrams's co-creator for the *Felicity* series, tells it,

> Well, *Felicity* was really a character piece, it was very intimate and had a lot of people in rooms talking to each other about relationships and stuff, but the thing that was important to me and JJ Abrams—who co-created it—was that we were always trying to go for a kind of naturalism. This was a college fantasy but there was a level of natural-ism with the actors and the situations we tried to create.[17]

Both Abrams and Whedon thus came to television with shows about young independent women but in environments that allowed for a stronger sense of reality and more serious subject matter than, say, Sabrina turning her roommate into a pineapple or revealing that England had been governed for two months by a bunny rabbit. This isn't to say that either Abrams or Whedon couldn't have pulled off such silliness in addition to covering serious issues such as date rape and addictive behavior. In fact, the genre-bending quality that embraced both the possibilities of the magical as well as thorny real-life matters was what gave both the series their strength.

The two series' universes are remarkably similar. The main characters of *Buffy* and *Felicity* each come as strangers to their respective schools. Buffy comes to a new high school after she has been expelled from the old one for burning down the gym because it was full of vampires, and Felicity arrives at the fictional east coast University of New York from California because she has followed a boy from her high school she wants to get to know better. Both programs feature blond California-girl protagonists with sweet but not cloying natures, who must come to terms with what it means to approach adulthood independently. Both confront expectations from the adults in their lives that conflict with their own personal desires. Felicity's parents want her to attend medical school at Stanford although she is more interested in studying art. Buffy just wants to have a normal high school life of dating, shopping, and hanging out, but as her generation's chosen "Slayer," she is under constant scrutiny from her "Watcher," who reminds her of her duties and obligations to hunt down demons and vampires. The young person's dilemma of how to combine the responsibilities of adulthood with the need for personal independence motivates the title character in each series.

Both shows also have similar constellations of supporting characters. The two heroines, for example, each have close girlfriends, who talk to them about issues more important than just boys.[18] Although boys figure as discussion topics, both series have meaningful conversations between named female characters that run the gamut of life and school issues and do not focus solely on relationships. Buffy has Willow Rosenberg, the shy, nerdy, computer-savvy friend who is picked on by the upscale clique of popular girls. Felicity has Julie Emrick, a girlfriend with musical talent and a history of abuse and insecurity. Both gal pals serve as sounding boards and supporters for the main characters, modeling positive friend behavior rather than the generic backbiting relationships so frequent in programs about women. Both pals, however, also do eventually become involved in issues of rivalry over boyfriends.

Triangles are the foundation of television drama, and both Abrams and Whedon deserve credit for not turning the female support figures into stereotypical enraged rivals. Instead, frictions are dealt with credibly and with the subtlety and ambivalence of real life. The women are genuine friends who must come to terms with where loyalties should lie. While at times this means that they are estranged or angry, there is reinforcement of the fact that frictions result from lack of communication and from the emotional confusion of adolescence, and the pairs remain genuine friends throughout the run of tensions.

Friction occurs in *Felicity* when Julie, with Felicity's permission, decides to date the protagonist's ex-crush, Ben. Both women recognize the complexity of the situation, coming to realize that their rational response to the situation may not reflect actual emotional reality. Despite the fact that Felicity believes she has disengaged from her attachment to Ben, it becomes clear to her and Julie that their mutual attraction to Ben is a problem for their relationship. Within the story, the women struggle to come to terms with the complexity of these emotions rather than allowing their relationship to devolve into a televised woman-on-woman mud-slinging and wrestling event. We viewers experience the issue with them sympathetically rather than as a schadenfreude-filled spectacle and pull for them to maintain their close relationship despite their shared interest in Ben.

Likewise Whedon shows Buffy's pal Willow pining for Xander Harris, who is infatuated with Buffy, but the women's interactions never involve bitchy competition over men. From the moment Buffy sees the popular and stylishly clad Cordelia Chase put down Willow and her choice of clothing, with "Good to know you've seen the softer side of Sears," Buffy and Willow become fast friends.[19] A rare exception occurs in the first episode of season 2, when Buffy has become full of herself and intentionally does things to annoy all of her friends, including doing a sexy dance with Xander to make someone other than Willow jealous. Even here, however, we are asked to identify with the feelings of the characters and understand the emotional costs of the situation rather than simply gape at Buffy on the dance floor. In short, Buffy and Willow do not fight over the same object of desire. Whedon, as a feminist, allows for many of his women, characters like Buffy and Willow, to engage in more complex emotional interactions that portray hurts, slights, and teenage slips of the tongue rather than the hackneyed "You stole my boyfriend, time for a catfight" scenes so familiar in television soap operas but not in the Buffy(uni)verse.

At the beginning of both *Felicity* and *Buffy*, we meet prickly female characters who intentionally give the heroines grief and thus risk becoming stereotypes, but even these characters end up being nuanced and carefully constructed. Over the course of the narrative, they are given credible and human justifications for their behaviors, and they also change and grow but not to an unrealistic extent. Male bullies also figure in these shows, particularly in *Buffy the Vampire Slayer*, which offers equal-opportunity bullying of sensitive, weaker characters both male (Jonathan, Xander, and Andrew) and female (Anne, Amy, and Marcy). In an interview with Jeff Bercovici, Whedon referred to his primary major theme:

> And that's helplessness. The empowerment of someone who's help-
> less. And that has everything to do with how I feel about myself. Buffy

was a pretty blond girl of whom nothing was expected, who didn't try
very hard at anything, and then suddenly became the most powerful
person around—that theme, whether it's empowerment or the discovery that one is powerless, that drives everything I do.[20]

A key idea in Whedon's work is that the mean pick on the weak, and
wouldn't it be great if the unempowered could arise and kick some bully
butt and even win an occasional battle or two!

In both series, even secondary female characters who start out as
bullies usually develop into complex, motivated individuals. Meghan, at
the start of *Felicity*, is a self-centered Goth party girl who sees her roommate as hopelessly naïve and uncool. She is vicious and self-serving in
her behavior but very gradually develops into a more nuanced character
and Felicity's close friend. Although Meghan does experience inappropriate jealousy and is often opaquely bitchy, her alienation from others is
a significant but not monolithic aspect of her character. Additionally, her
flawed nature brings a sense of realness to the series. We (and the fans)
all know, and live among, this kind of person. Meghan is allowed to
mature and develops kindness and moderate consideration for others,
while still retaining her egotistical core. She is a credible character with
negative traits who grows but does not alter her basic character.

Likewise, Cordelia Chase of *Buffy* starts off as a clichéd "spoiled rich
girl" character who is obsessed with her own self-importance. While
strong-arming Buffy into going to a frat party with her, she exclaims,
"These men are rich, Buffy, and I'm not being shallow—think of the poor
people I could help with all my money."[21] Cordelia is allowed to grow
and change because of her experiences while still retaining her fundamental personality. Like Meghan, she remains somewhat egotistical
through the run of *Buffy*, but she comes to care for the others and becomes an important member of Buffy's circle of friends, who call themselves "the Scooby Gang." In an episode where Mr. Giles (Buffy's mentor and Watcher) is in danger and has disappeared, the others immediately
list the things they will do to secure his safety. Cordelia responds, "What
about me? I care about Giles."[22] The beauty of the writing is such that,
even in this first instance of the audience getting a chance to see Cordelia
thinking of others, her utterance shows that she still comes first. Later she
has the opportunity to grow in a story arc of her own, when her family's
wealth is squandered and she finds herself trying to maintain her fashion-

able image with no real means of support. We sympathize with her even when we dislike her choice of action.

Our commitment to the *Buffy* characters is no doubt due to the fact that the writing stemmed from personal experience. Joss Whedon openly identifies with his characters and the difficulties that they go through. In interviews, he frequently speaks of relating to the character of Xander Harris. Xander is one of the eponymous heroine's best friends, a guy with a giant crush on Buffy, but also the geeky guy that girls always want for best friends but never as romantic ones. Buffy, um . . . rebuffs his advances, and Xander just can't win in the love department, variously finding himself unwittingly involved with a giant praying mantis, an evil Incan Mummy, and an ex-vengeance demon to whom he cannot quite commit. Not a good choice of someone to leave at the altar, by the way, as Xander will later find out. As silly as the stories sound, Whedon sells them beautifully and we take them to heart.

Viewers identify with Xander because we have all been "that guy" who says hopelessly inept things at the worst possible times. We have all been the one that complains, "Does every conversation we have have to come around to that freak?" just as the person in question comes up behind him.[23] We have all been the wrong person in the wrong place at the wrong time; the person who can proclaim, in horrified frustration, "Sometimes I shouldn't say . . . words."[24] That combination of terror and embarrassment is what Whedon aspires to and what makes the show so popular. *BBC.co* notes that Whedon's "storyline inspiration for Buffy involves not only his own experiences in school, but the universal woes of others."[25] The Buffy creator says, "When I get together with my writing team, I ask them 'What was your favourite horror movie? What is the most embarrassing thing that ever happened to you? Now, how can we combine the two?'"[26] Buffy manages this with unique success.

In the *Felicity* universe, Xander's counterpart is a character named Noel: a sensitive, kindly regular guy who is as taken with Felicity as Xander is with Buffy. No doubt creators Abrams and Reeves, who were both film geeks in high school, also pulled from their personal experiences. Starting off as Felicity's resident adviser and later graduating to a position as a university guidance counselor, Noel is hopelessly in love with Felicity, even though he knows she has come to the university because of her infatuation with Ben. Noel has a bit of Xander's ineptitude, mentioning Felicity's "overbearing parents" within their earshot, for example, and getting himself into predicaments where he can be black-mailed or placed in uncomfortable positions by other characters despite (or, more precisely, because of) his own best intentions. For both Xander and Noel, no good deed ever goes unpunished.

Both heroines, however, are more interested in "bad boys" than in the sensitive guy next door. Ben is a good-looking, popular sports star who, like Xander, comes from a troubled home. He has issues with commitment to both people and to his education; Felicity is disappointed repeatedly by his indecisive and erratic behavior over their four years together in college. Buffy makes an even worse choice, however, in falling for Angel—a well-intentioned two-hundred-plus-year-old vampire with a vicious history and a curse that does not allow him to experience happiness without major negative repercussions. It goes without saying that a Slayer, whose primary duty is to kill vampires, is in a rather untenable position if she falls in love with one, but over time Buffy falls in love with two. Buffy, like Felicity, is caught between the Byronic bad boy and the kinder, more sensitive partner that she deserves. This sort of triangle, and its eventual unhappy resolution, is in fact indicative of Whedon's prime directive, which insists that television must give the audience not what it wants but what it needs.[27]

Audiences seem to want the women to settle on the attractive and disarming bad boys, and indeed, in *Felicity*, viewers get their hearts' desire. The title character follows her sentimental inclinations and finally settles on Ben. Although Whedon claims he tried to give Buffy the kind of good-guy boyfriend that she deserved, he concluded that it simply didn't work.[28] Her fourth-season military dreamboat, Riley Finn, was despised by the fans, and his character was ultimately made darker before being phased out at the end of season 5. Whedon must have felt sorry for him because he let the character reappear briefly in season 6 with a better-matched mate, who genuinely appreciated him. After Finn's departure, Buffy returned to the dark side with a hot-and-cold-running relationship with Spike, another vicious vampire, who had killed two Slayers in the past. He had been rendered effectively harmless, but not uncruel, by a government-implanted chip in his brain. Spike, in his frustration with not being able to get Buffy to accept, let alone acknowledge, their relationship, eventually tries to rape her and thus permanently destroys all hopes for a serious relationship between the two. Whedon emphasizes here the fine line between our fantasies of bad-boyness and the reality of genuinely horrible things.[29] Spike goes on heroically to win back his soul and struggles, for the rest of season 6, with his feelings of guilt over having attempted this unforgivable action.[30]

Although Buffy chooses both the nice guy and the bad boy, she ultimately ends up with neither. This highlights a major difference between the two series creators. While Felicity Porter decides in favor of the latter, Buffy Summers rejects both, deciding she is not ready and is like an "unfinished batch of cookies" needing time to become what it will be.[31] Abrams gives audiences what they desperately want, while Whedon gives them what he feels they need: a woman hero who does not need to have a partner nor to fulfill the demands of the Hollywood dream machine.

The difference between Abrams's and Whedon's worldviews is especially clear in the way each deals with the hyper-romanticization of the female loss of virginity. Both heroines will find out that giving themselves to a man sexually is not the romantic act that our society likes to paint it as. Each auteur plays with this in terms of sexual initiation by both the bad-boy and nerd characters, and neither scenario offers satisfaction. In a very humorous episode, Felicity decides to have her first-ever sexual encounter with the sensitive and smitten Noel.[32] Everything imaginable goes wrong on two separate occasions, including the couple being burst in upon, interrupted by phone calls, and ultimately driven out by a fire, so the act is not consummated. Later with another man, illness, a mongrel dog adopted off the street, and rooming situations all interfere with hyped-up romantic hopes for union. The mood is one of wistful humor.

Scenarios involving the series' bad-boy figures are even less sanguine. Felicity and Buffy both think they have found the loves of their lives only to feel the men change after intimacy. *Felicity*'s Ben embraces his inability to commit at a Halloween party after his (as yet unconsummated) relationship with Felicity has gotten closer, by going off to pet with a different woman wearing a costume from the *Mighty Morphin' Power Rangers* television series. Felicity is crushed by Ben's response:

> Well, I can't live up to that, all right? I'm a guy in college. If I want to make out with a Power Ranger, I can do that. I mean, not everything has big meaning, okay? I mean, yes, we had a nice moment, but so what? It doesn't mean anything.[33]

Even though Felicity will not lose her virginity for another eleven episodes (and not with Ben), the insensitivity of certain men is clearly highlighted. In the end, she will sleep with an art student named Eli, with whom she has no real personal connection—a decision she will come to regret—just to get her virginity loss over with. The series suggests both what Ben says, that not everything is deeply meaningful, but also acknowledges Felicity's viewpoint by titling the episode in which she finally does sleep with Ben "The Biggest Deal There Is."[34] Them having sex together, the title hints, has extraordinary meaning—a point that reinforces Ben's earlier insensitivity.

Whedon emphasizes this theme repeatedly. Buffy's love interest, Angel, is cursed with a soul (that makes him good), but he will lose it and turn evil if he experiences a single moment's bliss. Buffy hears the same kinds of words that Felicity hears from Ben from the now-soulless Angel (called Angelus in his evil incarnation) after she consummates their relationship sexually.

> **Buffy:** But you didn't say anything. You just left.
> **Angelus:** Yeah. Like I really wanted to stick around after that.
> **Buffy:** What?
> **Angelus:** You got a lot to learn about men, kiddo. Although I guess you proved that last night.
> **Buffy:** What are you saying?
> **Angelus:** Let's not make an issue out of it, okay? In fact, let's not talk about it at all. It happened.
> **Buffy:** I, I don't understand. Was it m-me? Was I not good?
> **Angelus:** [*laughing*] You were great. Really. I thought you were a pro.[35]

Men are not monolithically insensitive in either show. Neither Noel nor Oz, Willow's boyfriend, would behave this way, but the clear message is still that men's behavior can change after sex.[36]

Buffy has to relive the demeaning experience again with a college student named Parker Abrams, who beds her to improve his hook-up score. Their conversation is very similar to the one with Angelus above.

> **Buffy:** You had fun? Was that all it was?
> **Parker:** What else was it supposed to be?
> **Buffy:** It seemed like you liked me.

> **Parker:** I do. But I'm starting to feel like you felt what? Some kind of commitment? Are you sure that's what you want right now?
> **Buffy:** I just thought . . .
> **Parker:** I'm sorry if you missed something. I thought things were pretty clear.[37]

Parker will later display his crass insensitivity in a conversation about Buffy with another college boy by saying, "[She's] definitely a bunny in the sack, but later on, well, you know the difference between a freshman girl and a toilet seat? A toilet seat doesn't follow you around after you use it."[38] At this point Riley Finn punches Parker, to the audience's great delight. Even the apparently nice Scott Hope in season 3 ends up spreading false rumors about Buffy's sexuality after he becomes frustrated with her inability to commit. Thus Felicity and Buffy both learn that their ideals of love and the way some men behave are not necessarily consistent and they need to be wary of ulterior motives and differences in people's value systems. The message is realistic and was unusual at that time for women-focused series, which were much more likely to highlight idealized romantic relationships as the most important aspect of life than to ask hard questions about what we tell young people about sex.

Both shows were also willing to take on other major issues. Felicity focused on difficult matters such as gambling addiction, alcoholism, and date rape, while Buffy looked unblinkingly at a variety of addictions and abusive relationships and also dealt with the effects of the death of a parent. *Felicity* featured an arc, for example, in which Julie was date-raped by an otherwise sympathetic and likeable character. The story line focused on the way she and some of the ignorant characters around her wanted to blame Julie for what had happened and on the inability of the boy to recognize the true ugliness of what he had done. This made for groundbreaking television.[39] The story arc was nuanced, complex, and painful.

Both creators approach the reality of difficult issues in different ways but still manage to strike at the deeper issues. Abrams indicated to *Seriable.com* that it can be quite difficult to keep momentum going in a realistic weekly show based on college life.

> It was so hard because when you got to Episode 3, you're like "um . . ." There were no bad guys, there were no monsters, [there were

literally only] grades. There was no way to do a show, the[re] were no crimes, there were no legal cases or medical cases. [40]

One of the things that set both Whedon and Abrams apart from some of the rest is that they had carefully thought about the long-term and short-term structures of the medium they were using. Abrams continued with his analysis of his problems in creating *Felicity*:

> A TV show typically needs a door that every week bursts open with [a] burden that the main characters have to hold, carry and deal with, and help people in a selfless way. The model . . . is a condition that characters can actually deal with stuff that's not just their own issues, college is only about your own issues. . . . There were things that were substantial; whether it was anything from date-rape to drug use—there were all these kind of things that were where you need to go to find stories, and of course there are things that are sadly very relevant to that age, but typically it was [very difficult] to come up with what's the "thing" every week. [41]

It was his and Matt Reeves's success in coming up with that *thing* that really resonated with fans.

Whedon also managed to touch on real issues in spite of the magical nature of his show's environment. Despite Buffy's ability to bring in bad guys and monsters, she was still also able to deal with themes similar to Abrams's heroine, from addiction to spousal abuse to emotional obsession. Whedon's tour de force may well be a look at the way the death of a loved one affects a community of people. *Buffy*'s fifth-season episode "The Body" breaks with the series' seemingly lackadaisical attitude about death by zooming in on its genuine effects. [42] When Buffy's mother dies of an aneurysm, Whedon, who wrote and directed the episode, featured the lifeless corpse prominently in numerous shots—a reminder of the difference between the fun of scary TV and the horrific reality of death. This is the death of a beloved character, not just some nameless demonic monster with a walk-on role, and *Buffy*'s creator shoves it in our faces to remind us that we need to take life seriously.

Abrams alluded to one of the primary differences between the two TV series when he noted that there were no bad guys or monsters on *Felicity*. The man infamous for supernatural aspects in his film and television oeuvre used the mystical very sparingly in his very first series. Lacey

Rose, writing for the *Hollywood Reporter*, quoted Abrams as saying that what he missed about the show after it ended was the straightforward nature of the relationship stories.

> "I miss writing for a show that doesn't have any sort of odd, almost sci-fi bend to it," he says, noting the challenge of having to come up with stories for a series that had neither high stakes nor a bad guy. "It was just sort of pure romantic, sweet characters who had crushes on one another and were dealing with which party to go to and if they had a part-time job or not—stuff that was kind of fun to write about."[43]

These sweet characters in moving relationships remained a hallmark of Abrams's work in series to come.

Only two parts of the show have much at all to do with the supernatural. The first is the stand-alone episode "Help for the Lovelorn," which was Abrams's homage to Rod Serling's ever-popular show *The Twilight Zone* (1959–1964).[44] The other is a series of five episodes more or less forced on Abrams and his team by a network that couldn't decide when to cancel the series. Expecting cancellation after seventeen episodes of season 4, Abrams and team produced a series finale that tied everything up with the characters' graduation and had everyone in tears, only to have the network decide they wanted five more episodes.[45] The solution that Reeves and Abrams came up with was for Felicity to go back in time in order to give her a chance to choose the other guy in her love triangle. Although many viewers were not fond of this plot device because they felt it broke with the spirit of the show, it was an inspired solution to a problem of what to do with a mere five episodes after the show had essentially ended.

Of course TV networks can be fickle, and Whedon was pitched a few curve balls of his own to deal with. One of these was a WB network decision that called for *Buffy* to concentrate on a series of stand-alone episodes rather than long, complex, multi-episode character arcs. Both Whedon and Abrams became quite adept at bending the genre rules, but Whedon deserves extra credit for initiating this undertaking with *Buffy* from the very beginning. His concept involved horror, relationship drama, humor, and action all in a single series, and although science fiction, humor, and action had already been done in TV series as diverse as *Lost in Space* (1965–1968) and *The Wild, Wild West* (1965–1969), Whedon was also able to take this mutant genre and add elements of musicals, serious drama, and fairy tales—with lengthy, intricate story arcs to make it feel like something beyond just a horror series, all while avoiding the dreaded territory of camp. [46]

Abrams, too, had longer story arcs. *Felicity*, however, never had the extreme mixture of genre conventions that Whedon used to add layering and depth to the narrative, delight fans, and confuse the network. Although this may make *Felicity* seem more overtly realistic, this adherence to principles of realism also, as noted above, hampered the story development. The choice of a university campus—even one in the center of New York City—isolated the characters and forced the drama to relate primarily to the kinds of relationship issues that featured prominently in soap opera and teen dramas. Although the characters were brilliantly written and delicately portrayed, the show in its later seasons suffered from a certain incestuous quality because the choices of action and interaction were limited and thus became repetitive. Two major themes connected to the campus arise: issues that affect the health and well-being of a character or relationship issues in which someone breaks up with someone else to form a new relationship with a different character. At a certain point in his or her college career, a student is done and it is time to leave, and by the fourth year, the whole "Felicity loves Ben; no, she loves Noel; no, she really loves Ben" thread had reached the limit of its possibilities.

Felicity's story arcs are straightforward, in that they follow the developmental process of a young female student growing to adulthood. The first season sets up the premise of the naïve girl who doesn't know what she wants but who sees limitless possibilities and then explores the possibilities of first relationships for Felicity and the other primary characters. In the second season, the focus sharpens and most of the episodes are loosely based on the question of developing values. When does one decide to do what one wants as opposed to what one should? This is prominently featured in Felicity's struggle to decide on a major, in the suffering she and other characters experience in unrequited and unacknowledged attractions, and in the agony of making decisions about when, and for what purposes, it is right to have sex with someone. The third season focuses on intimacy and trust. Ben struggles to believe in an undependable, alcoholic father, and Felicity struggles to trust Ben and vice versa. Molly, a student struggling with addiction and abuse, pushes the envelope in terms of the trust required of roommates, while Sean Blumberg, Ben's roommate, struggles with putting faith in God. These tests of faith help to

Felicity (Keri Russell) with her famously unpopular short haircut from *Felicity*
(1998–2002). *The WB / Photofest © The WB*

establish the characters' fundamental core and segue into the fourth and
final season in which they return to the issue of responsibility as more
mature individuals. The fourth season allows the characters to come to
final decisions about their values and their newly solidified identities and
ties up the multiple story threads in a nice, neat bow.

Buffy's seven seasons also have themes, but the series' genre-blending
made Whedon's job easier in terms of creating innovative arcs because he
had a much larger playing field than Abrams did with *Felicity*. Each
season, Whedon came up with a "Big Bad" antagonist to drive the plot
forward and to provide space and situations through which to explore the
season's theme. The first season of *Buffy* (as is so in all Whedon series)
sets up the characters and establishes the premise and theme for the year.
For *Buffy* the overarching theme is the metaphor of high school as hell.
The twelve episodes of the first season establish the basics of that premise: that adolescence makes everyone feel like geeky outsiders in high
school and that everyone suffers as they attempt to discover who they are
and who they want to be apart from their family and parents. The fight
against the season's nominal Big Bad, an ancient master vampire who

wants to open the portals of hell right under Sunnydale, still allows space for a popular girl to bully Willow, for Buffy to try to shirk her responsibilities, and for the geeky guy to pine for and ultimately save the new girl at school. The set of first season episodes was carefully structured to tell a self-contained story, in case the series was canceled, but also to allow the teen heroine to become empowered, to show the power of a community to solve complicated problems, and to allow the nerdy guy to be heroic. All these remained major themes of *Buffy* through its seven-season run, but later seasons explored them in light of the effects that the characters' growing maturity and personal development had on the decisions and actions they undertook.

The second season, in which the network ordered a full twenty-two episodes rather than just twelve, allowed for greater story depth and complexity and focused on the characters' first romantic relationships with "others"—both other students and, in some cases, other beings. Most of the main characters experience relationships with beings quite dissimilar from themselves, and the metaphor in season 2 is that lovers who at first seem normal and well-adjusted can turn nasty; in fact, they can turn into demons. Xander's big romance turns out to be with a decrepit Peruvian mummy, Willow finds herself in love with a werewolf, and Buffy discovers that the love of her life is a several-hundred-year-old vampire who loses his soul and thus his humanity after their first and essentially only sexual encounter.

The third season deals intensely with a topic already broached in season 2, parents, but focuses on it more intensely, with particular attention to absentee fathers and relationships with father figures. Buffy has to deal with the unreliability of her absent father. At the same time, Buffy's fellow Slayer Faith (a new character) finds herself bonding with Sunnydale's mayor—an apparently gentle soul who represents the caring father she has never had. Unfortunately her new surrogate dad is also the season's Big Bad, who wants to ascend to demonic power and destroy the world by becoming a giant snake. During this same season, Buffy's mentor and Watcher, Mr. Giles, continues to perform the role of Buffy's ersatz father and is in fact fired from the Watchers Council, the organization responsible for overseeing Slayers, for treating Buffy paternally rather than professionally.[47] The third season also begins to deal with mothers in all their complexity, introducing a topic that carries over into seasons 4 and 5.

Season 4 returns to the issues of relationships with "others," this time with the characters as young adults moving into the real world—some to college, some to the world of work—where they no longer have the protection and imprisonment of high school. Season 5 explores a concept of "family" that extends beyond accidental blood relations to include bonded groups. It also considers the realities that these groups change, that people are multisided, and that changes can have major unsettling repercussions. Season 6 investigates the necessity of friends, the need to accept both their darker and lighter sides, and the price we pay for our decisions—especially when we let ourselves and our friends down. Willow, Xander, Buffy, and Spike all, at some point in the sixth season, fail to support their friends and must then come to terms with how to find a road to redemption. The final season explores the power of community to get individuals through the problems of life even after they have let down particular friends and committed heinous acts against them. In the end, season 7 suggests, no matter how badly you have behaved, it is friends both individually and as a group that will get you through the really tough parts of life.

Whedon's use of such themes enables him, in the series and in the individual character arcs, to explore an issue from a variety of perspectives without insisting that there is necessarily a single correct perspective or answer. The season 2 episode "Ted" suggests that the "perfect father"—that is, the dad who does everything the way the 1950s sitcom dads do—may not really be the perfect father, that doing all the things a child might wish a father to do may be creepy and in fact evil if the father in question is merely going through the motions and doesn't really love the child.[48] Later we will see that sometimes the perfect father is not even a blood relative, but a human being with bumps and flaws, one who cares and gives the best advice of which he is capable. This describes Buffy's relationship with Mr. Giles and distinguishes him from in loco parentis figures like Buffy's later Watcher Wesley Wyndham Price, who is told to train and observe but not become emotionally involved with his apprentice. This also describes the relationship between Faith and the soon-to-be-demonic mayor of Sunnydale. Despite the fact that he is inherently evil, Mayor Wilkins is kind, supportive, and concerned about Faith. Whedon gives us a tender and touching relationship even though the things the mayor wants Faith to do are on the wrong side of the justice fence. Because the situations are complicated, there is room for disagree-

Television Buffy (Sarah Michelle Gellar) gets fatherly advice from Mr. Giles (Anthony Stewart Head) in *Buffy the Vampire Slayer* (1997–2003). *UPN / Photofest © UPN*

ment about which is the most salient aspect of a situation, leading fans with varied emotional, ideological, and political views to have equally varied perspectives on what episodes mean and what is the right course of action for the characters.

Realizing that the college show *Felicity* limited issues to personal internal ones, Abrams sought a means to inject more interesting external issues into his next show. He liked his *Felicity* characters, liked the focus on a young woman facing the difficulties of growing up, but wanted the benefit of outside threats that make for exciting television. He told *Seriable.com*'s Roco:

> While we were working on that show, I pitched "what if Felicity were a spy?" and I said it simply because it would answer every problem I have. Because she could go out on crazy missions, she could be in insane chases and fight scenes and be sneaking around, and the stakes would be literally life and death for the world, and she'd come back and no-one would know what she'd been doing and she'd still have the issues of Ben or Noel or whatever we were doing. And everyone looked at me as if I was insane, and I wasn't serious but I was looking for something to make that show [easier] in terms of finding ways to tell stories.[49]

Abrams was fortunate that about this time, ABC/Touchstone was looking for a new show centering on the challenges faced by a young woman, so he pitched the idea about a girl,

> who's a spy and she's in Grad school, because I know you can't in Episode 16 say "and Felicity's a spy," and they said "that sounds great why don't you write it," and so I put the *Run Lola Run* soundtrack on and I listened to it non-stop and wrote the Alias pilot . . . [and] they said "who do you want to direct it?," and I heard myself say "me," and they said "OK," and I thought "they're crazy," and we cast the show with Jennifer Garner who had been on *Felicity*, so it was fun.[50]

In a comparison of the Whedon and Abrams girl-power credentials, therefore, Sydney Bristow of *Alias* (2001–2006) also needs to be taken into account.

Alias's basic premise follows Abrams's original pitch (described above), and the show has the look of a stylish, techno-music-drenched spy film. The sweet and unassuming Sydney is a grad student who hides a secret: that in her free time, she is also a highly trained superspy for the secret intelligence organization SD-6. Early episodes of the show attempt to maintain a sense of reality by showing the difficulties she has in juggling her two jobs, but the narrative quickly turns away from school toward an intricate series of season-long story arcs, motivated by outside political events, in which enemy agents seek to create a network to control the world.

The show is active, fast paced, and filled with elaborate twists and turns. People held to be dead return with ingeniously contrived explanations, and the beginnings of the compelling web-of-mystery technique that Abrams would later employ in *Lost* (2006–2010) are visible in the baroque plotting of the *Alias* narrative. Sydney's estrangement from her father, and loss of her mother and fiancé, provide a good underpinning for her character, but *Alias* lacks the focused emotional themes of either *Buffy* or *Felicity*. Sydney has family issues, and undeniably we feel for her, but at a certain point her family baggage gets to be too much. Her difficulties are out of the ordinary and not the kind that average viewers can identify with. Few of us have been forced into spy training by our fathers at the age of six.[51] Not too many of us are confused about whether to trust our aunt or our mom or our dad or our other aunt, and certainly we don't vacillate wildly between liking and hating them in the course of a few months or years. Sydney's emotional issues finally become secondary (although contributory) to the thriller spy action enveloping her. After all, if you have to choose between saving the world and figuring out if your aunt is crazy, therapy must be put on hold. We watch Sydney, clad in colorful wigs and skintight garments, blow up targets with panache, escape tricky situations, and solve logistical problems, and these activities make us forget about the personal emotional stress of what she is going through.

The plot of *Alias* is complicated and becomes more so with every new episode. Sydney's father, Jack Bristow, is a double or perhaps triple agent and may have killed her mother (in fact at more than one point in the action). Her mother, Laura (aka Irina Derevko), is, or was, a super-spy bent on to destroying the world, or maybe isn't dead, so is (or isn't) one again. Or maybe her father is her boss at SD-6, Arven Sloane. We can identify with Sydney's estrangement from her real (we think) father, Jack; her insecurity with her new boyfriend; her close relationship with her work partner; and her suspicions about her kindly but eerie boss,

**Sydney Bristow (Jennifer Garner) in a typical disguise with Michael (Michael Var-
tan) in** *Alias* **(2001–2006).** *ABC, Inc. / Photofest © ABC, Inc.*

Sloane, but these are unstable situations that recur and repeat in a fugue-
like fashion over the run of the series. The constant resurrections and
relationship shufflings start to become tiresome in the fifth season. As
one disillusioned online reviewer named Kosinus put it, "People seem to
be transferring sides from one moment to another, people die, come back,
are cloned, copied, brainwashed . . . there is no clear story line left . . . or,
if there still is, this show really got me to the point where I gave up trying
to give it a chance."[52] The network announced its cancellation of the
series in November 2005, noting: "When we met Sydney Bristow, she
didn't know who she was. Now, at the end of this season, she may have a
family. It's time for her to move on to the next phase. That's what life is
about."[53] Sydney had been there (and there and there), seen and done it
all, and bought the T-shirt; there just wasn't much else left for her to do.

Sydney and Buffy both have superior strength and skill without having overtly unrealistic powers, and there is a joy in watching a strong,
capable woman in action.[54] With her expensive gowns and wig-of-the-
week hairstyles, however, Sydney rises to the level of female spectacle.
Each week she performs her spy duties in a different color and cut of wig

and an ever more egregiously slinky outfit. While Buffy might also be seen in skimpy outfits, the way she is photographed rarely invites prurience. In fact when a soldier she is about to help on patrol suggests she should change her clothes, Buffy immediately defends her right to wear what she likes for her slaying activities: "Don't worry. I've patrolled in this halter many times," she exclaims.[55] Be it extra-short miniskirts or teensy halter tops, she still wears the clothing of a real high-school- or college-age girl. Sydney, on the other hand, becomes a fantasy woman, dressed in stiletto heels and high-fashion evening gowns that hug her curves, and she crosses over the line from empowered woman to spectacle-object. Abrams's camera dwells on her movement in slow motion as she heads off on assignments, punctuating her walk with slick music, while Whedon's camera never ogles Buffy on behalf of the viewer. Sydney recapitulates the virgin/whore dichotomy with her sweet, naïve college student persona played off against her secret identity as a hyperefficient, gun-toting-assassin—a literal femme fatale. Any kudos Abrams has won for making Felicity a normally clad young woman, he loses in his objectification of Sydney. Buffy, on the other hand, manages to be strong without becoming a sexualized object for the audience.

Although both showrunners are known for their use of the supernatural, Whedon shows skill in making his fantastic worlds feel real and down to earth, while Abrams struggles with how to incorporate it into his early work. Its occasional appearances in *Felicity* are more subtle and always explicable by alternative means—dreams, illnesses, or hysteria—and enhance, rather than undercut, the seriousness of the subtextual message. The famous *Twilight Zone* homage in which Felicity imagines herself a captive in Meghan's mysterious box, with doctors trying to remove her heart, makes us even more sympathetic toward the lovesick characters and their metaphorical desire to have their hearts removed in order to avoid the suffering.[56] In *Alias* the supernatural undercuts the more serious plot material. The death of Francie, Sydney's roommate and best friend, so she can be replaced with a mystically produced clone saddens us, but her murder is played out solely in the context of a thriller.[57] The loss has no emotional effect on Sydney with which we can empathize, for she cannot learn of the death until season's end or else the clone plot makes no sense.[58] The death is used simply for its shock value, to jolt the viewers, and the supernatural element is purely incidental and sometimes silly.

Abrams is certainly not the only one to kill off primary characters in his shows. Whedon is famous for annihilating important figures unexpectedly and to the great dismay of viewers. The effect is always personal. When Buffy's mother dies suddenly, the whole point of the episode is to explore the effect a recent death has on the people left behind. When Tara is shot and killed, it is a key plot point but also a painful experience for characters and audience alike. We see these events through the hearts and eyes of the characters and not just around the characters, and although the supernatural universe allows for the possibility of resurrection, Whedon never uses it frivolously. Buffy is raised from the dead at least twice, and yes, it would be hard to have a series called *Buffy the Vampire Slayer* without the title character, but the point is that Whedon makes room for more interesting narrative developments by returning a confused and now miserable Buffy to Sunnydale from a blissful existence in the afterlife. Such methods represent a crucial part of Whedon's philosophy of giving the audience what it needs instead of what it wants. [59]

Relationships between sons and their mothers are famously a dramatic trademark of Steven Spielberg. Family is naturally also important in Abrams's and Whedon's television shows about young women, but they use parent figures differently from Spielberg as well as from each other. Spielberg tends to focus on younger male characters who have been separated from their mothers and are trying to return to or reunite the family. Whedon's and Abrams's older female characters are struggling with their independence and moving away from parents who misunderstand and alienate them.

Both Barbara Porter (Felicity's mom) and Joyce Summers (Buffy's mom) strive to understand their daughters. Abrams deserves kudos for his very sensitive portrayal of the prickly interactions that can develop in otherwise close mother–daughter relationships. After Felicity impulsively decides to go to the University of New York for school, instead of Stanford, her father is full of his own practical solutions to his perception of her problem, while the mother tends to take Felicity's efforts at independence more personally. We can presume an earlier, closer relationship between the mother and child because their backstory includes a tradition of having Tuesday dinners out together. [60] The Felicity–Barbara story line depicts the kinds of miscommunications that cause pain and rupture in relationships, such as Felicity inadvertently hurting her mother's feelings by clumsily alluding to the great sense of freedom she experiences when she now goes out on a Tuesday night on her own. The dialogue and acting skillfully portray lack of connection as the mother tries to be supportive, exclaiming, "You're feeling the rush of independence. That's wonderful," but also voices the personal hurt she is experiencing: "I didn't know Tuesdays were such a problem for you."[61] For viewers invested in Felicity's narrative, the exchange is doubly painful: she recognizes she has hurt her mother, but Barbara does not grasp the importance this event has for her daughter.

Buffy's mother, likewise, is in the dark about the true nature of Buffy's problems, but Team Whedon's approach is less direct and lays on a healthy dose of irony and humor. It is a truism that teenagers' parents simply do not understand that teenagers' problems feel urgent and that every issue seems like the end of the world, but for Buffy this is literally the case. Her mom tries to ground her at inconvenient times, as when hordes of demons are overrunning the town or when there is about to be an apocalypse that only her daughter will be able to prevent. Whedon heightens the humor, while not undermining our sympathy for the teenage characters, by having Buffy's mother insist that she's read the parenting books and understands these feelings, but the experts insist she must put her foot down. In the second episode Joyce tells her daughter, "The tapes all say I should get used to saying it. No. . . . I know. You have to go out or it'll be the end of the world. Everything is life or death when you're a sixteen-year-old girl."[62] The viewer easily recognizes the teen's exasperated feelings as a personal experience. Although such writing does tend to flatten the mother figure a bit by putting her in the shoes of a typical and thus somewhat superficial mom, she does not remain this naïve throughout the series. She in fact becomes a nuanced and sympathetic character whose death crushes viewers as much as it does Buffy.

Joyce Summers also suffers from other adult failings in her dealings with teens. Team Whedon includes instances, particularly in the early seasons, in which she is so preoccupied with her work and personal life that the she does not listen to her daughter or see the danger Buffy faces even though it appears literally before her eyes. Nor can Joyce see her daughter's point of view when she begins dating Ted, who seems to be the perfect man but by whom Buffy feels (and genuinely is) threatened.[63] Joyce's behavior is always logical and reasonable, but Buffy's viewpoint—shared by the audience—is generally confirmed to be the more accurate viewpoint when all is said and done. She is, after all, the show's hero!

Both mothers become deeper characters over time. In Barbara's case, we learn that she became pregnant with Felicity when she was quite young and her subsequent marriage and motherhood interfered with her professional plans. We will see Barbara casting about for her own independence and seeking the perfect job in real estate, which she then tries (again parent-like) to foist onto Felicity as the answer to her daughter's problems.[64] Sydney's mom in *Alias* is eventually revealed to have had a similar situation and made the opposite choice—not allowing Sydney to interfere with her career as a spy. Sydney, who sees this as a rejection, suffers because of it, suggesting that Team Abrams notes the difficulty for women who get pregnant early but, given our sympathies with Sydney, sees a woman's duty as falling on the side of motherhood.

Joyce's career advancement in *Buffy* also suffers because of her daughter. The Summerses have had to move to Sunnydale because Buffy has been kicked out of school for burning down the gym in an attempt to rid it of vampires. For a while Joyce's efforts to open a gallery keep her preoccupied and unquestioning about Buffy's late-night absences and erratic behavior, but eventually she becomes a three-dimensional character who tries to negotiate the difficulties of single-parenthood and an ex-partner who continually fails her daughter. Joyce is portrayed as a caring individual who becomes aware of the complexities of life in Sunnydale and their effect on Buffy. You cannot almost marry a fiendishly perfect robot who hates your daughter without learning a thing or two, no matter how naïve you are when you start off.[65] Joyce is also relieved of any maternal guilt because the audience recognizes that Buffy's father is not good husband material, that he cheated on Joyce and has let down his daughter many times. When Joyce dies, we are informed he is somewhere in Spain with his new flame and cannot be located.[66]

In *Buffy*, mothers are not always good nor necessarily evil, which helps to make the show feel more realistic. Willow Rosenberg's mother also has difficulties connecting with her daughter and ends up (along with Joyce) supporting a campaign, MOO (Mothers Opposing the Occult), which effectively persecutes her own child.[67] Buffy has a kind of inverse mother in her university professor Maggie Walsh, an authoritarian taskmaster, who turns out to be a mad scientist in the throes of birthing her own Frankenstein monster. Adam, her creation, will become the favorite son against whom Buffy must compete in battle to win her surrogate mom's attention—and, once again, save the world—at the conclusion of season 4. When Spike turns *his* mother into a vampire to save her from a miserable death by tuberculosis, she turns on him—criticizing his timidity and his poetry and saying she could not stand to spend an eternity with him.[68]

Even when mothers turn bad, the writers give them strong and believable motivations to do so. Willow's mom is motivated by what she believes to be the best interests of her daughter (and magic will, later in the series, develop into an addiction for her daughter), and Walsh is a scientist with a professional agenda. Spike's kindly and caring mother turns nasty as a vampire but is redeemed when Spike realizes that it is not she who treated him badly, but the demon that had taken over her body.[69] This kind of experience must strike particularly close to home for anyone who has experienced a relative going through the process of brain damage or Alzheimer's as the disease takes over the personality and body of the loved one. Despite the magical aspect of the show, it is precisely these types of underlying connections with the real that make the series so meaningful to its fans.

The mother seems a bit more problematic in *Alias*. Laura Bristow starts out as a missing figure and fond memory for Sydney, who believes her mom was killed in an accident when she was a child. Laura is a source of estrangement and antagonism between Sydney and her father because Sydney blames him for the accident that caused her mother's death. Later, the antagonism intensifies after Sydney begins to believe that her father had her mother intentionally killed because Laura turns out to have been a Russian spy named Irina Derevko. As is so common in the world of *Alias*, however, Laura turns out to be still alive and maybe—or maybe not—a more loving and trustworthy parent than Sydney's taciturn father, Jack. Both Jack and Laura waver, over the course of the series, between being kind, loving parents and untrustworthy, dispassionate (that is, evil) assassins. What's a girl to do?

The structure of *Alias* is one of doubling. There are two agencies; Sydney, as a double agent, must play two roles; and spies in general live two lives—one public and one secret. Sydney also has two partners (one at each agency) and two aunts (the Derevko sisters), who double her mother. It comes as no surprise, then, that the role of father is also doubled. Jack Bristow, Sydney's biological father (we think) is uncommunicative, hard to read, and himself a double agent. He is reverse-mirrored by the smarmy but somehow likeable Arvin Sloane at the evil agency SD-6. Sloane alternates between angelic protector and evil mastermind with every added twist of the plot (a frequent occurrence given that this is a J. J. Abrams production). Although suspicion is cast upon Jack Bristow many times, in the end it will be he—not Arvin Sloane—who will be the (mostly) good guy, while the majority of women in the series (Sydney's mother, aunts, and archnemesis Anna Espinosa) are revealed as power-hungry manipulators who cannot be trusted. [70]

Biological fathers in *Felicity* and *Buffy* are likewise problematic. Dr. Edward Porter is an unreliable presence in Felicity's life, having developed chronic depression after divorcing Felicity's mother. Buffy's dad is disloyal to her mom and is shown standing Buffy up on her birthday in what we take to be a repeated behavior. Xander Harris's father is a drunk and abusive, and the father of Willow's girlfriend Tara Maclay is a tyrant who maintains that the women in his family are demons who need to be controlled and "protected" from themselves. For Whedon, blood relations are not necessarily good, and family is not necessarily about blood relations. Characters must reach beyond the narrow definitions of the familial and find real connections. Buffy has a good father in Mr. Giles. She just doesn't happen to be related to him.

Rupert Giles is all the things a perfect father should be. He is kind, caring, and of course squeamish about sex and demonstrations of impropriety. He tells the truth at appropriate times, even when it is inconvenient to do so, and is flawed enough that his caring will cause him to act unethically for the greater good. He kills an innocent person to protect his adopted family and prevent a worse evil from being loosed upon the world, having explained earlier that: "I've sworn to protect this sorry world, and sometimes that means saying and doing . . . what other people can't. What they shouldn't have to." [71]

The action Mr. Giles refers to—killing a young physician named Ben to prevent his evil alter ego, a hell-demon named Glory, from taking over the world—is juxtaposed with Buffy's refusal, in the same episode, to kill her magically created sister, Dawn, in order to prevent the apocalypse. [72] It may be that the role of father requires certain distasteful but necessary acts that new father Whedon was reflecting on. On the other hand, it may simply be the creator of the series speaking to his fans about ethical ambiguities he feels they need to consider. Regardless, it is evident from the episode that family consists of the people one chooses to be close to and that perfect fairy-tale fathers cannot exist. The good father, however, (just like the rest of us) keeps striving to overcome his flaws and do the best he can. Although the acting of Ron Rifkin and Victor Garber give Sydney's two fathers in *Alias* gravitas and extreme glamour, they are not intellectually complex. Whedon's Buffy ultimately gives us a more complex and nuanced version of parenthood than Abrams's *Alias*.

Whedon also deserves credit for figuring out how to end a long-running series in a meaningful manner. Abrams's creation of an alternate timeline for the extra five episodes of *Felicity* was inspired but gave rise to unexplained elements in the narrative (such as what happened to Elena, who mysteriously appears in the final episode—after she has supposedly died—without a clear explanation of her presence). Season 7 of *Buffy* returns to earlier themes, but it does so in order to underscore the original messages of the first season. The empowerment of women is featured prominently, as Buffy decides to reject the tradition of a single Slayer, a concept devised and directed by the original male Watchers. She contrives, through Willow's magic, to disperse the Slayer's power to all potential Slayers, thus acknowledging the synergistic power of the group (another of the series' main themes).

Whedon empowers women here without disempowering men. He recognizes that the equally maligned non-macho male has a significant role to play and that the geeks of the world (regardless of gender) rally to contribute to saving the world. Mr. Giles with his good counsel, Xander with his caring, and Andrew, who (like Joss Whedon) tells stories that people need to hear, all play meaningful roles as part of the community necessary to vanquish the evil of the series' final villain, who is simply called the First in reference to original evil. The weak and geeky men end up saving the girl, just as Xander does for Buffy at the end of season 1 when he performs artificial respiration on Buffy to bring her back from the dead and again for Willow in season 5 when he disables Willow's evilness with his love of her as his best friend. Here too, Spike, the long-suffering vampire, is finally able to make good on the promise of his soul by sacrificing himself to the Hellmouth out of love for Buffy and maybe even respect for humanity. Felicity's reunion party and Sydney's home life with her child are both satisfying endings for their respective series but do not constitute the emotional and moral tour de force that Whedon achieves in *Buffy*'s final episode, when all the Slayers and geeks join together to combat evil.

Buffy also takes more risks in its format and story line. By combining stand-alone and arc stories, it is able to have the best of both worlds. Much has been written about Whedon's experimentation with the story format, but two episodes in particular stand out as breaking new ground in TV history. Season 4's "Hush," for example, features a set of villains, "the Gentlemen," who steal everyone's voices, leaving the characters to communicate—and Whedon, known above all for his dialogue, to tell the story—visually rather than aurally.[73] It is a brilliant, and simultaneously poignant, episode that shows Whedon has truly conquered the milieu. Other innovations include his musical episode, "Once More with Feeling," in which a spell forces the gang to sing out their feelings, which they have been hiding over the early part of the season.[74] "Normal Again" may or may not take place in the mind of a feverishly mad person, and "The Body" is deadly serious, looking at the real meaning of death.[75] Abrams's *Twilight Zone*–homage episode is compelling TV, with the characters ending up inside Meghan's mysterious box and struggling with heartbreak, but Whedon's *Buffy* experiments are more daring and edgier and outnumber those by Abrams.

In terms of the contest to fill Spielberg's sneakers, Whedon comes out ahead in fan and critic popularity, working the business in his complex dealings with Fox, innovation, and personal growth as far as directing, writing, and producing. Abrams garners slightly better marks for visual creativity with regard to the look of *Alias*'s world and *Felicity*'s New York and for dealing with a series that is canceled and brought back for five episodes. While both Abrams's and Whedon's writing is exquisite, Whedon has more memorable lines and more biting witticisms in *Buffy*, so he wins the points there, although both deal with weighty subjects in deft and poignant fashion. Felicity and Sydney together are almost but not quite a match for Buffy. The race is neck and neck, but Whedon is ahead five points to Abrams's two. In the long run, both auteurs, still at the beginning of their careers, are already showing their potential brilliance, but Whedon must be judged slightly better at "getting" the girl.

3

WHAT FRESH HELL

Devils, *Angels*, a *Firefly*, *Lost* on a *Joy Ride*

A hero is someone who understands the responsibility that comes with his freedom.—Bob Dylan

Coming off successful series, both Abrams and Whedon had a little more freedom and money to pursue other projects. Both auteurs moved in darker directions with their new shows, which is hardly surprising given the surrounding events of the 1990s and early 2000s. The United States was embroiled in domestic political scandals while capitalism spread in conjunction with the ongoing wars in Afghanistan, Bosnia, and Yugoslavia and bombs went off in Ireland, Buenos Aires, Oklahoma City, and, infamously, Manhattan. Whedon proceeded with a spin-off of *Buffy*, the film-noir-influenced series *Angel* (1999–2004), and then with the sci-fi dystopia *Firefly* (2002–2003). Abrams had one more co-written script produced—*Joy Ride* (2001), a mixed-genre film about a vengeful truck driver pursuing some college students who had pranked him—then turned his focus to television and a mystery/science adventure series about survivors of a plane crash, called *Lost* (2004–2010).

Although *Angel* and *Lost* did not broadcast at the same time, they bear similarities in terms of where their creators were in their careers and what they were doing. Abrams's and Whedon's TV shows became more adult and more philosophical, and even *Joy Ride* felt much more serious in tone than Abrams's earlier films. The new productions were also more strongly flavored with the personalities and worldviews of their creators. The freedom provided by prior success meant being able to explore new topics for television series, but of course, bigger projects also create the possibility of bigger obstacles. Both Whedon and Abrams ran up against limitations, which revealed some of the differences in their attitudes and personalities.

Joy Ride was a low-budget movie co-written by Abrams and Clay Tarver. Costing an estimated $23 million, it did not break even financially in the United States but eventually pulled in some $37 million when overseas receipts were taken into account.[1] The film was ambitious in concept—both a character study and a suspense film, with elements of horror—but the character elements somehow got lost. In their DVD commentary, Abrams and Tarver say that they intended *Joy Ride*, like Steven Spielberg's *Duel*, to show as little as possible of the vengeful truck driver, to keep the viewers riveted and wondering what would happen next.[2] It took the pair about four years to finish the script, and Abrams, who also co-produced the film and hoped to direct, became busy with his television work. Eventually, he had to turn what would have been his first film-directing job over to John Dahl.[3]

The structure *of Joy Ride* is designed to interrogate the way behaviors change with the anonymity made possible by the Internet.[4] Tarver and Abrams hoped to make the viewer complicit in the bad behavior of the college men, who—because they can do so anonymously—pose on the CB radio as a woman and invite a lonely trucker to meet at a hotel. Abrams wanted the audience to laugh about the prank, "so that you as a viewer were as invested and as present and enjoying as much as possible this prank so that when stuff got dark you felt somehow guilty yourself, that you had participated in it and not just observed it."[5] Sadly the film tries to do too many things at once. In not seeing the truck driver, he becomes a monstrous other for whom we cannot really feel compassion. The antiquated CB radios do not remind us of the Internet, and the film ends up being the B horror film with which the writers originally said they would be satisfied.[6]

Joy Ride, despite director Dahl's "American noir" feel (per Abrams DVD commentary) and its horror film tropes, does contain typical Abrams elements. The film centers on questions of identity, relationship issues between estranged brothers, and young adults growing through mistakes. Much of the dialogue between the brothers is nuanced and speaks to how easily we can be persuaded by siblings to do things that we

Brothers Lewis (Steve Zahn) and Fuller (Paul Walker) make the fateful CB transmission to psychotic truck driver Rusty Nail in *Joy Ride* (2001). *Fox-Regency / Photofest © Fox-Regency*

otherwise might not. The film tries to hold on to the mystery by keeping the truck driver a disembodied voice and is an unmistakable homage to Spielberg's *Duel* (1971). It strives for what Abrams calls "a moral center" by asking us to regard how our unconsidered behaviors may affect others. [7] The DVD overplays the film's importance, however, having not only a twenty-nine-minute alternate ending, but "4 new endings in all" according to the box, along with three full sets of commentaries. Still, the film was a pretty decent thriller and it made money and even spawned several sequels, which is pretty much the measure of any horror film's success. Abrams, as co-producer, had the beginning of a minor franchise.

Whedon, meanwhile, was already looking ahead to a franchise by *Buffy*'s second year. Coming off Oscar, Hugo, and Saturn nominations (and an Annie win) for his part in writing *Toy Story*, he had reason to be optimistic. He had started his production company, Mutant Enemy, before *Buffy* aired in 1996 and by 1997 was considering both Willow, Buffy's best friend, and Angel, her vampire lover, as characters who might be able to anchor a spin-off series of their own. [8] Whedon ultimately chose to make *Angel* for several reasons. Willow, although adorable, had not yet found her center in *Buffy*'s second season. David Boreanaz, on the other hand, had shown the versatility of skills needed to anchor a weekly show of his own, and he was popular with fans and quite marketable due to his good looks. Whedon told *Fresh Air*'s David Bianculli,

> I have always been of the opinion that any one of these guys could sustain their own show. I think they're that good. . . . But . . . everyone else was normal, mortal, whereas Angel was kind of a bigger-than-life character. . . . He was gonna have a kind of heat that would certainly make the network interested in making a show about him.[9]

Finally, it had become clear to Whedon there was no longer space for Angel on *Buffy* given the show's dynamics. He could see that the romance between the circa 250-year-old vampire and the teenage Slayer had limitations.[10] As he told Bianculli, it could only "go so far before it became incredibly tired. . . . We knew that there was gonna come a time where there wouldn't be as much of a place for Angel on the show, so it made sense to give him his own."[11] Although the creator/producer appeared to be thinking in terms of the strategy for selling the idea to networks, the choice was really driven by character. For Whedon everything revolved around character.

The producers understood that *Angel* as a show would make an interesting counterpart to the *Buffy* story. Whedon describes the two titular characters as almost opposites.[12] As David Greenwalt, executive producer, director, and writer on *Angel*, explained it, "*Buffy* is about how hard it is to be a woman and *Angel* is about how hard it is to be a man."[13] While that was an obvious starting point, there were other significant differences between the two shows. Whedon was interested in exploring the developments necessary to adulthood, the frustrating details of everyday grownup life as opposed to the teenage relationship angst of the Buffyverse.[14] He therefore created a show about the vampire with a soul, who leaves a doomed relationship with the mortal woman he loves and moves to Los Angeles, where he can devote himself to helping the helpless as a form of redemption for the evil things he did in the past.

Whedon found *Angel* harder to work on than *Buffy* for a variety of reasons. One problem was that he was busy, stretched too far between his old series, his new series, and his plans for a third series, *Firefly*. Interviews at the time stress how tired he was. He told *Bullzeye.com*, "I was so exhausted by what had happened with *Firefly* and with the fifth season of *Angel*, which I worked a lot harder on than I had expected to."[15] It was,

Vampire private detective Angel (David Boreanaz) in his element (nighttime L.A.) from *Angel* (1999–2004). *WB Network / Photofest © WB Network*

however, not simply the increase in the workload. The new shows meant bringing in new people, with all the inevitable friction and human-inter-action issues.[16] Furthermore, whereas *Buffy* was about revenge for the wrongs perpetrated against the young and innocent, *Angel* was about redemption for having done such wrongs. Stacey Abbott points out that "while *Buffy* reflected on the future, *Angel* explored the past and its often painful impact on the present."[17] Part of the problem was that Whedon identified with the *Buffy* character as the one who gets bullied, but An-gel's past was instead as the bully. Whedon and his team had to be able to look at and write the other side, and it didn't come easily.[18] He admitted in the Q and A of his Harvard Humanist Award speech that "I had no idea what to do with this guy."[19] The handsome, sophisticated heroic type was less easy to identify with. "I didn't know how to write him, uh, I had a little bit of trouble with that, because, you know, those were the guys, they would beat me up," but luckily Angel was also dark and brooding and no doubt that made it easier.[20] Between changes in staff, lack of time, and figuring out how to approach these different issues, though, it took a while for the show to find its stride.

Lost came to Abrams and his Bad Robot production company in a completely different fashion and at a much quicker pace. He had founded Bad Robot in 2001 when making *Alias*, but while *Angel* developed as a part of Whedon's own creative process, Abrams was brought in as an outsider and asked to take a quick look by an ABC producer who had proposed a series that he just could not make work the way he wanted. TV executive Lloyd Braun championed the idea of a "Castaway" series for TV and then farmed it out to writer Jeffrey Lieber to produce a script. After months of work, Lieber came up with a "carefully plotted, fact-checked realism" that was somehow unsatisfying and so Braun asked Abrams to look at the script "as a personal favor."[21]

As Alan Sepinwall points out in his hilarious description of the process of getting *Lost* off the ground, Abrams was already overloaded because he was doing another favor for Braun in trying to develop a script for a series called *The Catch* (unrelated to the 2016 series starring Mireille Enos and Peter Krause), but he set that (and other) work aside to take a brief look.[22] Abrams wanted a supernatural element in opposition to Braun's more realistic concept, and only when Damon Lindelof, a potential collaborator "possessing a healthy dose of sci-fi geek cred," was brought in did things click and lead to a brainstormed outline that the two rushed out in the matter of a week.[23] The Studio Powers-That-Be (at this point Disney) loved it, and suddenly they were set to go.[24] The whole production went on what Sepinwall describes as "an absurdly accelerated schedule."[25] Lloyd Braun set Lindelof and Abrams to work at once. "We were shooting this thing in the end of March," says Braun, "and I didn't even call J. J. until January. This whole thing was done in 6 to 8 weeks. Never ever have I heard of anything like it in the TV business."[26] As if Abrams didn't have enough to do, besides working on *The Catch*, he was preparing to direct his first major motion picture, *Mission: Impossible III*. Somehow he managed to give Lindelof and *Lost* the time for imagining an exciting set of characters and a supernatural premise that included the island itself as a character and a mysterious hatch.[27] He did not, however, have time to follow through after his work on the initial pilot.

This means that an examination of *Lost* as part of the Abrams oeuvre must move forward with care. After co-writing and directing the pilot, Abrams maintains that he essentially left the production to work on other things. He did return two years later to co-write the opening episode of season 3 before leaving once again and was involved in giving notes on scripts.[28] He told Tim Molloy, "He and his production company, Bad Robot, lean heavily on the writer-producers who lead their shows day-to-day. But he reserves the right to weigh in, often in unexpected ways."[29] This chapter will therefore focus as much as possible on what can be established as Abrams's actual involvement in the initial creation of the series and on the three episodes for which Abrams wrote. We know that he was busy with his other story children and simply did not have much time to dedicate to *Lost*. Luckily the series fell into competent hands that produced a series that took us on a fantastic ride.

Angel also suffered from middle-child syndrome. Whedon had an older, dearer child in *Buffy* and a younger one, *Firefly*, on the way. He had to put together a new writing team, which did not have the benefit of growing up together, like *Buffy*'s writers. This metaphor of creative works as children comes straight from Whedon. Michael Patrick Sullivan reports he lamented,

> "I have this series and I have this son and between the two of them, one of them is always crying," Joss Whedon started our discussion, referring to his only show currently on the air, *Angel*, and his nearly one-year-old child. "That's not true," he clarified. "My son hardly ever cries, but the series. That's another story."[30]

There were understandable concerns from the writers at *Angel* that the old hands at Buffy might get more of Whedon's attention and time. Additionally the *Buffy* staff were often leaned on for *Angel*'s early material and writing, making the fledgling *Angel* staff feel, as first-season writer Tim Minear put it, "like the red-headed stepchildren."[31] There was disillusionment, but Joss still held his different teams together, managing to write episodes for every season of *Angel* and stay involved with the story lines and polishing of scripts.

Part of solving the problem of too much to do was figuring out how to hire well and then to trust the people with whom he worked. Whedon told Jim Kozak,

> What I would do with *Angel* was more break the story and then take a
> polish pass, as opposed to take the script and completely rework it.
> Because I had David [Greenwalt] at the helm, he could be the guy who
> had to do the all-night frantic version and I could just sort of help.[32]

This was a vital lesson for both Abrams and Whedon at the time. Both
learned what happened when they took on too much, but Whedon deserves credit for managing to stay involved actively in all the projects he
originated and see them through to the bloody end!

Still, on Abrams's side, *Lost* was popular and had a wildly dedicated
fan base. Abrams played a large role in creating a compelling story and
getting the series off the ground. For those few people living on . . . er . . .
another desert island all their lives, who are unfamiliar with the very
complicated story, the premise that co-creators Abrams and Lindelof established for *Lost* is as follows: a group of plane-crash survivors find
themselves stranded on a mysterious island, where something furtive,
threatening, and quite possibly supernatural (don't tell Lloyd Braun) is
afoot. Any attempt to unravel Abrams's contribution from the work of the
other highly talented people who worked on *Lost* can be, at best, hypo-
thetical. Nonetheless, by using the co-written pilot, a second-season-
opening script credited to Lindelof alone, and a third-season-opening
script credited to both Abrams and Lindelof, it is possible to tease out
some information about the types of contributions made by each of the
partners.

The two-part first-season opener directed by Abrams and co-written
with Lindelof is by far the best work on the show. The pacing is magnificent, and there can be no question that the pilots benefitted from the $14
million budget (one of the largest, according to Sepinwall, ever to be
given to a TV pilot at that time), from Larry Fong's fantastic camera
work, and from the skilled editing of Mary Jo Markey. Still, the quality of
the episode comes from more than the expensive effects, the great casting, or fancy cinematography. The writing and direction shine.

One need only compare the opening episodes from the first three
seasons of *Lost* to see that Abrams is a gifted writer and director when he
chooses to concentrate his energies on something. It is possible that the
quality is due to a synergy that occurs from teamwork with Lindelof, for
neither of the other two independently written season openers are quite as
sharp or quite as compelling. Abrams is given more credit by virtue of
having both written and directed the season opener, but putting one's

finger on good direction is quite the art and not something easily done. Part of directing skill involves choosing and trusting one's team, exemplified in the pilot by the choice of Larry Fong as cinematographer and Mary Jo Markey as editor. With their help, Abrams produced a visually gorgeous, furiously paced episode that still provides the necessary space to introduce memorable, clearly defined characters.

Take, for example, the opening seven minutes of the pilot. The audience is so engrossed that it barely notices the passage of time. After an initial shot of an opening eye, Abrams begins with an overhead shot of the main character—Dr. Jack Shepard, a surgeon—regaining consciousness in a forest glade. As he rises and stumbles, we, the viewers, through jerky camera work experience his discombobulation and confusion and then, along with him, watch events unfold that display his heroic qualities.[33] It is completely convincing to watch Shepard move swiftly from one character to the next, taking the lead in tending to the survivors. Immediately he dislodges someone pinned under wreckage, using a tourniquet to stanch the bleeding, and then moves on rapidly and efficiently to calm a pregnant woman who may be having early contractions and to get people away from an engine that will indeed eventually suck in someone careless enough to venture too close. Then we watch him administer mouth-to-mouth resuscitation after sending the unhelpful lifeguard who is botching the job off on a useless errand. This allows him to work in peace but still make the lifeguard feel useful. The viewer is breathless after the first seven minutes as Jack moves mostly from right to left across the screen, intercut with straight-on, forward motion shots and Larry Fong's restless camera work that slowly but repeatedly arcs around characters in order to give a sense of reeling and an adrenaline-charged need to look for ways to provide emergency help.[34] The camera comes to rest only when Jack does, framing him in a triangular window made by wreckage lying on the beach.

The beauty of the sequence, beyond the fact that it is exciting, is that it reveals the characters by the way they behave in this time of stress. Kate's willingness to close up Jack's wound with sewing thread despite her lack of experience with medicine shows us her grit. Boone's lack of expertise in resuscitation, even though he is a lifeguard, will help us see him as a well-intended but inexperienced wealthy slacker. Hurley's inadequate attempts to take care of the pregnant woman, Claire, show us his kindness, his pessimism, and his ineffectuality. After the first seven minutes, the show continues to deliver unforgettable scenes to make memorable characters that we will not confuse with each other: Locke sitting on the beach with an orange peel showing instead of his teeth, drug-addicted musician Charlie's desperate attempt to get a heroin fix before the plane goes down, and loyal wife Rose kissing her husband's ring and insisting that he is still alive although he is nowhere to be found among the survivors on the beach. Sepinwall stresses that what Lindelof and Abrams did in the weeks preparing the pitch was to get the characters down pat, and this shows in the opening sequence.[35] Abrams as director gets his cinematographer and actors to put the characters into sharp focus, and this is the difficult work of a good pilot.

The writing sparkles. In one sequence aboard the plane, our hero Jack responds to the flight attendant asking if his drink is okay. "It wasn't a very strong answer," she remarks after he seems to indicate it is. "It wasn't a very strong drink," comes his reply. This is a set-up to give a reason why he might have alcohol in his pocket for a later scene when Kate sews up his wound.[36] Another example is Jack talking about how one sometimes has to let fear in for just a short time:

> Well, fear's sort of an odd thing. When I was in residency, my first solo procedure was a spinal surgery on a sixteen-year-old kid, a girl. And at the end, after thirteen hours, I was closing her up and I, I accidentally ripped her dural sac. Shredded the base of the spine where all the nerves come together, membrane as thin as tissue. And so it ripped open. And the nerves just spilled out of her like angel hair pasta, spinal fluid flowing out of her and I . . . And the terror was just so . . . crazy. So real. And I knew I had to deal with it. So I just made a choice. I'd let the fear in, let it take over, let it do its thing, but only for five seconds; that's all I was going to give it. So I started to count: one, two, three, four, five. Then it was gone. I went back to work, sewed her up, and she was fine.[37]

This is Abrams at his finest: beautiful narrative writing that reveals a lot about the character.

The episode is written visually too, an area for which the director and cinematographer are usually given credit. The sequence in which Kate takes the shoes of a dead passenger so she can go with the others across rough terrain to test the radio is stirring because as viewers we have a distanced-enough view to contemplate the deadness of the feet from

Kate (Evangeline Lilly) and Jack (Matthew Fox) tend an ailing Charlie (Dominic Monaghan) in *Lost* **(2004–2010).** *ABC, Inc. / Photofest © ABC, Inc.*

which she removes the shoes but are also close enough to see the complex play of emotions that run across her face. These are nuanced to show resolve and discomfort rather than broadly disgusted or emotionally overplayed. Other odd visual elements add lyricism, like a shot of a single shoe lodged in a tree or Locke with the orange peel in his mouth. While any of these elements could have come from someone other than Abrams, the director made the decision to use or emphasize them within the rhythms of the story and these same kinds of elements do not appear in the other season openers.

By comparison, the script of the second-season opener, credited to Lindelof alone, is solid but less memorable. It promotes the story. It works with the philosophical issues grounding Jack, and it contains humor, like the lava lamp in new character Desmond's living area and Hurley's protest that Jack's bedside manner "sucks." Dialogue sequences are terser and more straightforward, but they do not convey the poetry of the pilot.

The episode's pacing is understandably different because it has different goals. Lindelof has no interest in introducing the character of Desmond at the episode's start. We see him only from behind as he goes through his morning routine. Instead his presentation is saved as a way of surprising the viewer with a reveal of a person Jack had met in the States before the infamous plane crash. Lindelof's scenes are longer, frequently containing more characters, so that they do not seem as intimate, and transitions do not flow as smoothly from character to character.

Lindelof's second-season opener is entitled "Man of Science, Man of Faith." The story in flashback to the pre-crash world builds on the emotion of the miraculous. The viewer is shown how one of Jack's patients (his future wife) escapes a life of paralysis thanks to Jack's surgery and her own persistent hope. The dialogue is believable but not as facile, probably because it is designed to emphasize the ideas and philosophical aspects of the characters. When Jack's father tells him to let his patients experience more hope (instead of honestly assessing their survival chances), Jack, the man of science, says curtly: "That's false." The father replies: "Maybe, but it's still hope." One cannot help but wonder if Abrams would have made the conversation zing a bit more, but nonetheless the sparse words get the points across. Still, the filmic impact is not as strong as Charlie's line in the pilot, "How does something like that happen?"[38] The directing works with the writing here because the line is tied to a bird's-eye shot of the foregrounded dead pilot in a tree with the crash survivors made small and ineffectual in the distance.

The initial episode from the third season suggests the power of Abrams's collaborative writing. Bonnie Covel cites Abrams as saying that "writing the first episode [of season 3 with Damon] was just an absolute joy—to get to write those characters again and be inside the heads of those characters."[39] Alas, the DVD commentary on this episode is unrevealing about the amount of work done by each collaborator. Lindelof, who does the commentary, rarely mentions Abrams and makes references to "when I wrote this" almost as if he had penned the entire thing himself.[40] Nonetheless, the episode is very different in character from the season 2 opener, hinting at elements Abrams may have brought to the collaboration. The episode's set-up is that the three main-character survivors—Jack, Kate, and cynical con man Sawyer—have been seized by the shadowy "Others" and are held captive in their camp. The episode makes a good comparison piece to the opening episode of season 2 because it focuses on Jack, but this time on his jealousy and obsessiveness rather than his lack of faith. While season 2 opens with Desmond's morning routine in the hatch viewed from behind so we cannot see his face, season 3 opens with new character Juliet's morning with her in full sight.

The writers and director give Juliet, who is one of the "Others," issues to deal with and highlight her facial reactions. She is trying to cheer herself up and thus we see her looking at herself in the mirror while listening to Petula Clark's rendition of "Downtown."[41] She is having a bad day: she burns her muffins and then her hand and has to deal with esoteric criticism in her book club by members of the most snobby kind. Her book club choice is Stephen King's *Carrie*, which another character, Adam, denounces because there is "no metaphor. It's not even literature. It's science fiction, by-the-numbers religious hokum-pokum!"[42] Adam goes on to insist that the community's leader, Ben, refuses to come to the book club because she has chosen so poorly. This humor, intellectually astute but snide, sounds like Abrams winking at his own geekiness and taste. Abrams's love of weird science/fantasy/horror tales like *The Twilight Zone* (1959–1964) is well known, and doubtless Stephen King also falls into this category.[43]

Other humor that feels like Abrams's touch surfaces later on in a scene about Sawyer, whom the Others have imprisoned in a bear cage. Lindelof's one mention of Abrams's addition to the script is a sarcastic line by

Sawyer to one of his captors that he was hoping for a blow dry.[44] Sawyer finds himself in a B. F. Skinner–inspired bear cage, which contains levers and buttons separated by the length of the cage, and he figures out the not-so-easy combination of levers to pull and buttons to push concurrently in order to be delivered a reward of music and what turns out to be animal food.[45] Tom Friendly, his guard, compliments him warmly, and the dialogue is classic Abrams—snarky and hilarious:

> **Friendly:** Hey, you got a fish biscuit!
> **Sawyer:** Looks like I figured out your complicated gizmo.
> **Friendly:** Ha ha! It only took the bears two hours.
> **Sawyer:** How many of them were there?[46]

The humor seems just a tiny bit smarter and more biting than that in other episodes.

Finally, the way the first season 3 episode ends is markedly different from the season 2 opener. The payoff at the end, rather than being a reveal, focuses instead on making a solid emotional impact. While Kate and Sawyer have had difficulty with the Others, Juliet has seemingly tried to help Jack over the course of the episode. The story hinges on Jack's attempts to face his failure to break his obsession and jealousy vis-à-vis his ex-wife, during which Juliet is portrayed as sympathetic and supportive. Intercut with Jack's story is interaction between Juliet and Ben, the leader of the Others. Ben has been snide and superior to Juliet in response to her fondness for Stephen King, and noticeable tension exists between them. This sets up the ending for greater impact. Ben fails to cajole Kate into submission with his offers of fine food and a dress, while we discover in the final scene that Juliet succeeds in breaking Jack. Juliet's expression at the end of the episode as she "reports" to Ben is complex because she has beaten Ben by getting to her prisoner while he has not. It is also clear from her facial expression that she is not particularly happy with what she has had to do. The opening scene has come full circle as we realize she has done what she needed to do, and her comment, which we felt was supposed to comfort Jack earlier, takes on an added, more sinister meaning in its newfound irony: " It doesn't matter who we were. It only matters who we are now."[47] As viewers, we sense that that is not always a good thing as we shift our focus from this as advice to Jack to understanding it as a self-reflexive statement Juliet pronounces in reference to her moral decline. This is the kind of emotional pathos that was the touchstone in *Felicity*.

This is not to say that Lindelof is undeserving of credit. He and Carlton Cuse deserve more credit than anyone else for the continued success, fascinating complexity, and weird turns of *Lost*. Abrams is careful to stress that when he stepped away from the series to do other things, he left things in capable hands. He told On Demand Entertainment:

> I left work on the show in the first season after I started doing *Mission Impossible 3*. . . . So anytime someone says that they love like the latest episode, I always say, you know, it's what Damon [Lindelof] and Carleton [Cuse] and Jack Bender, it's what they've done. I mean they've really taken this thing that we created into a place. . . . I'm like the audience now; I watch what they do and think, oh my god, like, look where this has gone, because you could never have predicted at the beginning where they've taken it. It really is a testament to the work that they did.[48]

While he may have had little to do with where the series ended up, there is no doubt that Abrams deserves credit for strong writing and contributions to early episodes.

So even though most of the complex, supernatural plot elements were not planned at the series' beginning, we can still give Abrams credit for his work in establishing strong, unique characters; for originating the idea of the locked hatch, a mysterious sign of prior life on the island; and for wanting to make the island itself a character. While *Alias*'s Sydney can be Sydney in Sydney or Melbourne or in any major city, *Lost* can only be *Lost* on this particular island. Place has become a more complex and interesting element in the Abrams oeuvre.

Place is also important in *Angel*. Whedon conceived of Los Angeles as a character in much the way Abrams imagined *Lost*'s island. Whedon's film theory training makes L.A. a natural location for a series that was partially envisaged as a high-concept cross between *Batman* and film noir.[49] While this was not a new idea in the world of graphic novels— Batman had already become the noir-ish Dark Knight in the comic books of Frank Miller in the mid-1980s—it was a new idea for television, coming six years before *Batman Begins* (2005). The setting does not, however, represent growth on the part of Whedon. Sunnydale, a peppy little California town sitting on a hellmouth, was also a vital part of *Buffy*, and moving to the big city simply gave *Angel* other ways to mature. David Fury, a producer, director, and writer for the show, tells us that what differentiates the two is that in L.A., "the evil's more insidious, you know, it's more there, it puts on fancy clothes and talks in big words."[50] Benjamin Jacob, who has analyzed this relationship, also stresses the schizophrenic nature of the city known for the Beach Boys and sunshine (both used in the *Angel* series) as well as being the "place of pain and anonymity, alienation and broken dreams and an almost omniscient darkness."[51]

Angel is also more daring cinematically than other shows of the time. Particularly when Whedon directs, its episodes have the look of a film rather than a TV show. One need only glance at the opening montage of Los Angeles in the first episode ("City Of") to see the meticulousness with which the shots have been captured and edited. A series of overlays creates restless oppositions of movement. A scene that follows gives a prime example of the care taken with shooting and editing.

A series of shots of Angel in a bar keeping an eye out for potential bad guys displays movements of background characters to heighten anxiety. Characters move behind Angel as he speaks, coming alternately from one direction and then the other to create visual tension, while primary characters and the camera work together to complete a clockwise circle around the character of Angel. A second circle is completed when the movement is then picked up by Angel himself, who closes the circle by rising and turning his face and then body clockwise as the camera follows him up and left as he heads toward an exit. The sequence finishes on an up-angled shot of Angel striding powerfully on this path out of the bar. This intentional movement of camera and characters heightens the visual tension in preparation for the confrontation about to occur in the alley. These kinds of shots are rare in television and unlikely on typical TV studio stages, which generally have two cameras filming simultaneously from different directions.[52] *Angel* clearly has greater aesthetic goals than just being a scary TV story.

Whedon also pushes the envelope with regard to the creativity of the premise. Episodes written or inspired by Whedon, such as "Smile Time," "Spin the Bottle," and "Waiting in the Wings," all break with the typical *Angel* format, making us feel that our TV sets are taking us into some kind of Outer Twilight Limits Zone.[53] "Waiting in the Wings" deals with the repercussions of love triangles (of which the episode has no fewer than three).[54] The regular characters get caught in a time warp caused by a nineteenth-century ballet troupe leader who is jealous of his primary dancer's lover. Through magic he forces her and the entire troupe to repeat the exact same performance nightly. As a metaphor for obsession, the episode works beautifully. By its end, the Angel Investigations team resolves not only the dancer's dilemma but also its own triangle of Fred, Wesley, and Gunn, which had been brewing in prior episodes. (Wini)Fred chooses Gunn, and the audience is teased with the possibility of a relationship between Angel and his assistant Cordelia, only to have Cordelia's prior "Prince Charming" show up from another dimension to sweep her off her feet and reconnect a new triangle. The episode stands on its own but also contributes to the season 3 story arc about love and delusion. Whedon giveth with one hand and taketh away with the other, to the delight and agony of his viewers.

"Spin the Bottle" also feels like a step into the Outer Twilight Limits Zone, as the main characters are turned back into teenagers—younger versions of themselves, familiar to faithful viewers from episodes of *Buffy*—by a memory spell gone wrong.[55] Angel, for example, an eighteenth-century teen, neither knows that he is a vampire nor has any understanding of modern conveniences such as cars, which he takes to be big, shiny demons. The episode allowed Whedon to inject much-needed levity into a season that would go on to include an apocalypse brought about by the obstruction of the sun and a season-end disaster involving human race's enslavement and loss of free will at the hands of a needy god.

An even more bizarre and entertaining episode was "Smile Time," which turns Angel into a puppet.[56] Reactions were mixed, but the BBC praised the show as "one of *Angel*'s most inspired and laugh-out-loud episodes," noting, "How such an innovative show can be canceled after producing something like 'Smile Time' is baffling."[57] Amy Pascale notes that Whedon had always wanted to do an evil Muppet story but had been unable to come up with the right gimmick.[58] The story explores the relationships between free will, knowledge, and control, forcing characters to think about how we learn new things and the price we pay for doing so.

The humor notwithstanding, both *Lost* and *Angel* share a serious common theme: that of redemption. The ways the two series deal with the topic underscore differences between their two creators.[59] Whedon told the *New York Times*,

> Redemption has become one of the most important themes in my work and it really did start with *Angel* . . . probably with the episode "Amends," but even with the character itself and the concept of the spin-off was about redemption. It was about addiction and how you get through that and come out the other side, how you redeem yourself from a terrible life. [60]

Angel is not the only one whose terrible life needs to be redeemed.

Jack, Kate, Sawyer, and Locke in *Lost* are also coming off of difficult lives. [61] Jack was originally supposed to be the first victim of the Smoke Monster, but this fate fell instead to the pilot, played by Greg Grunberg, because the producers did not want Abrams to yank the rug out from under the viewers' feet so soon. They feared it would harm the ratings. Had Jack—who was to be played by Michael Keaton—died, the plan was to have Kate take over the role of the primary seeker of redemption. [62] The premise that each character has a reason for not wanting to return to the mainland is important in keeping the action of the show centered on the island, but it also interferes with the characters' search for redemption. They can come to terms with their pasts, but they have no way to interact with the world beyond the island, in which they failed the first time. Thus, they have no way to achieve any kind of fitting restitution. The mechanics of the flashbacks that reveal the characters' pasts work as exposition, but they rarely give these individuals the chance for epiphanies. In other words, it is the audience rather than the characters that seem to experience this past and have the "aha!" moments in *Lost*.

In *Angel* there are also flashbacks to the past (and often very far back in the past), but, because of the magical nature of the show, the characters may quite possibly (like the eighteenth-century vampire Slayer Holtz or the nineteenth-century vampire Penn) show up after many years of absence. The flashbacks may on some occasions be merely explanatory, but on others are shown to be the result of the memory, dreams, or even delusions of the characters or else they lie close to the surface of their memories. When we see Angel's past with his sire (the vampire that turned him and thus serves as a kind of father) and lover Darla in season 2, it is because he is having dreamlike experiences with her. He is being affected by this past and feels confusion in the present, since she had been killed in an earlier episode of *Buffy*. When we see Angel's past again in season 4, it is merged with the hallucinogenic state of another character and thus psychologically potent but not necessarily historically accurate.

This way of reviewing the past thus not only provides moments of revelation for the audience but also affects the behaviors and understandings of the characters rather than simply explaining past motivations. It both expresses and foments change.

Lost has many characters who need redemption, but they do not generally seek it until they are forced to do so. Jack's experiences with his alcoholic father and ex-wife explain his behavior on the island. The portrayal of Angel's past does this too but also leads to change in his actions, thus it goes beyond the explanatory. *Angel*'s crew members are consumed with the unfairness of the existence of evil in the world and constantly seek to atone for things they themselves have done, or contributed to, in the past. They look into themselves for the villainy and beyond themselves for redemption. *Lost*'s figures have exterior enemies, thus their focus is primarily outward. Jack, Kate, Sawyer, and Locke never seem to have a bad conscience about the way they are, while Angel and his team never seem not to.

That said, however, Abrams does not follow his characters through their developments over the years in *Lost*, and so has little opportunity to show them in search of redemption. Angel, on the other hand, is shown— almost from the beginning of the series—unsuccessfully in search of something to ease his conscience. The character of Doyle, who is half-human and half-demon but passing as human, is introduced in the very first episode to suggest to Angel that he can be a do-gooder and save all the people he wants, but there is no redemption if he keeps himself emotionally aloof from the people he is helping and only goes through the motions. Doyle points out if one does not feel one's penance or really care about others, then it does not really matter what one does.

Like other Whedon series, *Angel* has a different theme each season, with the first one establishing Angel's emotional investment in his world, forcing him to interact with others who have lost their faith, and asking what it means to be a hero. Season 1 must therefore assemble a team, and Angel acquires a group of supporters: a vampire Slayer named Faith (who has lost faith and thus lost herself) and Cordelia (both from *Buffy*); a street fighter named Charles Gunn, who must cope with the loss of his sister to the vampires: Angel's half-demon helper Doyle; and Wesley, an ex-Watcher from *Buffy*. All will struggle in the first season with what it means to perform an act of heroism and to what extent such acts can bring redemption.

Season 2 looks at the significance of families, both those we choose and those into which we are born. Whedon brings us some interesting characters: Kate Lockley, a disillusioned, hard-boiled cop who is the daughter of a disillusioned, hard-boiled cop and who returns from season 1, and the horned demon Krevlornswath of the Deathlok Clan from another dimension, the host of a karaoke bar dedicated to peaceful existence between humans and demons. Angel, Gunn, Lorn (for short), and Kate Lockley all find themselves individually exploring the nature of familial bonds. The Angel Investigations team—a chosen family, like Buffy and her circle of friends—undergoes a similar process when Angel deserts them, leaving them to carry on his work without him. Season 3 focuses, much more specifically, on parenthood. Angel confronts his own paternal vampire sire, becomes a father, and is hunted by a vengeance-seeking time traveler named Holtz, whose family he destroyed in the 1700s. Season 4 returns to inner demons as Gunn, Fred, Cordelia, Wesley, and Angel embrace and examine their own dark sides. It ends with a recognition that a world without dark sides is no better than one in which we let our dark sides get the better of us.

The final season reinforces themes from the beginning of season 4 and provides an answer to why heroes keep fighting the good fight. In season 4, Angel explains,

> Nothing in the world is the way it oughta be. It's harsh and cruel, but that's why there's us: champions. Doesn't matter where we come from, what we've done or suffered, or even if we make a difference. We live as though the world were as it should be, to show it what it can be. [63]

He tells this to his son, adding, "You're not a part of that yet. I hope you will be." Although the episode's writing is credited to Steven S. DeKnight, it is hard not to believe this is something Whedon might be thinking about saying to his own son.

Whedon voiced similar sentiments in his script for an earlier episode called "Epiphany." [64] In fact, he referenced this particular line after a screening of his film *Serenity* in Australia: "One of the few times I really got to sort of say exactly what I think about the world was in the second season of *Angel*, when [Angel had] gone all dark . . . and he basically decided . . . 'the world is meaningless. Nothing matters.'" [65] The speech is one that Angel gives Kate Lockley, whom he has just saved from a suicide attempt:

> **Angel:** Well, I guess I kinda worked it out. If there's no great, glorious end to all this, if nothing we do matters . . . then all that matters is what we do. 'Cause that's all there is. What we do. Now. Today. I fought for so long, for redemption, for a reward, and finally just to beat the other guy, but I never got it.
>
> **Kate:** And now you do?
>
> **Angel:** Not all of it. All I wanna do is help. I wanna help because I don't think people should suffer as they do. Because if there's no bigger meaning, then the smallest act of kindness is the greatest thing in the world.[66]

After quoting the exchange, Whedon summarized his belief that "morality comes from the absence of any grander scheme, not from the presence of any grander scheme."[67] This helps to explain the series' open-ended finale, which many fans found unsatisfying. When it is all over, the war has not been won, nor can it ever fully be. The existence of free will—ensured, at the end of season 4, by the defeat of the goddess Jasmine—implies the opportunity to choose between good and evil and the impossibility of doing away with either. Thus the fight will always go on.

Whedon developed a similar theme in the short-lived "space Western" series *Firefly*, which debuted midway through *Angel*'s third season and was canceled the same year. Here, too, Whedon wanted to go dark, but the network interfered constantly.[68] Fox executives insisted that Whedon rewrite the pilot; change the nature of the main character, Captain Malcolm Reynolds; de-emphasize the Western elements; and add more guns and action. Even after he did what they asked, however, Fox scheduled the program in a Friday-night time slot that rarely produced successful shows, aired the episodes out of their intended order, and canceled the show after less than half a season.[69] Amy Pascale writes that Fox told Whedon that Mal Reynolds needed to be more sanguine and that the show should be less dark and have more action and thus more shooting.[70] The incongruities of a jolly captain shooting off his revolver all the time were disturbing, however, and according to Whedon, "[Fox's] insistence that it be less dark made it, on some level, more offensive." He ultimately felt he was being asked to compromise his morality.[71]

Whedon's idea for the series had come from reading about the American South after the Civil War, and he decided to put together a show that dealt with the regular people trying to survive after being on the losing side of a revolution, "not the people who made history, but the people history stepped on—the people for whom every act is the creation of civilization."[72] Taking that viewpoint also made the series—at least in theory—less political because the story was not going to be about the rightness of who lost or won but simply present a view from the other side. Whedon came up with a version of *Stagecoach* (1939) in outer space: nine people on a little transport vehicle who were mostly outsiders to the larger world of civilization.[73] He told Mike Russell that *Firefly* and *Serenity* (a 2005 feature film about the same characters) were

> about how politics affect people personally. And the personal politics are the only politics that really interest me. I'm not going to make this big, didactic polemic—I'm just going to say, "When there are shifts in a planet, those tiny little guys are the ones who are affected. So let's hang out with them, not the Federation heads or the Jedi Council."[74]

In Whedon's hands, however, *Firefly* could not help but be political in the broader sense. Our rebel protagonists in *Firefly* live and seek to survive through illegal activities under the shadow of a corporate government entity called the Alliance. The Alliance would turn out to be more like Jasmine in *Angel*, the goddess who seemed simply to want the happiness of all her worshippers but actually was sucking them of their life blood. The Alliance likewise, no matter how well intentioned, turns out to be willing to torture and oppress a minority to achieve its goals of what it feels is the greatest good for the greatest number. Even "*Stagecoach* in a spaceship," when Whedon did it, had political criticism of government control written all over it.[75]

Despite all its dystopian elements, serious topics, and grim depiction of the government, *Firefly* was a fun series. Despite the grimness of the world, the characters had hope, persistence, and joie de vivre, and Whedon's wit had a splendid stage for display. Short exchanges in the pilot episode, "Serenity," reveal both character and Whedon's famed humor. Zoe Washburne, second-in-command of Mal Reynolds's crew of smugglers on the small transport ship *Serenity*, tells her husband, Hoban "Wash" Washburne, that something is not right. He replies, "Sweetie, we're crooks. If everything was right, we'd be in jail."[76] Another scene

Captain Malcolm "Mal" Reynolds (Nathan Fillion) confronts shipmates Hoban
"Wash" Washburne (Alan Tudyk), Zoe Washburne (Gina Torres), Jayne Cobb
(Adam Baldwin), Inara Serra (Morena Baccarin), and Dr. Simon Tam (Sean Maher) in *Serenity* (2005), the big-screen sequel to the television series *Firefly*
(2002–2003). *Universal / Photofest © Universal Pictures; photographer Sidney Baldwin*

from the same episode provides another classic Whedon line as Wash sits
in *Serenity*'s pilot seat, playing with plastic dinosaurs and giving them
voices the way children do with their toys. "Curse your sudden but inevitable betrayal!"[77] he growls, voicing a plastic Stegosaurus's response to
being attacked by a plastic Tyrannosaurus rex. The T-shirts were printed
and available on eBay before you could say the name of villain "Adelai
Niska," along with versions of the dinosaurs themselves!

Firefly would voice sentiments that approached the serious moments
in *Angel*. "Bushwhacked," for example, deals with the horrors of post-
traumatic stress, while "Safe" broaches the issues of fear of difference
and the human reaction of wanting to oppress it.[78] Although neither of
these episodes was written by Whedon, we know that he was actively
involved in all aspects of the show. He is always the first to give others
credit for their brilliance and hard work but also exasperatedly told Jim
Kozak when they were talking about the role of the TV producer, "Sometimes it's a little dispiriting, when you see, 'Well, Joss had nothing to do

with that.' Well, there's nothing that goes on screen that I have nothing to do with."[79] In an episode written by Whedon called "The Message," we hear a refrain of the need to help others despite surrounding conditions.

> **Tracey:** When you can't run, you crawl. And when you can't crawl, when you can't do that . . .
> **Zoe:** . . . you find someone to carry you.[80]

The episode has Mal and Zoe dealing with a rebel buddy from the past. As with *Angel* and *Buffy* before it, the family one chooses becomes the important thing in one's life and one must keep trying no matter what.

One of the most interesting and serious episodes of *Firefly* is "Objects in Space."[81] Whedon both wrote and directed what would turn out to be the series' finale, and in the DVD commentary, he indicates that the episode represents one of his "favorites that [he] ever shot" because it comes so close to things that he personally believes.[82] While Abrams's *Lost* flirts with all manner of philosophical approaches and philosophers, this episode of *Firefly* focuses on the existentialist worldview taken by French existential thinkers such as Sartre and Camus. The epiphany that Whedon experienced from watching Steven Spielberg's *Close Encounters of the Third Kind* (1977) combined with a friend giving him Sartre's *Nausea* had a major impact on his understanding of his world.[83]

The episode centers on bounty hunter Jubal Early, whose fascinating name was most probably borrowed from a short-tempered Confederate general. The bounty hunter was a character whom Whedon based loosely on *Star Wars*'s character Boba Fett. "Take one extraordinarily strong element, in this case a preternaturally cool, nearly psychic bounty hunter who is able to board their ship from the middle of space," insists Whedon on the DVD commentary, "and mess with the entire crew and see what it has to say about our people when you add that element."[84] Jubal is there to capture River Tam, a preternaturally gifted teenage girl who has been smuggled onto the ship by her older brother, Simon, and traveling with him under Mal's protection. The siblings are fugitives from an Alliance facility where—because of River's brilliance—she was the subject of medical experiments that left her traumatized and mentally unstable (a significant issue, since she appears to have off-the-charts psychic powers).

It is commonly agreed that "Objects in Space" deftly portrays the existential nature of Whedon's worlds.[85] Caroline Preece describes the set-up:

> Both Early and River are outsiders of the group . . . shown in full light when they both listen in to conversations, above or below the ship's meeting place. As much as the show places River in direct contrast to Mal, . . . here she is compared to the enemy, both of them damaged by some past trauma . . . that has somehow heightened their sense of space, matter and the truth of those around them.[86]

This outsiderness is something Whedon describes as aloneness: "Not loneliness, but aloneness, is the most common theme in everything that I feel and do, and hers is so painful."[87] River's acceptance by the group, the episode's main theme, occurs just in time for the network to cancel the series.

Donna Bowman explains the Sartrean nature of the story in a retrospective of the episode.

> The backdrop for this philosoventure is a thought experiment. What would happen to our freedom if someone had the psychic power to discern our true selves? . . . We might decide to *feel* trapped by the existence of such a power, he says, but in actuality we *wouldn't be*— because no matter what message came across those spooky wires, it would still need to be interpreted. It means what you think it means, no more (there's no permanent, eternal, involuntary meaning to a life), but also no less (there's no getting away from the necessity of choosing a meaning moment by moment).[88]

The bounty hunter tries to get at the essence of objects, and in fact to treat people like objects, as he attempts to impose his will upon the things around him. He is unable, however, to get beyond the fact that meaning is an interpretation and that objects in space are beautiful and they have intrinsic meaning, but how we understand that meaning is always an act of interpretation.

Whedon is attracted by the beauty of these objects, he says, precisely because he has no metaphysical plan or expectation of them. To him, the script addressed the pain of being aware of things and their existence, outside of their meaning. Just the very fact of objects in space. That we cannot stop existence and we cannot stop change . . . that we have to accept these things. And again, if we see no grand plan in them, we have to accept them as existing completely on their own and existing totally. [89]

On the other hand, this suggests that we are not limited by the metaphysics of the absolute.

Whedon continues his explanation in terms of a scene in which the camera shoots River as she sees and picks up an object that she perceives to be the branch of a tree. As we cut to the perspective of those around her, we see she is holding a gun.

What makes objects so extraordinary is the fact of them. The very fact of them. It's mindboggling. I believe that whether you have faith or not, to think about consciousness, our ability to understand these things exist and to think about the fact of existence. But what's equally extraordinary, is our ability to, and I use this word specifically in the show, imbue them with meaning. And not just with function . . . [for example] the way River imbues the gun with a different meaning than Early does. [90]

In the sequence in which River holds the gun, it has significantly different meaning to her than it does to those around her who are worried about what she might do with it. This is a phenomenally complex idea to try to get across in a serialized television show, and although he insists there are other ways to enjoy the story, Whedon still undertook this complex narration, which was accepted, comprehended, and embraced by many, many of his fans.

A shot of the planet at the beginning of the show comes back in an image at the end of River playing the children's game jacks as she holds up a multicolored planet-like ball and pauses to experience the object in its function and its pure being as an object in space. Whedon concludes the DVD commentary clarifying that the match shot of the ball, "held up in frame, [is] to really just take a moment to experience it, and feel the connection between it and the ship and the world they're in, and there's no better statement about mankind's fate or quite frankly, the fate of this show." River gives us a chance to sense a rapture with the object, that amazement with the fact that things exist and humans experience them.

Lost is to be lauded for alluding to different approaches to life with its characters named for famous philosophers: the man of rational belief, Jack, facing off against the man of faith, (not well represented by the name) John Locke, and the pilot is perhaps the best writing Abrams has ever done. Whedon, on the other hand, creates an entire universe that echoes an absurd existentialism. It's a hard-fought tie for writing.

Joss Whedon and J. J. Abrams start to show genuine maturity in their work at this point in their careers. Abrams has less material to fall back on as proof, but his growth is apparent in his scripts and his direction and writing for *Lost*. In terms of sheer numbers, by the age of thirty-two, Whedon has directed thirty TV shows compared to Abrams's eight and has written some fifty-one episodes to Abrams's thirty. On the other hand, he has been bested by Abrams in terms of production. At the same age, Abrams has branched out to produce 304 television episodes compared to Whedon's 268. Whedon gets the point for writing and for his innovation in new genres, but Abrams wins the chapter's point for working the business.

Their experience with the television industry no doubt plays a significant role in each man's creative growth. Both reveal maturation by developing works in a new genre and by increasing their abilities to take on multiple complex projects and still turn out stellar work, but Whedon seems to have been more intimately involved in the day-to-day work of television. Whedon wins the points for growth, while Abrams wins for both popularity and profitability. The latter's name became a household word after *Lost*. The contest for visual creativity is a tie. Abrams's opening sequence to *Lost* is visually stunning. Whedon matches him with his noir look and camera expertise on *Angel*. Whedon, however, also shows the desire and ability to stay the course and stick with his shows, even when the Powers That Be turn out to be dark and evil instead of supportive and beneficent. For his determined follow through, Whedon pulls a wild card point. The chapter ends in a 4–4 tie, but of course the contest has only just begun.

4

WHO WE ARE AND WHO WE WILL BE IN *DOLLHOUSE* AND *FRINGE*

Nearly half of the American population is eagerly anticipating the end of the world. This dewy-eyed nihilism provides absolutely no incentive to build a sustainable civilization. Many of these people are lunatics, but they are not the lunatic fringe.—Sam Hall

In comparing these two creators, it would be perfect to be able to compare side by side two similar texts created in a similar time period using similar structures to discuss similar themes. Such a situation would give an opportunity to really explore the differences between the two artists. Luckily, we have precisely that. Before the concluding year of *Lost* (2004–2010), J. J. Abrams jumped into a new science-fiction series, *Fringe* (2008–2013), with Whedon getting his new science-fiction/thriller series *Dollhouse* (2009–2010) off the ground a year later. Both series featured a new conceptual focus on procedural drama, a science-fiction-based story that veered into the fantastic, and strong female characters fighting for their integrity in a mostly male-run corporate world. Furthermore the series had almost identical structures. The protagonists' worlds each included a mad scientist of dubious ethical integrity; a female authority figure who was the forbidding, but also somewhat maternal, director of a massive corporate entity; and an outsider love interest to play a pivotal role in the woman's life but not usurp her power and authority. Each also had a murky and missing father figure, who would later turn up to cause difficulties. Both shows also shared a focus on the theme of the importance of family.

The resemblances between the two series offer a great opportunity to look at where Whedon's and Abrams's individual strengths and weaknesses lie. Of interest are the two as authors and creators, but at the same time, many of the shows' dissimilarities must be credited to the different teams each creator put together to bring the stories to fruition. Series creators are only a part of the final product. Abrams and Whedon get credit because after coming up with the ideas for the show they both, as shown in prior chapters, maintained major influence despite turning much of the writing, production, and direction duties over to carefully chosen others.

To complicate matters, some directors, crew, and artists that were part of these shows crossed over from Whedon series to Abrams ones and vice versa. David Fury, for example, wrote for and served as an executive producer on *Buffy* and *Angel* before becoming executive producer for thirty-five of one hundred episodes of *Fringe* as well as taking on writing duties. Zack Whedon (one of Joss's brothers) was production assistant on *Angel*, wrote for *Dr. Horrible's Sing-Along Blog* (2008), and went on to write a couple of episodes for *Fringe*. David Straiton directed shows not only for *Angel* and *Dollhouse*, but also for Abrams's *Fringe* as well as the Whedon-produced series *Agents of S.H.I.E.L.D.* (2012–).[1] Abrams took a writer's credit on only six of one hundred *Fringe* episodes and Whedon on four of twenty-seven (counting the unaired pilot) of *Dollhouse*, but Whedon also directed three of the episodes he wrote. In *Dollhouse* and *Fringe*, nonetheless, the signature brushstrokes are quite evident, and the two creators' fingerprints lie heavy on the production values, characters, and story lines, which had been worked out fairly extensively in advance of shooting.[2]

A quick look at the characters shows us similarities but also interests peculiar to our individual creators. When we first meet Anna Torv's Olivia Dunham in *Fringe*, she is an emotionally closed but intelligent interagency liaison. The pilot hammers home her persistence and grit as she counters hegemonic turf battles and blatant disrespect. The "special agent in charge of Homeland Security," Phillip Broyles, sees her liaison assignment as government interference and calls her not by her name but, with snide hyper-articulation, "Li-ai-son" or sometimes "Honey." Through her competence and creative thinking, we get to see her make a place for herself in the FBI's "Fringe Division," a very *X-Files*-like FBI subgroup that investigates strange and scientifically unexplainable events.

Dollhouse's Eliza Dushku, on the other hand, is Echo, a mind-wiped "doll" (also called an active). This means that on the surface she lacks Dunham's persistent determination and intellect. She is a blank-minded body, being used by a nefarious corporation for their own profit.[3] Rossum Corporation sends Echo and others like her out on assignments with other people's personalities imprinted into their brains. These jobs vary from being the frivolous plaything of a wealthy "patron" to being an international hostage negotiator or an art thief or even a bodyguard to the rich and famous. The main character's lack of personal agency does not, however, prevent Whedon from making strong political statements about the treatment of women and in fact allows room for the character to develop and grow and eventually to stand up for herself. Over the course of the series, Echo seems to retain minute traces of the imprinted personalities, and she will ultimately develop into a strong, independent woman with both persistence and integrity. Both creators wisely provide their characters with flaws at the beginning of their series and thus with the room for growth that is vital in film and much rarer in series television.

Despite having such disparate premises, *Dollhouse* and *Fringe* share several similarities, the first and most important of which is that they reflect their creators' new artistic maturity. Their themes are intellectually and philosophically complex but well integrated with their action/adventure drama pacing. Both series are extremely well crafted, both in their handling of their central concepts and in their execution of the details. Both focus strongly on themes of identity and memory and their interconnection. The series' narrative twists and turns are kept exciting not only on a visceral and emotional level but also on an intellectual one, as they interweave popular science and current events in order to explore what makes us human beings the individuals that we are. In the long run, character is the primary focus of both shows.

Abrams made several wise changes from structures he used in *Lost*. He improved on the series' comprehensibility, for example, by limiting the number of characters. *Lost*'s forty-eight survivors made keeping straight the mythology and story lines both a delight and a nightmare for us and probably also for the writers. He limited primary figures in *Fringe* to Agent Olivia Dunham; her boss, Philip Broyles; her assistant, Astrid Farnsworth; the Timothy Leary–influenced mad scientist Walter Bishop;

Echo (Eliza Dushku) and mad scientist Topher Brink (Fran Kranz) in the mind-wiping chair from *Dollhouse* (2009–2010). *Fox Television Network / Photofest © Fox Television Network*

and his son, Peter. This magic number of five increases to six with Nina Sharp, executive director of the ominous uber-corporation Massive Dynamic. Two other significant but more minor characters appear in *Fringe*'s initial episode—Dunham's lover and partner, John Scott, and her friend and fellow agent Charlie Francis—but both die early in the series.

The great reduction in cast size, compared to *Lost*, gives room within the episodes for characters to reveal idiosyncrasies and attractive quirks. Each character is imperfect and not immediately likeable, but for viewers who stay the course and pay attention, clues to the origins of those flaws gradually come into view. As with *Lost*, the focus is on looking back at what has shaped each individual. Olivia's emotional reserve and her ability to bluff with a straight face are shown to hide a strong emotional and intuitive underside. Peter's rejection of his father is explained and understandable as we see Walter's erratic behavior and learn Peter has no idea that his father did not work for a toothpaste company. Walter's insanity and anguish are tempered by, well, his insanity and anguish, by having us

Olivia Dunham (Anna Torv) and Peter Bishop (Joshua Jackson) investigate a scientific anomaly in *Fringe* (2008–2013). *Fox Broadcasting Co. / Photofest © Fox Broadcasting Co.; photographer Liane Hentscher*

see the suffering he has experienced in the mental hospital from which he has just been released and by his comical schizophrenic actions—conversing normally one moment and then suddenly calling for a strawberry milkshake or announcing that he has "pissed himself, but just a squirt."[4] His need of a cow, which became a recurring character in the lab, was ingenuous but must have given the prop people nightmares.

Whedon has always been careful about the numbers of characters he utilizes and tends to limit numbers of primary characters particularly in his pilots. Although *Dollhouse* is based on the idea of a brothel giving clients numerous choices, the first episode—"Ghost"—focuses on one doll/active: Echo.[5] Thus at the beginning we have Echo (former student Caroline Farrell); her handler, Boyd Langton; and FBI agent Paul Ballard, who is trying to blow the whistle on an underground (literally) and unknown corporation known as the Dollhouse. Additionally there is the head of the Los Angeles house, Adelle De Witt, and the (yes, another) mad scientist Topher Brink, who does the programming. Two other employees, head of security Laurence Dominic and staff physician Dr. Claire Saunders, bring the number of significant characters to seven. The doll Sierra, whom we see in passing during the episode, and the male doll who shows up with her at episode's end round out the regular cast to nine. This number increases (and at times decreases) over time as the viewer has a chance to get to know and recognize characters. Thus, what the pilots tell us is that Abrams and Whedon have both settled on seven to nine as the right amount of character material an attentive audience can handle at any given time.

The pilots of both series reveal TV writing at its finest. Abrams's *Fringe* pilot may, in fact, be the best thing he has ever written. It is beautifully paced, precisely constructed, and sets up the primary issues and characters for five seasons' worth of shows without seeming artificial or tenuous in the way so many series premieres do before actors have grown into their roles. Abrams knows the problem, indicating to Geoff Boucher that "anytime you go back and look at the very first episode of almost any series there's a charming incongruity to it. . . . It's not the show you've come to know. It's all promise but no clear trajectory."[6] It would seem Abrams is selling himself and co-creators Roberto Orzi and Alex Kurtzman short. Many of the first episode's themes and issues resurface over the next five seasons, and interviews show that Abrams, Orci, and Kurtzman had a very clear idea of the overarching themes that the show would cover, even if they were unclear on the number of episodes they would have to develop them. Kurtzman says,

> We knew that when we went to series we were going to have to reach a certain end point, that end point is very flexible in terms of when we get there. If they let us run for 12 seasons, we'll see it in season 12. If they take us off the air by nine episodes, you'll see it in episode nine.[7]

Episode 1 begins with an eerie incident leading to a familiar Abrams scenario of an airplane in trouble.[8] The opening introduces the frightening and fantastic transformation of people (on this occasion into corpses with flesh melted via scientifically engineered chemical agents) and sets up an *X-Files*-flavored universe for our soon-to-be-introduced FBI characters to inhabit.[9] It then moves immediately to those characters.

In a series of carefully plotted scenes, we see agent Olivia Dunham negotiate her way through the situation, despite the intransigence of hard-ass FBI head Phillip Broyles, institutionalized (and thus certifiably mad) scientist Walter Bishop, and his son, Peter. Naturally she must also overcome the episode's real bad guys. Dunham's talent and resolve allow her to win respect in all quarters. Both Broyles and the younger Bishop begin the show by treating Dunham with the dismissive epithets "Sweetheart" and "Honey," but we are shown how the men begrudgingly come to respect her persistence and intelligence by show's end.

Abrams, who is credited with penning the pilot, focuses simultaneously on character and setting up the vital motives and themes that are integrated throughout the upcoming seasons and that tie into the series' season 5 finale. He provides complex characters with whom the viewer can identify but also raises the topic of love as central. This is made prominent both in terms of Olivia Dunham's efforts to find out what happened to a man she finally realizes she loved, as well as in terms of parenthood, which is highlighted in the broken relationship between Walter and Peter Bishop. Both aspects of love are crucial themes that permeate all five seasons of the show and that are satisfyingly transformed and modulated before being resolved in the series' poignant finale. Abrams and his team succeed in closing the series far more cleanly than was the case with *Lost*. They end with a tidy tying up of the questions of what it means to be in a family, how it feels to be a father, and how connection to others emotionally is what makes us human.

Comparing Whedon's *Dollhouse* pilot to Abrams's *Fringe* pilot is no easy matter because there is no simple one-to-one correspondence. Whedon's original pilot, with which he pitched the show, was unaired, and a second episode had to be written for the dissatisfied network to open the season with after the series was picked up. In an interview with Brian Ford Sullivan, Whedon indicated the network people showed a lack of excitement about the show,

> so we talked about why and why and why and I figured out what they wanted . . . and it was obvious they wanted more of an action feel than a noir feel. What I had done was very sort of dark and moody. And they wanted . . . a first episode that absolutely laid out the structure of the show, which is—Echo is at the Dollhouse, she is imprinted for an engagement, she goes on the engagement, she comes back from the engagement. . . . This is how it works. . . . The first thing I wrote was sort of laying out how that would happen . . . in the next episode. They were like, "No, we want it to happen in [this] episode so people get it from that." And then, you know, upping the action and deciding to . . . change certain events that ultimately made it so that I just junked the other pilot.[10]

To Whedon's credit, he was open to the network ideas, and it made the viewer's entry into the series easier. Later in the interview he adds, "I realized, you know . . . you don't pitch *Buffy* with 'The Body.' You earn that. You pitch it with the premise and then you get to all the stuff that you're really doing it for."[11] On the other hand, he told David Kushner that this was his last TV show because "I'm beginning to wonder how viable the medium of television, as it's run right now, will be a few years down the road."[12] Clearly Whedon was able to listen to the network's advice and make his series more accessible because of it, but doing so hampered the statement he had hoped to make about women's rights—a significant cost for the hoped-for but as-yet-hypothetical audience.[13] Both pilot episodes are quite well written, but each has a unique plot with quite different emphases. The unaired pilot sets up the basis of the themes to be developed over the course of the series' run, while the aired episode adds more network-encouraged action and makes the series' future direction less clear. It additionally explains the complicated set-up for the series, establishing the primary characters and their situations just as a pilot needs to do.

Unfortunately, to introduce Echo's diverse types of assignments, she is given two tasks of different natures, and this cuts the episode into two hard-to-reconcile parts. Although the original script was evenly divided into four acts of similar length, somehow the divisions as filmed do not feel equal.[14] Jill Golick, basing her analysis on an early version of the script, speaks of the genius of the script's structure, noting she understands why Whedon has such a huge fan base.

> Hour-long TV shows are usually 5 or 6 acts. . . . Four acts is pretty unusual. Also unusual is that the *Dollhouse* acts are almost even in length. . . . With only three act breaks to worry about, Whedon doesn't have to force the drama up into unnatural cliffhanging pre-commercial moments. He gets into the story quickly and . . . by eliminating the short final scene or tag, Whedon can play out the real story right to the end, weaving together the final beats of the story with the final emotional moments, rather than playing them in separate scenes.[15]

In theory this is true; however, the first episode simply does not feel balanced.

We begin with a short clip of Echo's original identity before she has had her personality erased. It is such a short segment, however, that we hardly have time to register the strong, willful, and glorious person that was Caroline. We then move to Caroline's new (non)identity, the doll Echo, who is shown on a fabulous date, full of motorcycle racing and partying. We learn that Echo's programmed persona is madly in love with her client, only to watch her be yanked out of the situation by her handler and erased for her next job. The pathos here is similar to what we experience in *Fringe* with Agent Dunham's loss of the lover she has just realized she is in love with, because we see the programmed doll telling her handler that she thinks she has at last met the right man.[16] Both women, who have been marked as emotionally distant types, have stumbled onto something that feels very genuine, only to have it ripped away in the initial quarter of the first episode. This is effective writing. In *Dollhouse*, we feel for Echo as she is being imprinted and we see her hand release the necklace she has been given on her date with Mr. Right, watching it fall to the floor as the Dollhouse steals away her imprinted personality and memories of the evening. It nonetheless feels abrupt to then see her in one (and only one other) imprinted personality for the rest of the episode. We become so engrossed in the kidnapping story that follows that the first scenes involving the mechanics of the Dollhouse seem to jar with the more compelling second part. The character's transformation is necessary for the series set-up and probably could not be done any better given the one-hour format, but it makes an episode with otherwise very tight writing and great pacing feel a bit choppy at times.

Using the metaphor of a ghost, the story revolves around the ways that memory affects us and is, in fact, titled "Ghost." At first we understand this idea as pertaining to the experience of Echo's new character imprint. The personality injected into Echo's head is from a (now dead) hostage negotiator named Eleanor Penn, who herself had been abducted as a child. In order to make the abducted child feel powerless, the kidnapper had told Penn that he was "a ghost, and you can't fight a ghost."[17] Penn went on to become a successful hostage negotiator but one who never got over her abduction as a child. This wound was thus both the source of her strength and her weakness. Echo has been given Penn's personality in order to help negotiate the release of a child who has been abducted from a wealthy client. Penn's imprint comes complete with this mental ghost of her past haunting and driving her.

Whedon skillfully turns the mantra about the ghost around so that by the end of the hour it represents empowerment instead of powerlessness. As Whedon explains, "There are two things that interest me and both are power. Not having it and abusing it."[18] Here we see both as well as the common trope of the apparently weak woman turning the power inequity around. The imprint in Echo's head is metaphorically another form of ghost because the negotiator is deceased, and she, through Echo/Caroline's body, is able to tell the abductor that this time *she* will win because "you can't fight a ghost." The poetic justice in this act of empowerment is the kind that should make viewers jump out of their seats and cheer.

The early reviews of *Dollhouse* were not attuned to the complexity of the writing. Of course part of the critical ambivalence was likely due to the fact that it is hard to identify with a character who has no personality and who changes personalities every episode, and the success of the show depended on the audience buying the change of personality as sincere. Unlike Sydney Bristow in *Alias*, when Echo was on assignment, she was not merely in disguise. She genuinely experienced her new personality, meaning actress Dushku had to create convincing new transformations of personality without the benefit of glitzy costumes and brightly colored hair. In that regard Dushku did well. Her society dame Margaret has different carriage and expression from her blind fundamentalist, Esther Carpenter. Using body language and nuanced expression, her "broken" art thief Taffy shows her insecurity, while the prudish Internet mogul's wife, Rebecca Mynor, is in love but dubious of her husband's successes. The characters had to be different, but the premise also depended on the fact that part of the experience lingers with dolls after the engagement. With each successive imprint, a little bit of the previous personality adhered. Dushku had to make each character different but also connected in a subtle manner.

The show was also hard for many viewers to stomach because of its darkness and because the faults of the supporting characters made them hard to like. As audiences learned their motivations and began to grasp the show's structure, the characters became more interesting and likeable, but Whedon's pilot, even the simpler, faster-paced version created to satisfy the network executives, hit the viewer with a lot—a lot of complexity, a lot of darkness, and a lot of character nuance without sympathetic shading—all right off the bat.

The network banned all mention of the word "prostitution" on the show, but doing so did not destroy all opportunities for the series to interrogate the oppressiveness of prostitution. Whedon, in his sneaky way, still managed to raise the issue on several occasions. "Stage Fright," for example, considerers how we allow ourselves to be easily bought and sold.[19] The episode explicitly remarks on the way we repackage and market our media stars in order to make money and fame at the cost of identity. The main guest character, a singing superstar named Rayna, begins her stage performance inside a large cage, singing about how everyone thinks they know her because she is a superstar and in front of the public so much. She tells Echo, who has been hired as a bodyguard: "I don't exist. I'm not a real person. I'm everybody's fantasy. God help me if I try not to be. I know you weren't grown in a lab, but I was."[20] The irony of this statement is that she says this to a doll, a Rossum Corporation lab rat, who like herself has been repackaged, remade, and marketed for money. Living the dream results in misery that causes the singer to seek her own death at the hands of a psychotic fan. The point is that we are all dolls in a way, all manipulable by the ways our socially constructed fantasies tell us what a lover will find sexy or what friends or employers will think of us based on what we wear or eat or own.

We also see prostitution in other forms. In season 2, for example, we meet Senator Perrin's wife, who is working with the Dollhouse's parent corporation, Rossum. She loathes her husband physically and emotionally and marries him to advance her own aspirations for political power. Because the senator is actually an active, a doll programmed to give Rossum Corporation more control over the world, Cindy Perrin believes she will soon be erasing the senator's mind, so she hurtfully tells him outright, "I can't stand you. Having to be your wife, letting you touch me, pretending that it doesn't disgust me, it doesn't bore me, that has been really hard." This character, who has clearly sold her body for wealth and power, is coded as thoroughly negative. She is mean-spirited and willing to kill to advance her ambitions. The worst prostitutes are those who voluntarily join the power structure and abuse those who have less choice in the matter. We find a wide spectrum of volition with regard to how people end up selling their bodies, and with this comes a wide variety of culpability. Harry Lennix, who played Echo's handler, Boyd Langton, says as much in the DVD featurette "A Private Engagement," when he suggests, "I think we're all in a Dollhouse,"[21] and Topher Brink would have driven the point home if Whedon's original pilot had ever aired: "You wear the tie because it never occurred to you not to. You eat eggs in the morning but never at night. You feel excitement and companionship when rich men you've never met put a ball through a net. . . . Your stomach rumbles every time you drive by a big golden arch, even if you weren't hungry before. Everybody's programmed."[22] The show that made it onto the airwaves may not have been exactly what Whedon intended, but if one scratches the surface, the original intent can still be found.

The *Fringe* pilot also got mixed reviews from critics for a variety of reasons including its lack of restraint, its extraneous flashlight use, and its bad science.[23] Criticism of the science in these shows, however, seems a little unfair. Admittedly *Fringe*'s opening credits highlight science. In capital letters, imposing scientific fields float from the foreground into the distance, highlighting areas like cellular rejuvenation, clonal transplantation, neural partitioning, quantum entanglement, all of which are entirely real fields of science.[24] These titles are accompanied, however, by mysterious *X-Files*–influenced piano arpeggios (composed by Abrams) and other scientific-sounding words floating past that refer to less-accepted areas like astral projection, pyrokinesis, teleportation, cryotozoology, and retrocognition. These wonderfully scientific-sounding areas would not be accepted as genuine fields by the majority of scientists and should signal to viewers with a scientific bent that there is a strong dose of the fantastic in the mix.

If that isn't warning enough, then the pilot's initial sequence should clearly announce that this is not *The X-Files*, where an alternative, rationally acceptable explanation will most always be available, albeit wrong. Already in the show's first minutes, people on an airplane are turned into mushy cell masses by an airborne substance within a matter of seconds. In the second episode, a pregnancy develops from fetus to full-grown man in hours without benefit of sustenance, breaking (among other things) the laws of thermodynamics. No matter what cable pseudo-science reality shows might suggest, the kinds of events taking place on *Fringe* are imaginary. The show takes on topical issues, but it is interested less in reality than in playing with ideas.

Dollhouse, likewise, toys with providing a scientific basis for its scenarios. Whedon admits indirectly to doing research on neuroscience for the show to improve the plausibility of the premise. He told Alan Sepinwall from the *Star-Ledger*, "What's exciting is finding out stuff about how the brain works and realizing anything is possible, and there's a reason for it. That stuff is exciting: that we're so close to science with our science fiction."[25] This indicates that the show's emphasis was not on scientific accuracy but on science fiction. For this reason, it is only fair to accept the parameters set by the creators for the events in their series. There is no presumption of reality. Science is fantasized about in order to provide an opportunity to play with the larger implications socially and personally. This is not a case of TV's Batman just happening to have a can of shark repellent in his utility belt when he unexpectedly gets thrown into shark-infested waters. Both creators define the parameters of what is possible within their science-fictional worlds early on, and then they pretty much stick by their prescribed rules.

Science fiction in these series is thus clearly not about looking at the realistic implications of science. While horror might tend to hit us more personally, since its intent is to horrify or scare the viewer, science fiction is generally much more about what might happen with unusual scientific developments within our society. It is about the values and attitudes generally of groups of people. Whedon and Abrams's shared love of mixing the two will be explored more thoroughly in the chapter on *Super 8* (2011) and *The Cabin in the Woods* (2012), but basically, with science fiction, while we fear for the characters personally because of the threat of the horrible, we also—and perhaps more importantly—think deeply about the implications of social changes related to the science. It is the mixture of these two effects added to the puzzles of the police procedural that gives both series a freshness not seen since *The X-Files*.

Looking specifically at the episodes written by Abrams and Whedon for *Fringe* and *Dollhouse* respectively, it is reasonable to ask what they achieve. What can we clearly credit the series creators with, and how do they stand in relation to one another? It is not surprising that the characters in both shows are fascinating and anchor the center of the series. Both creators have already shown their ability to create mesmerizing personalities in *Felicity*, *Lost*, *Buffy*, and *Angel*. In the case of the new series, however, it is the relationship between the characters and the situations that shows growth and difference on the part of the creators.

Abrams has sharpened the significance of location. *Felicity* suffered from the limitations of being set in and around a college in New York City, but using the entire world as a backdrop for *Alias* did not really deepen the nature of the stories that Abrams could tell. If anything the constantly changing worldwide locations and chic clothing emphasized the inconsequentiality of the environment with regard to events in the story. Whether Sydney was in Berlin, Kandahar, Sovogda, Mexico City, or Paris didn't really matter. The locations were trendy and exciting but interchangeable. We were focused on the activity and not the significance of the environment. We learned that villains hung out in exclusive night-clubs and that we should fear parking garages no matter what famous city they were to be found in.

Lost was limited to some extent by the island on which everyone was stranded. Like some kind of gothic mystery house, however, Abrams imbued it with a sense of claustrophobia and then expanded it with secret tunnels through not only space but time. Although most of the action occurred on the island, new areas opened up as the writers wrote in newly discovered trap doors to a mysterious lab or an unsuspected other village on the island. Later they would get even more creative and fold the time line of events back onto itself in flashback and flash-forward segments, so actions in the past and future on the mainland were also allowed. This was effective but frequently confusing given the large cast of characters and the constant shifting of relationships. In *Fringe*, Abrams kept it smaller and realer. He learned his lessons and did better.

While the home base of the main characters in *Fringe* is Boston, there is enough space and diversity of location to give them a variety of environments to inhabit and by which to be affected. Settings like the corporate headquarters of Massive Dynamic, Walter Bishop's antiquated Harvard lab, and FBI headquarters are important elements of the story, affecting the way the viewer "reads" the characters and feels about the situations. The parallel universe introduced in later seasons allowed for additional environments that included alternate versions of characters, showing how changes in characters' histories, situations, and environments can have a direct effect and connection to who they are.[26] This makes the story easier for the audience to keep straight, making it more believable, and thereby creates a greater impact on the viewer.

Whedon's locations for *Dollhouse*, in contrast, became more variable than in *Angel*. Both series take place in Los Angeles, but *Angel*'s Los Angeles is decidedly noir-ish, with the events taking place either in the detective's historic hotel residence or in the L.A. night outside. The Los Angeles of *Dollhouse* conversely is more varied and attuned to its wider spectrum of characters. The primary set, the Dollhouse itself, is made clean and elegant as a place representative of the Zen-like empty minded state of the dolls. The space is open and sparsely fitted, with soothing colors. The locations to which the actives are sent—unlike the settings of Sydney's missions in *Alias*—are not anonymous, chic discotheques and clubs emphasizing "cool" but environments that reflect the actives' new personalities. Echo, imprinted as Rebecca Mynor, for example, is brought to a brand-new suburban home befitting her flowered shift and prim personality. Eliza Dushku plays a literal version of blind Faith when, as a sightless, hyper-religious true believer, she goes to investigate a David Koresh–like cult leader in a bone-dry landscape with a colorless housing compound. Likewise, wealthy socialite Margaret Bashford's estate sets the tone for her difficulties with her heirs and helps explain and define the nature of Echo's hoity-toity imprint.

One major difference between the two writers is the tone of their writing. In the six episodes that Abrams wrote for *Fringe*, there is unmistakable emphasis on terror and the revulsion of the monstrous. As Kurtzman tells it, "JJ loves Cronenberg. He loves *The Fly* and loves, those kind of . . . where medical science or something like that goes just slightly wrong and becomes kind of horror." Five of the six episodes written by Abrams contain disturbing transformations reminiscent of those that—

through films like *Scanners* (1981), *Videodrome* (1983), and *The Fly* (1986)—became David Cronenberg's cinematic trademark. The pilot episode shows the planeload of people having the flesh melted off their bodies by an airborne contagion. Abrams's second episode, "The Same Old Story," shows us a baby (and later man) with a progeria-like illness, who develops and dies of old age within a space of hours.[27] In the last episode credited to Abrams, "A New Day in the Old Town," alien visitors crush their own skull bones so that they can plug themselves into people and transform into the shape of their victims. Each show has a high yecch factor; no less so Abrams's other two episodes, which have actual slimy, icky monsters.[28] "Bound" features a highly enlarged cold virus that suffocates its hosts and comes wiggling out of their mouths before skittering off like the monster from *Alien*.[29] "In Which We Meet Mr. Jones" includes a disturbing parasite that locks around a victim's heart and sends out tendrils.[30] Only "The Arrival" steers clear of monstrous transformation.[31]

Dollhouse is, likewise, a step forward for Whedon. His past series always allowed an easy out when necessary in terms of plot inconsistencies or character development because of the existence of magic or futuristic science. *Dollhouse*, however, sticks close to the present and thus moves more cautiously in terms of the plot. Whedon's signature humor pervades his episodes but without going over the edge. In the last episode Whedon wrote for the series, the head of security is shown speaking with Adelle DeWitt—the Dollhouse's director—about an upcoming assignment that concerns him. After much discussion he concludes, "But this engagement, honestly, this one's sick." Cut to classical music as Echo as bride is shown traipsing to the altar of the perfect fantasy wedding.[32] Elsewhere in the episode, the security chief mentions one of the Dollhouse's stranger customers: a client who wants to be dipped in eggs and flour. DeWitt's dry response is pure Whedon, "Ah Tempura Joe, such a lonely soul."[33]

Abrams's humor is also very funny and often depends on the interjection of the unexpected. Mad scientist Walter Bishop of *Fringe*, for example, suddenly switches from discussions of a deadly disease to his desire for a root-beer float. Or we see a cow being led into the lab: part of a list of "necessary equipment" he reeled off in an earlier scene. By comparison, however, the edge goes to Whedon, who sets up the situation, perfects the right moment, and then lets fly a zinger that sends it out of the ballpark.

Decisions about how to handle the mad scientist characters are a perfect example of the differences in the way Whedon and Abrams work. In both *Fringe* and *Dollhouse*, scientist characters have worked for large corporations that expect them to put ethical issues aside, but each represents a different way of looking at the relationship between morals and science. Abrams chooses Walter Bishop, an old burnout from the sixties, and by doing so looks back with nostalgia to the days of *Twilight Zone* and monster movies. Bishop's son, Peter, even comments in episode 1, "So you're telling me, what? My father was Dr. Frankenstein?" Walter is well aware of the nightmares that scientists have wrought by ignoring the larger ethical picture. This theme is explicitly raised in season 2 when scientist Carla Warren, in 1958, cites the words of J. Robert Oppenheimer on seeing the first atomic explosion—"I am become Death, the Destroyer of Worlds"—and (echoing *Frankenstein*) insists that some things are not theirs to tamper with.[34] The final *Fringe* episode also references the 1964 campaign commercial for Lyndon Johnson in which the voice of a child counting the petals on a daisy echoes a countdown to a nuclear explosion that we see reflected in her eye. In *Fringe*, we have seen Olivia and Peter's child in a park full of dandelions on several occasions to hint at the happiness of family life. She blows away the seeds (a motion reminiscent of the wave of energy released by a nuclear explosion) just before being captured and taken away by the ominous, bald-headed Observers who periodically appear unobtrusively in the series.[35] Director Joel Wyman further hints at the familial devastation by upping the brightness of the shot of the seed head being blown away to make it resemble a nuclear blast. For anyone familiar with the Johnson advertisement, the connection is clear.

Whedon chooses to look forward rather than back, making his mad scientist a precocious geek. Topher Brink, the Dollhouse's resident scientist, has no fully developed sense of ethics and clearly speaks to what Whedon perceives as the missing ethical framework of present-day science. He is less sanguine about possible resolution of problems brought on by science being rectified by it. In the episode "Man on the Street," a person interviewed on the street relates:

> Imagine this technology being used. Now imagine it being used on
> you. Everything you believe, gone. Everyone you love, strangers, may-
> be enemies. Every part of you that makes you more than a walking
> cluster of neurons dissolved—at someone else's whim. If that technol-
> ogy exists, it'll be used, it'll be abused, it'll be global. And we will be
> over. As a species, we will cease to matter. I don't know, maybe we
> should.[36]

Eventually Brink will recognize the questionable morality of what he
does, and it will eat away at his sanity until he is barely able to function.

Whedon's episodes also return some of the feminist perspective of the
series minimized by Fox's marketing department out of concern over
offending people with the mention of prostitution. By putting words in
interviews of people on the street, Whedon can remind us in "Man on the
Street" of the extent to which corporations involve us in prostitution,
either as salable objects or eager purchasers of unrealistic dreams.[37] Most
of his episodes deal directly with the abuse of power when women are
objectified for body work. In "Man on the Street," for example, Agent
Ballard is abusive to Mellie, a doll programmed to keep an eye on his
Dollhouse investigation, and in "Vows," we learn of the rape of one of
the actives by her handler, the person who is supposed to protect her.[38] In
no sense can we agree with a woman interviewed who thinks being a doll
would be a great opportunity because "so, being a doll, you do whatever.
And you don't got to remember nothing. Or study. Or pay rent. And you
just party with rich people all the time? Where's the dotted line?"[39] We
are reminded by another person on the street that this is slavery: "There's
one thing people always needs is slaves."[40] Money has corrupted science
within a structure that allows for the abuse of people in general and
women in particular.

The final episode of *Dollhouse* springs forward in time into a dystopian future created by scientists who have not considered the implications
of their science. Most of the population has been remotely wiped and runs
wild in the streets. The idea of trying to correct science through science is
represented by a gang of revolutionary "Tech-heads," who (like the Observers in *Fringe* a few years later) voluntarily jettison the emotional
parts of their brains in order to fit themselves with up-to-date technology
in an attempt to combat those that now run the post-apocalyptic world of
L.A. Viewers are moved to reject this option. They see the precious
relationship and family of Sierra and Tony destroyed by his emotional

loss in becoming a Tech-head because the new technology takes up the space in his brain reserved for his emotional connections to them. This same devastation occurs in the brains of *Fringe*'s highly evolved Observers as they discard emotion to give the brain more room for rational and analytic ability. For both shows, the solution to the woes of inhumanity is more humanity, not less of it.

As a final point of comparison, both series conclude by emphasizing that the locus of humanity is the family. The primary arcs of both series end with families torn asunder by heartless governmental uber-structures that must be brought down by the action of united family units. Abrams's production emphasizes the optimistic possibilities but also indicates the sacrifice that must be made by parents for the sake of the next generation. Abrams's team will have the father voluntarily sacrifice himself for his children, not once but twice, in the final episode. In order to save the future, a special boy must be taken back to the past. A character from the future named Donald will die in preparation for taking his son back to the past in order to preserve human life, and our scientist Walter will decide to take Donald's place at the price of extinguishing all memory of him for everyone in his own present, including his son and family. Walter's sacrifice thus compensates for his own history of poor fathering, and he is able to make it up to his progeny by ensuring them a future even though they will have no memory of him.

Whedon stresses the problems of absent fathers but is less forgiving. Sacrifice and absence cannot serve as restitution for those who have committed ethical transgressions. They must instead turn over a new leaf, and it is the younger generation of scientists that ends up making the sacrifices. Both physician Claire Saunders and scientist Topher Brink will lose their minds over the ethical transgressions of the Dollhouse. Saunders, as an outsider, will sacrifice herself for the well-being of the others in a true act of altruism. Brink—not only the doll programmer, but the father of Dollhouse technology—also sacrifices himself but in penance for the harm he has inflicted upon others. A makeshift family of those humans left behind will be the ones who must carry on in a ruined world of mind-wiped humans and Tech-heads—albeit in a world made better by the sacrifices of the scientists, who will be able at least to disable the technology used to wipe the minds of the human public.

Lost, *Fringe*, and *Dollhouse* demonstrate that Abrams and Whedon used very similar themes, and even very similar solutions, in their explorations of dark, dystopic worlds. The series examine fears about the dangers of science gone wild and concerns about what older generations do to those that follow. They suggest that the family is the best source of protection and that an overly rational approach threatens to erode emotional health and well-being, traits that are valued as an important source of familial strength. Whedon introduces children only in the final episode of *Dollhouse*, where they are seen as the victims of their father's embrace of technology. Abrams uses children more consistently, using a younger, divorce-torn version of Walt in multiple episodes of *Lost* and including flashbacks of a youthful Peter—along with a significant character arc for Peter's daughter, Etta—in *Fringe*. The less-prevalent role of children is consistent with Whedon's emphasis on people choosing their own family groupings as they get older, while Abrams (like Spielberg) is more prone to manipulating sentiment by showing the emotional effects of trauma on children within families.

Abrams gets a Spielberg point for the greater popularity of *Fringe*, a long-running, successful series with a techno-dystopic edge. *Fringe* also wins him the points for working the business and for profitability. Both creators' writing here favors the humanitarian heart over science, but Whedon's carefully paced humor and fine sense of nuance and irony lend him the points in the innovation and in the writing areas. His frustrations with the studio and maturation in learning how to play nicely with those with power also earn him the personal growth point. Both men show fascination with the darkness of horror and dystopia, but Abrams succeeds in creating visible, truly disquieting horror, and thus he takes the point for visual creativity. In the end Abrams takes the lead with four points to Whedon's three.

5

TV OR NOT TV

No Success Like Failure

Our great weakness lies in giving up. The most certain way to succeed is always to try just one more time.—Thomas Edison

Coming off a series of remarkable successes, both Whedon and Abrams suddenly found themselves at loose ends. After 2004, *Buffy* was over, *Firefly* and *Angel* were canceled, and Whedon took a break from television. Abrams, likewise, went through a dry spell. He kept pitching series, but somehow they withered and died instead of creating the sensations he had achieved with earlier shows such as *Felicity*, *Alias*, and *Lost*. David Lavery, in his book *Joss Whedon: A Creative Portrait*, uses Howard Gruber's work on creativity to help understand Whedon's creative development. He argues that creative people follow many directions in terms of creativity and that, metaphorically, when some doors close, other (usually quite different) ones open; that (citing Gruber) the end of a project might effect "such a change in the focus of attention from the newly achieved pinnacle to the next morass."[1] This applies equally to Whedon and Abrams. At this point in their lives, both creators had reached one of those pinnacles and now found themselves deeply embroiled in the new morass. One thing that defines both Abrams and Whedon as creators is their resilience in the face of failure, and this chapter examines a variety of failed undertakings, across a spectrum of media, from 2004 to the present.

Firefly was probably one of the biggest disappointments of Whedon's career, but he had already started exploring other opportunities long before the series' cancellation. One new avenue for him was comic books. Starting in 1998, he premiered his *Buffy the Vampire Slayer* comics with Dark Horse, an Oregon-based manga and comic-book publisher. Whedon and some of the series' writers provided the comic with stories interstitial to the events taking place on the TV show. The *Buffy* comics ended up exploring many different aspects and time periods of the Buffyverse, from the life of the original Slayer years earlier to the future of Slayers hundreds of years later, and eventually this led to a new comic series called *Fray* (2001–2003).

Fray (named after its main character: street-wise young woman Melaka Fray) took place far in the future when Slayers had long been forgotten, although the world was still in need of them. Fray would, to her own surprise, turn out to be one of the chosen. Whedon had been a big fan of comic books ever since his father brought some home for research in the anticipation of writing for comic-book-character segments on *The Electric Company*.[2] In his foreword to *Fray,* Whedon writes about his dreams and ambitions to someday do a comic book and their fulmination at a time when "I was near death from too much creating, [so] I decided I needed to fulfill my childhood dream of writing a book on top of everything else."[3] And so he did.

Fray was a different world than he had described before but had most of the trademark Whedon elements. "My visions of the future," he notes in the foreword, "are always pretty much the standard issue: The rich get richer, the poor get poorer, and there are flying cars."[4] These motives are repeated in many of his works (okay, maybe not the flying cars), but he also detailed the elements that recur to audiences' great delight: "Keeping it simple. Slayer. Family. Strength."[5] These themes are at the center of *Buffy*, of *Angel*, and, of course, of *Fray*.

Whedon wanted to produce a series that was inflected with his feminism, and he indicates that he told Dark Horse he had one requirement for the book:

> No cheesecake, no giant silicone hooters, no standing with her butt out in that bizarrely uncomfortable soft-core pose so many artists favor. None of those outfits that casually—and constantly—reveal portions of thong. I wanted a real girl, with real posture, a slight figure . . . and most of all a distinctive face.[6]

He seems to have achieved that goal, although the result was still not perfect. The opening image of Melaka Fray is an upward "shot" of her squatting (knees spread) on the top of a skyscraper with the pointed corner of a building blocking her crotch. The lines of the building in the foreground thus point relentlessly and phallically at this part of her anatomy, which is centered in the drawing and thus the visual focal point. Fray may not be giant-breasted, but the blowing of her blouse on this splash page creates the sense of a gigantic bosom that just might come into view with a little more updraft. Likewise, the first image after the prologue to chapter 1 is a full two-page image that shows Fray falling from a building: sailing through the air on her back, legs splayed, with her crotch fully and prominently visible and a large male hand reaching out toward that same central focal point.

Admittedly, the rest of the series is more careful about Fray's positioning, and these types of images do not recur. The series ends with a return to the top of the skyscraper. Fray once again squats atop the building, but this time we see her from the side, her knees closer together. She sits before sunset skies holding an ax, victorious and no longer the sexualized object of the opening frame. The change certainly reflects a change in empowerment, but it seems unlikely this was a conscious theme in the first panels. More likely, someone (perhaps Whedon himself) caught the character's earlier sexualization and asked for a change. For the most part, though, Whedon got everything he stipulated for Fray and proved himself in this very different medium.

The writing itself is pure Whedon. The themes are there: the way the unempowered are taken advantage of in a dystopian world; the strong young woman, rough around the edges, fighting to put things right; the importance of family and chosen friends; and even the killing of a beloved character. The comic takes place in an appropriately apocalyptic future and focuses on family in terms of Fray's relationship to her sister and to a young one-armed child with cataracts, who is close to Fray and who will be bullied and eventually killed before the story's finale. These kinds of relationships will seem familiar to those who are fans of Whedon's other series.

Comic-book artists (that is, the people who actually draw the images) sometimes worry that when successful writers turn to comic books, they will be overly wordy and likely to crowd out the art. This is not a problem with Whedon's writing, for he is able to use his own invented slang to keep commentary short and pithy. A conversation between Melaka Fray and her sister is curt and to the point. Melaka (shown in a hospital bed) says, "It was a lurk [vampire]. . . . I tried to—" The sister says, "You were grabbing" (indicating that she knows Melaka was stealing things for someone else). "You took him on a grab and got our brother killed." The images deliver the emotional poignancy of the acrimony and loss, and because of the careful wording, they have the space to do so. Panels are generally spare in words and leave plenty of open space for action drawings. Only occasionally does a conversation overfill a few panels, but this happens in most comics at some point in the action, and Whedon also leaves abundant room for purely image-laden splash pages and wordless expository art.

In 2004 Whedon also did a series for Marvel called *The Astonishing X-Men* (2004–2006, episodes 1–24). The world itself was getting darker with the reverberations of the terrorist attacks in September of 2001, the American wars in Afghanistan and Iraq, issues of government and military autocracy, the Abu Ghraib scandal, George W. Bush's presidency and re-election as president in 2004, and the Bush administration's inability (or as Whedon, a self-proclaimed liberal, might say, lack of intention) to allay public fears. It is hardly surprising, then, that the comic world of the *Astonishing X-men* would be dark, complex, and dystopic. The story that mutants are being targeted and that the primary villain, Danger, will use the heroes' own fears against them echoes the fearfulness of the early 2000s.

Whedon's incarnation of the *X-Men* comic featured, also unsurprisingly, the return of Kitty Pryde. Pryde, the youngest member of the X-Men, came to the Xavier School for Gifted (that is, mutant) Children when she was thirteen. In Whedon's story, she returns to the academy to teach. That Pryde, a strong-willed teenage girl, would be a favorite Whedon character should come as no surprise.[7] Whedon, as writer, teamed up with John Cassaday, who did a phenomenal job with the art. Not a panel is rushed or rough, and it is no wonder that the story arc won the 2006 Will Eisner Award for Best Continuous Series.[8] The majority of fans loved it. A smaller number of detractors felt Whedon's version was too much of a throwback to the earlier days of the X-Men, which of course other more enamored fans felt had been the glory days of the franchise. An IGN video timeline about the X-Men credits Whedon with an X-Man resurgence and "a hit," recognizing "Whedon's trademark ability to meld great character work with cool action and of course plenty of humor."[9] In eighty-three Amazon reviews, nine people (11 percent) rated the arc three stars or lower (out of five stars), and most mentioned the new series felt like a throwback to the seventies, missing some later character growth. On the other hand, seventy-four respondents (roughly 89 percent) gave it a rating of four to five stars.[10] Writing for the X-Men was a great moment of success for Whedon. He told a friend, Lisa Rosen, with whom he had attended Wesleyan, "That was probably the most straight-up fantasy fulfilled. . . . As a child this was the holly bibble."[11] Whedon had fulfilled a lifelong dream.

Whedon went on to make contributions to a range of other comic projects that were not his original creations, such as *Giant-Size X-Men* (2005–2008), *Stan Lee Meets Spiderman* (2006), and *Runaways* (2007–2008), and also worked on the end of *Civil War* (2006–2007). Reception as might be suspected was mixed but generally successful, and Whedon's early comics stories allowed him to continue the narrative of his abruptly canceled television series *Firefly* with a comic series titled *Serenity* (after Mal Reynolds's ship).[12] Teaming with Brett Matthews, he produced *Serenity: Those Left Behind* (2005) and *Serenity: Better Days* (2008). Then he joined his brother Zack in 2008 to work on *Serenity: The Shepherd's Tale* (2010), which filled in the previously mysterious back-story of Shepherd Derrial Book, one of the nine principal characters in *Firefly*. These stories filled in spaces between the TV series and the feature film *Serenity*, released in 2005. With the film, Whedon was able to fulfill his promise to the fans not to let the *Firefly* universe die. After the cancellation of the original series, they had been extremely supportive and vocal about him continuing the characters' story. The comic books helped, but they were not enough. Whedon told the *A.V. Club*, "I love the comics, and I'm having the time of my life, and when this comes out, there will have been a new comic unveiled, and it's great, but that's not enough for me, and it's not enough for the fans, either. I need to film some people."

Whedon's respect for his fans meant they could feel inspired to take things into their own hands, and they did! One fan, for example, set out to undo the death of a beloved character in the *Serenity* film by showing that the laws of physics made the death impossible.[13] The fans, who called themselves Browncoats after the coats worn by *Firefly*'s defeated rebels, campaigned vigorously to reverse the network decision to cancel the show, and what is more, they were willing to put their money where their mouths were. In 2011 Nathan Fillion, who played Captain Reynolds, tweeted if he ever won the lottery he would buy the rights to the series so they could continue the show. Fans sprang into action, ultimately raising thousands of dollars in donations for "Browncoat redemption." They organized and even wrote stipulations for what they called—in reference to a frequently quoted line of dialogue from *Firefly*—their "Big Damn Plan":

> 1. The idea here is to create a limited partnership to be owned by the fans. Anyone who invests in the company has a voice.
> 2. The purpose of this partnership will be to enable . . . the production and distribution of more of our favorite show. Obviously, there are a lot of things to figure out before we actually get to that point.
> 3. We're going to create a system through which anyone can invest in the organization. If we can't raise enough money, or if we can't acquire the rights we're after, we return the remaining funds. No hassle, no questions, no worries. There might be expenses like hiring a veteran negotiator, but we're going to keep expenses minimal. We're fans and will be investing too, so we will make it as safe an investment as we can for all involved. [14]

Unfortunately, the idea turned out to be unfeasible. The sets had been destroyed and the actors and creative staff were contracted out elsewhere, but the devotion and persistence of fans were palpable. [15] According to Thor Kuhn, who posted a history of the movement, "Once the Pledge hit over $1,000,000 dollars at an average of just over $85 per pledge it was also locked down." [16] The money was returned or fans had the option to donate their contribution to the charities such as Kids Need to Read, and more than $4,000 of the money was channeled in that direction. [17]

The fans have continued to hang tough. One group funded their own prequel version of the *Firefly* universe, a short film project called *Browncoats Independence War*. The group used Kickstarter to rake in more than their $16,000 original budget request and charged ahead with a filmed story about the lost war for independence, which grew through successive Kickstarter campaigns from a short to a full-length feature presentation. [18] J. J. Abrams has been saying that today's technology enables anyone to do a film in their backyard and that people who want to make a movie should just make their movie on their own. [19] Whedon would go on to do just this with *Much Ado about Nothing* in 2014, but his fans did so as well. *Browncoats Independence War* premiered at the 2014 San Diego Comic-Con on July 24.[20] Score yet another Whedon award for extremely devoted fans.

Whedon's *Buffy Season 8* (2007) and *Angel: After the Fall* (2007) comics would carry on the stories of the shows after their cancellations. Both series continued the themes and characters of the shows but with fewer restrictions on fantasy and action because the pen can summon up settings and magical inventions that are not cost-effective for television. The Buffy comics—again going beyond what TV would allow—also reveal her bisexuality, as she sleeps with one of the Slayer trainees. Fantastical things that would be difficult or too expensive for television, but which can be included in a comic, ranged from turning Buffy's sister Dawn into a giant and then later into a centaur, through large armies of zombies, swarms of werewolves, and masses of vampires, to depictions of the fanciful experiences Buffy has in her dreamspace.

The first Buffy comic arc deals with questions of connection, given that the role of unique Slayer has now—according to the introductory panels—been split and shared with 1,800 women across the world.[21] Green explanation bubbles describe how the relationship between Slayers and Watchers has reversed, that "there were hundreds of watchers and one slayer, [but] scales have tipped of late."[22] A Watcher from the original television show, Giles, underscores the salient problem, telling an ineffective group of new Slayers as they train: "It is of course useless. You're all fighting alone. Getting in each other's way, not protecting each other's flanks . . . failing to use your single most valuable asset . . . " and Buffy finishes his sentence " . . . each other."[23] Once again, we see the theme of supporting the people you choose as family found throughout so much of Whedon's work. These early panels set up the larger dilemmas for all the individual characters but focus on Buffy and her relationship to the new structures of the Slayer world. She is isolated from her trainees as well as from her former friends. Her sister feels estranged and is physically distanced by having been turned into a giant. Xander stands by Buffy as her second-in-command but also admonishes her for her treatment of her sister, while Andrew has been sent away to Italy with one of the now ten squads of Slayers. Buffy's closest friend, Willow, is also abroad, training in her craft of magic. The once inseparable Scooby Gang has been scattered across Earth.

The story structure for *Long Way Home* tells of how Buffy is awakened from her dissociative state, eventually made metaphor in a magically induced, coma-like dream life from which she cannot escape without the kiss of someone who loves her. Home is where the family is, and this center has not held. Events eventually pull Willow back to the group, give Buffy space to connect with one of the new Slayers, and drive home to her how distant she has been from her sister, who tells Buffy that Willow, rather than Buffy herself, has been like a mom to her.[24] Buffy must refocus on her family in order to grow and do better.

Written by Whedon, *Buffy Season 8* displays a variety of themes and techniques common to his oeuvre. In addition to the theme of connection, there is also the motif of an evil governmental militia, along with the figure of the geeky guy who is ever unlucky in love. Xander, who has always had a crush on Buffy, must watch her be awakened by someone else who loves her rather than being allowed to play the hero himself. Whedon also adds little crossover moments between *Buffy Season 8* and the last season of *Angel* on TV when, in a humorous episode, Angel and Spike head to Italy to try and find Buffy, who is supposedly dating a demon called the Immortal. In the comic we learn that the woman that the two jealous ex-lovers see dancing in a discotheque is one of several decoy Buffies conceived to make the real Buffy safer. In the television show, we never get to see her face, although a blond woman is featured dancing in a disco having a wonderful time to the dismay of her lovelorn former lovers.

Whedon was involved in three more Buffy comic arcs, although he no longer wrote the words. In *No Future for You*, characters are asked to deal with their secret fears. Here a different Slayer from the TV show, Faith, faces her fear of not being able to be accepted. *Wolves at the Gate* allows geeky guy Xander to come to terms with his lack of agency. Not only does he finally discover requited love, but he must deal with losing it, as well as with facing the age-old vampire Dracula, who had enslaved him—as a kind of Renfield replacement—in the television series.[25] By the end of the comic series, Xander expresses his own agency, telling his ex-master, "If you call me manservant again, I'll kick you in the teeth." The last panel has an image of two women making love and then a tilted ("dutch angle") drawing of Xander saying, "We have a cold journey ahead of us. . . . Find what warmth you can for now. . . . And I'll stand watch alone." This statement affirms his status as an outsider who accepts his role on the outside, thereby underscoring his growth toward self-acceptance. It also punches the reader in the emotional gut but in a good way—the way that makes Whedon's fans treasure his material.

Willow, too, grows and changes in the comic series. *Time of Your Life*, the final arc conceived by Whedon before leaving the series to others, centers on Willow trying to come to terms with the fact that she feels she chose Buffy's life over her own lover's when (in the TV series) an evil antagonist tried to gun down Buffy and hit Tara instead. Whedon sends Buffy and Willow into the future where they encounter Melaka Fray in a crossover story that forces the three of them to come to terms with Willow's anger and her potential for vengefulness.

The *Angel* comics work similarly, telling the story of what happens after Los Angeles is sent to a hell dimension by the evil law firm Wolfram and Hart. The comic provides many insider ("Easter egg") references to the television series for hardcore fans. The characters face a succession of separations that interfere with their fight against the powers of darkness and time leaps and resets, making the story convoluted but also allowing for the resurrection of beloved characters who die during the story arc.

The *Angel* comics sexualize women far more than those focusing on Buffy. Every one of the stipulations that Whedon gave to Dark Horse for *Fray* is broken in the earlier *Angel* issues drawn by Franco Urru. This is especially so in issue 2, in which Spike, Angel's vampire competitor for Buffy's love, pretends to be a Hugh Hefner–like Hell lord, surrounding himself with particularly scantily clad buxom female characters in thongs who moon over him slavishly. Although later issues reveal he is merely playing a role, it does not diminish the fact that these women are highly sexualized for the comic readership and also featured conspicuously on two alternate "collector's covers." Although later issues by other artists dodge this kind of objectification and avoid sexualized posturing by women, the impression has already been made.

Other, more important female characters like Gwen Raiden and Illyria are depicted in the Urru issues with much larger and more prominent breasts than they had on the TV series. Admittedly the character of Raiden is portrayed on TV as the type of woman who acts out visually because of her tough past and the fact that she cannot touch anyone without electrocuting them. Thus, she dresses provocatively in a kind of overcompensation. The Urru issues focus on Raiden's prominent cleavage or buttocks, while the TV show suggests her sexualized dress and actions result from her difficult childhood and thus does not normalize her behavior the way the comic does.[26] Television highlights her hypersexualization or specularization of herself as being due to insecurities, while the comic suggests it is what a woman of power does or can do. Notably, when Urru returned to draw the last three issues of the series, this sexualization of female characters was mostly absent.

The character arc of *Angel: After the Fall* is more complex and interesting than the *Buffy* comic arcs. The adult issues of the *Angel* series have always been more intricate than the teenage ones of *Buffy*, and the characters are allowed to engage in complicated interactions that relate to identity and the flawed human condition. In a typical example, a highly principled ex-Watcher named Wesley Wyndam Pryce is resurrected as a ghostly liaison between Angel and the evil law firm Wolfram and Hart. He must deal with a variety of problems that connect with his past from the television show, but, being a ghost, he is now incorporeal and can act through words alone. He faces divided loyalties and the lack of trust by Angel and those who know the law firm has sponsored his return to Los Angeles from the dead.

After the Fall brings both major and minor characters back from the TV series and, as noted by IGN, "doesn't have much of the new reader friendliness that its sister series Buffy does, and seems geared almost exclusively toward the moderate to hardcore Angel fan."[27] It seems a bit like deus ex machina to have law firm Wolfram and Hart reset the whole time-space continuum at the end, so that our characters can go back to where they were before the comic series and then continue on to new stories without further input from Whedon.[28] Time leaping is a relatively common comic-book ploy for returning dead characters to life, and—since Whedon had already set up the time jumps in the last year of the TV series—what occurs in the comic book can be seen as merely a continuation of, and a kind of baroque embroidery on, the many possibilities that time travel provides.

Whedon's volume of the *Runaways* likewise contains the typical elements of his other work. He described the book to *Newsarama* this way: "Group of kids find out their parents are supervillains, then they (this is where the title so brilliantly comes in) run away."[29] Kevin Chiat notes many Whedon-like themes in the comic book (even before Whedon took it over, it was reputedly one of his favorite series), such as choosing one's own family, an abundance of good (and young) female characters, a doomed love affair, and the message that adults are not necessarily to be trusted.[30] Whedon spoke to *Newsarama* about hopes for bringing new fans to the series, praising the work of Brian Vaughn and Adrian Alphona on earlier volumes:

> This series has a freshness and whimsy that are unique, but the great interpersonal stuff, the voices, the sense of self-discovery—that does resemble the classic X-stuff. Runaways is the new voice of the Marvel Universe because it thinks the Marvel Universe is a bunch of old guys, and treats them accordingly.[31]

So while Whedon took the X-Men back to their classic forms, he was also able to think about what would make other comics cool to upcoming generations.

At about this time, both Abrams and Whedon were invited to guest-direct episodes of the television series *The Office* (2005–2013). As it turned out, their episodes aired back to back, a sneaky plan fomented by the network for sweeps month, when advertising rates are determined and numbers of viewers are counted as particularly important. Brian Chu tries to compare the directing of the two, but this is a difficult task, for as Whedon points out on commentary for the DVD, the key to successful direction of *The Office* is to be invisible.[32] Indeed Whedon's camera direction is a trifle less dynamic than Abrams's, but both deliver on the typical *Office*-style shooting of characters talking directly to a restless, wandering camera. Neither director wrote the episode he directed, although each relates to themes that its guest director favored.

Abrams's *Office* episode features dating material of the type that might have been found in *Felicity*, while Whedon gets to lampoon business school and show what happens when a bat (possibly of the vampire variety) gets loose in the office. Whedon notes in the DVD commentary to "Business School" that the cast and crew were very open to changes that he wanted made.[33] Evidently he was unhappy with the paintings that Pam was to be showing at her art opening and so all work halted while the crew drew new versions.[34] Whedon says he loved the show and getting a chance to direct it. He later went on to direct a second one, "Branch Wars," which dealt with Art-with-a-capital-A by having Pam ground the "Finer Things" book club and also with social exclusion because she rejects some people as members.[35]

As a friend of Ricky Gervais—the star of the original, British version of *The Office*—Abrams says he was slow to come around to the U.S. version. "I resented it before I saw it, because I thought, 'well, how are you going to do what Ricky and Steve did,'" he told *Total Film*.[36] Chu's comparison comes down to:

> *The Office* usually gets by on the strength of its writing, but Whedon does a fantastic job of getting some truly genuine moments from the stellar cast. Most notably, the final scenes between Pam and Michael at Pam's art show. J. J.[s] episode, "Cocktails" . . . centers on a cocktail party where Jan and Michael plan to take their secret relationship public. There is nothing overtly "J. J. Abrams" about how this episode was directed (not a lens flare to be seen). But much like the previous episode, Abrams jumps right in with these actors and pull[s] out some great performances from them.[37]

Chu gives the edge to Abrams in his review because he likes "Cocktails" better.[38] Audiences disagreed. The Nielsen rating for "Cocktails" was "4.2/10 in viewers eighteen to forty-nine in age, with 8.3 million viewers watching (in competition with *American Idol*). Whedon's "Business School" did somewhat better: 4.4/11 (for ages eighteen to forty-nine). This was a 7 percent increase in ratings when compared to *The Office*'s earlier fall ratings. Whedon's episode garnered 8.8 million viewers, despite having *Survivor* (4.4/11) as its primary competition. The Whedon episode, in fact, won the slot for men ages eighteen to forty-nine.[39] This is a close contest, but Whedon got the higher viewer numbers in the back-to-back *Office*-directing competition.

One of Whedon's big experiments came during the Writer's Guild of America strike of 2007–2008. With his family (brothers Zack and Jed and Jed's wife, Maurissa Tancheroen), he produced a three-act musical drama and released it on the Internet in installments. *Dr. Horrible's Sing-Along Blog* (2009) involved a small investment of personal funds (about $200,000) and brought Whedon returns of as much as $3 million.[40]

Dr. Horrible was groundbreaking for a wide variety of reasons. First it allowed people to work during the writers' strike because Whedon paid very careful attention to the legal side of what could and could not be done during a strike. As Lisa Rosen explains it,

Joss and his line producer David Burns went to the WGA and SAG to work out deals. It was especially important during the strike to show how that could be done without screwing people. "For original content for the writers there was no model," Joss says. "The Guild said, 'This is what we would ask per-minute for reuse or repurposing or for a webisode spun off a show.' So that's what we used as our model." They also worked out the DVD fee and are still trying to figure a rate for theatrical showings, so people can have sing-alongs to the Sing-Along.[41]

None of this had been done before, so Whedon was making it up as he went along. To make a long story short, Whedon did a serialized set of three episodes shot in three days that eventually went up on Hulu over two-day intervals. After withdrawing the material from Hulu, it went up for sale at Amazon and the iTunes Store (where it was number one for five weeks) and was hugely popular.[42] Whedon had been told the audience wouldn't have the attention span online for the kind of story he wanted to present but analyzes his success to Jeff Bercovici in this way:

> I do think *Dr. Horrible* was particularly right for where people were with the internet at that time because it was a little bit more than they were used to, three 12-minute segments, but not so much that they couldn't make the commitment. And it had songs and superheroes and it was silly. It's very audience-friendly. And it also had to do with people who are in the culture of the internet.[43]

People made the commitment and in fact swamped the website. Whedon kids that they "broke the Internet" because the site had so much traffic.[44] This was the motivation for founding the new micro-studio with wife, Kai Cole, and it would go on to produce small, financially successful independent films *Much Ado about Nothing* (2012) and *In Your Eyes* (2014) a few years later.

In Your Eyes became a test model for selling a full-scale film over the Internet. Whedon had worked on the script in the early 1990s even before his *Buffy the Vampire Slayer* series came to TV.[45] After his success with *Much Ado*, he was ready to test the pay-per-view marketing method by charging $5 through Vimeo to watch the film online. The *International Business Times* called it "a bold move that's never been tried before for a feature-length film by a director of Whedon's stature, and the move is not without significant risks."[46] Certainly with his fan base this is less likely, but the *Times* explains potential difficulties of the Internet model:

> Traditional film distribution, however frustrating and complicated, does have its benefits. When a movie debuts in theaters, the studio typically keeps between 80 and 100 percent of the gross take in the first week, a percentage that shrinks for each film the longer it remains in theaters, according to the Independent Film Project. In addition, distributors take a roughly 50 percent cut of the profits, and sometimes there are deals to pay out shares of the profits to actors, writers and others. Vimeo's terms are much easier to swallow: If "In Your Eyes" is subject to the same split that has been standard for most other Vimeo projects, 90 percent of the profits will go to Bellweather [*sic*], Whedon's production company.[47]

Although the IMDb estimates Bellwether's budget at a million dollars, that seems a bit high for a micro-budget production. Cole and Whedon have remained mum about the financial specifics. The film nonetheless has ratings by more than 18,251 users on the same website, which at 90 percent of the now $4 price on Vimeo would still yield more than $65,000 gross. While one cannot be sure how many saw the film through bootlegs as opposed to paying the original $5 price, a DVD was also produced, and the combined profits most probably put the film at or near a break-even level depending on its original budget.[48]

The film itself is a sweet homage to classic Hollywood screwball comedy. A New England trophy wife susceptible to psychological fits and an ex-con in New Mexico share a kind of psychic link that allows them to communicate across the distance with each other and feel each other's feelings as long as their sentiments are spoken out loud. Talking to oneself is not generally acceptable to the average person and so goofiness ensues, as does the likelihood that the heroine's husband will try to put her into a mental institution. Up until the climactic end, this is a surprisingly sweet and romantic love story, almost reminiscent of the youthful, romantic work of J. J. Abrams. Despite its rewrites, the work is the product of a young Whedon inspired by classical Hollywood traditions. The film is able to combine humor and a sense of imminent threat as the ex-con, Dylan in New Mexico, is pressured back into a life of crime and his soul mate in New Hampshire, Becky, is dragged off to the mental hospital. Whedon even as a young writer shows nuance in writing isolated underdog characters, making us fall for Becky and Dylan. Likewise his penchant for killing off major characters helps to preserve a sense of suspense about whether the young lovers will survive to the end of the film.

With *Dr. Horrible*, Whedon's choice of the Internet as a distribution channel was vindicated in many ways, even if the verdict is still out about his later projects. *Dr. Horrible* received numerous tech and creative awards including the 2008 People's Choice Award for "Favorite Online Sensation"; a 2009 Hugo Award for Best Dramatic Presentation, short form; a 2009 Creative Arts Emmy Award for "Special Class, Short Format Live Action Entertainment Program"; and seven Streamy awards.[49] *Time* honored it twice by listing it as one of its top ten series of 2008 (number 4) as well as featuring it as number 15 in their list of Top 50 inventions of the same year.[50] In 2009 the Producer's Guild of America honored Whedon with the Vanguard Award. Quoting David Friendly and Laurence Mark, co-chairs of the PGA Awards, *Variety* reported, "Joss Whedon has mastered the art of melding the newest technology with inspired storytelling, truly exemplifying the spirit of the Vanguard Award." Although the ceremony had to be postponed, no one doubted the veracity of what the co-chairs said.[51]

Nor was it just a lame-brained musical comedy. In typical Whedon style, *Dr. Horrible* asks questions about hero worship and the costs of trying to impress people, all with catchy tunes and humorous lyrics. While Horrible's love interest, the sweet young Penny, swoons for the handsome Captain Hammer, the viewer discovers through song lyrics that Hammer is arrogant, conceited, and self-serving. Horrible, in his struggle with Hammer, will indirectly cause the death of the very person he most wants to impress. Thus several Whedon characteristics are present, including the death of a beloved character, fiendishly clever wordplay, and silly humor, along with a social commentary about the negative effects of norms of masculine behavior.

The year 2009 was one of great ups and downs for Whedon. Undoubtedly one of the high points must have been receiving an award from Harvard University's Humanist Chaplaincy: the 2009 Outstanding Life Achievement Award in Cultural Humanism. Whedon has never made his atheism a secret, but to receive such a prestigious life achievement award at the relatively young age of forty-five speaks to the cultural mark he has made on those around him. Harvard student Lewis Ward, who introduced

Whedon at the event, stressed they were not giving Whedon the award because they felt "his career is over," but rather that in his works, "we really see an expression of what Joss believes" and that "everyone of us can be a good person without having to believe in God."[52] Andrew Maher, the vice president of the Harvard Secular Society, observed that "what stands out about Joss is his explicit integration of his value system into both his work and his activism."[53] Indeed, his activism is another significant aspect of his creative opus.

Whedon's acceptance speech justified their decision. "Faith in God means believing absolutely in something with no proof whatsoever," he said at the climax of his talk. "Faith in humanity means believing absolutely in something with a huge amount of proof to the contrary. We are the true believers." In general he stresses inclusivity and tolerance of all worldviews, along with the importance of political action against oppression, showing himself to be a humanitarian deserving of such an award.[54]

The Writers' Guild of America strike also brought out the political activist in Whedon. His work with *Dr. Horrible* had driven him to find other mechanisms for producing and making public creative work and also gave him the chance to blog about why the writers should be supported. He had joined the picket line despite being extremely ill but also used *Whedonesque*, a website devoted to all things Whedon, to remind people that though writing is fun, it is also "hard work." He even wrote a 1950s-style protest song in support of the writers' activism.[55] In response to the *New York Times* description of the striking writers on the picket line, he blogged,

> Oh my God. Arty glasses and fancy scarves. That is so cute! My head is aflame with images of writers in ruffled collars, silk pantaloons and ribbons upon their buckled shoes. A towering powdered wig upon David Fury's head, and Drew Goddard in his yellow stockings (cross-gartered, needless to say). Such popinjays, we! The entire writers' guild as Leslie Howard in *The Scarlet Pimpernel*. Delicious.[56]

The target of his mockery was the *Times*'s description of the strike as having "the trappings of a union protest," which he felt trivialized it and betrayed the prejudice that real work was sweaty manual labor. "You see how that works?" he asked readers.

Since we aren't real workers, this isn't a real union issue. (We're just a guild!) And that's where all my "what is a writer" rambling becomes important. Because this IS a union issue, one that will affect not just artists but every member of a community that could find itself at the mercy of a machine that absolutely and unhesitatingly would dismantle every union, remove every benefit, turn every worker into a cowed wage-slave in the singular pursuit of profit. (There is a machine. Its program is "profit." This is not a myth.) This is about a fair wage for our work. No different than any other union. The teamsters have recognized the importance of this strike, for which I'm deeply grateful. Hopefully the *Times* will too.[57]

The writing has the strong rhythms and flow of a 1960s protest statement. Amy Pascale, Whedon's biographer, says political activist "was a role Joss was born and bred to play."[58]

Along those lines, Whedon would receive an award from the international human rights organization Equality Now in 2006 "for his courageous support of women's rights."[59] In the speech, he responded to the question he got repeatedly over the years, "Why do you write these strong women characters?" with the now-famous retort: "Because you're still asking me that question."[60] Seven years later he would be asked to speak at a rally to "Make Equality Now." His activist commitment was made clear in the conclusion of his presentation: "And I say to everybody on the other side of that line, who believes that women are to be bought, or trafficked, or ignored, . . . we will never not be fighting. We will go on. We will always work this issue until it doesn't need to be worked anymore."

The speech caused a controversy, particularly with some old-school feminists. Whedon began his talk with an etymological interrogation of the word "feminist," arguing that it betrayed an ideology because of the "ist" ending. One is not, he argued, born believing in ideas that end with "-ist." Thus, "feminist includes the idea that believing men and women to be equal . . . is not a natural state." He continued:

You can't be born an atheist or a communist or a horticulturalist. You have to have these things brought to you. So feminist includes the idea that believing men and women to be equal, believing all people to be people, is not a natural state. That we don't emerge assuming that everybody in the human race is a human, that the idea of equality is

Joss Whedon on the set of *Buffy the Vampire Slayer* in the spring of 1997. *WB Television / Photofest © WB Television*

just an idea that's imposed on us. That we are indoctrinated with it, that it's an agenda.[61]

"Equality is natural," Whedon argued in response. "There's no fuzzy middle ground. You either believe that women are people or you don't.

It's that simple." He then concluded with the comment quoted above, about staying committed to the fight.

What disturbed many feminists about the speech was the idea of a man telling them that they should abandon a word for which they had been fighting for many, many years to make acceptable. There were quite a few online rants in response as well as thoughtful reaction. Noah Berlatsky pointed out the long history of women having to fight arguments that it is natural for them to be the inferior sex and concluded: "Saying equality is natural sounds like a good thing, but Whedon uses it rhetorically to ignore the entire history of feminism."[62] Melissa McGlensey, writing in *Ms.*, concurred:

> I hate to break it to you, Joss, but the progress toward gender equality that we've enjoyed in this country did not happen naturally or without struggle. It was fought for by generations of strong women and men who opposed what the patriarchy told us was our *natural* role as women. It did have to be brought to people—and it still does.[63]

Katie McDonough at *Salon.com* added:

> I wasn't born a feminist. I chose to become one. And that becoming has meant a continuous and rigorous doing, not to mention a lot of listening and learning from other feminists. Because feminism isn't just the idea that men and women are created equal, it's the process of interrogating what assumptions we bring to that idea in order to get us all somewhere closer to justice.[64]

The opinions run the gamut from full-tilt adulation to unapologetic bashing.

Whedon's tweets and public commentary on Gamergate are a further example of activism that strengthens the case for Whedon's feminism. An anonymous poster on 4chan sent out the call that next time she came to a conference, female video game developer Zoe Quinn should be given "a crippling injury that's never going to fully heal . . . a good solid injury to the knees. I'd say a brain damage, but we don't want to make it so she ends up too retarded to fear us."[65] Whedon was quick to comment with regard to the sexist behavior of trolls against women on the Internet, how such behavior always surprises him because he wishes we were past that point:

Every time . . . I'm stunned. I'm like, Really? That's like, I don't believe in airplanes. It's like, What century are you from? I don't get it. So usually I'm shocked, then occasionally amused, then occasionally extremely not amused, but once I get over the shock, it's very clear that misogyny in our own culture—and not just where they perform genital mutilation and marry off 10-year-olds—runs so deep.[66]

In an interview with *Vulture.com*, he advised men who are shy about saying they are feminists to get involved and donate money. He told interviewer Kara Warner: "A guy who goes around saying 'I'm a feminist' usually has an agenda that is not feminist. A guy who behaves like one, who actually becomes involved in the movement, generally speaking, you can trust that."[67] Whedon seems to be following his own advice. He has not wasted a lot of energy defending himself against detractors and he does continue to donate money and time to the cause.

Five years after the writers' strike, Whedon would again put his creativity in the service of a political cause when he created a satirical YouTube video suggesting that (then) presidential candidate Mitt Romney would be a perfect leader during the zombie apocalypse. Romney, he explained with mock seriousness, "is a very different candidate," ideally suited for the job because he

is ready to make the deep rollbacks in healthcare, education, social services, reproductive rights that will guarantee poverty, unemployment, overpopulation, disease, rioting—all crucial elements in creating a nightmare zombie wasteland. But it's his commitment to ungoverned corporate privilege that will nosedive this economy into true insolvency and chaos, the kind of chaos you can't buy back. Money is only so much paper to the undead. The one percent will no longer be the very rich. It will be the very fast.[68]

The video, which went up just a couple of weeks before the election, immediately went viral. Sarah Parnass of ABC News reported it received more than 800,000 hits within the first twenty-four hours of showing up on YouTube.[69] Two days later, according to *Wired*, there were more than 1.1 million hits.[70] Humor was certainly a key element of the video's popularity. Whedon plays his part to the hilt, sardonically opening a cabinet full of canned goods and asking viewers to ask themselves: "Am I ready for the purity and courage of Mitt Romney's apocalyptic vision? Let's all embrace the future. Stop pretending we care about each other and start hoarding canned goods."[71] The piece ends with a campaign-style graphic showing a zombified Romney before a blurred American flag and the words "Zomney, he needs brains." *Wired* wrote about the tactic as occurring "in the midst of what has become a very internet-influenced election year," which shows once again that Whedon is at the forefront of using the new media.

Sugarshock! (2008), an online comic about a rock band in a sci-fi universe that Whedon produced around the time of the writers' strike, won him another Eisner award.[72] *Sugarshock!* is composed of Dandelion Naizen, the Asian lead singer; a plumpish female drummer, Wade; a bass guitarist, L'lihdra, who is a tall, thin woman in pinstripes; and robot Phil, who also plays guitar. They are accompanied by a single male groupie, whom Wade has commandeered as a sex toy. The plot follows them on an intergalactic mission involving a genuine battle of the bands that could get them all killed. Dandelion, the lead character, is a tad bizarre in that she tends to go off on wild tangents and paranoid rants and thinks she is working for a secret government agency. Whedon claims, "I think, [she is] more like me than anybody I've written. She's insanely bipolar and completely capricious but very dedicated to something or other, and has a particular dislike of Vikings. . . . No one knows why, but she doesn't like Vikings.[73] It would be interesting to find out if Whedon also hates Vikings. Presumably not, given his work on *The Avengers*.

J. J. Abrams, meanwhile, kept writing but increasingly turned his attentions toward producing. He had attempted to relaunch the Superman franchise in 2002, but his script was criticized for taking too many liberties with the canon.[74] The idea was intriguing. Abrams told H. Shaw Williams that he envisioned Superman's human adopted parents

> had to immediately begin teaching this kid to limit himself and to not be so fast, not be so strong, not be so powerful. The result of that, psychologically, would be fear of oneself, self-doubt and being ashamed of what you were capable of. Extrapolating that to adulthood became a fascinating psychological profile of someone who was not pretending to be Clark Kent, but who was Clark Kent. Who had become that kind of a character who is not able or willing to accept who he was and what his destiny was.[75]

Evidently the producers wanted something else because the franchise would finally end up being reinvigorated by Christopher Nolan and David S. Goyer some ten years later with *Man of Steel* (2013). Perhaps it was the right idea at the wrong time.

Abrams had previously also initiated a series of not terribly successful television shows. He had already experienced problems with *What about Brian* (2006–2007), a show his Bad Robot Production Company launched in 2006. *Brian* began as a midseason replacement in 2006 with six episodes but—although it was renewed—only made it through nineteen episodes rather than the twenty-two originally contracted. *Brian* was a kind of *Felicity* for the postcollege years: Brian is a lovable but socially awkward video game designer in love with his best friend's fiancée. Abrams worked on the idea with Dana Stevens but neither directed nor wrote any episodes, although he certainly advised on scripts and kept an eye on the dailies, the footage shot each day. Still, the series bears all the characteristic relationship turns of *Felicity*. Brian is caught between women, and the audience wonders if he will end up with the "wrong" one. The friends have bumpy relationships and fluky misunderstandings, but everyone has heart.

In July 2006 it was time to renegotiate the home base of his productions. According to the *L.A. Times*, Abrams left Disney, having been able to negotiate a satisfactory deal elsewhere.

> At midnight Thursday, at Paramount's Melrose Avenue lot, Abrams' representatives finalized the terms of a five-year movie deal with the Viacom Inc.–owned studio. Then they drove across town to the private Regency Club in Westwood to hammer out the details of a six-year TV pact with Warner Bros.[76]

Things were looking hopeful and the money was good. Claudia Eller and Meg James of the *L.A. Times* noted that this deal placed Abrams in the same league as producers like Jerry Bruckheimer and John Wells.

> The TV deal cements Abrams' status as what one Warner executive dubbed "an A-plus" talent. . . . Two sources said Abrams would receive at least $4 million a year for six years guaranteed and overhead costs that would average about $2 million a year for his Bad Robot production label. Two other sources close to the negotiations said Abrams' annual fee was closer to $6 million a year, which when combined with the movie deal would bring the total to $68 million.[77]

The article also cites Paramount Pictures' Chairman Brad Grey as saying, "We think J. J. is the next Steven Spielberg. . . . He's a triple threat: a great writer, producer and now, a first-class movie director."[78]

Bad Robot's six-year deal with Warner Brothers Television led to the floating of several projects that never became series. The first was a medical show based on Harvard professor Jerome Groopman's book about a hospital cancer ward, called *Anatomy of Hope*. Abrams directed a pilot that aired on HBO, but it was not picked up. Another project, according to *Hollywood Reporter*, was "'Boundaries,' [which] centers on a failing cable access psychologist who rediscovers her true purpose when she is forced to take a job as a mobile notary."[79] The network must not have signed on the dotted line as "Boundaries" bounded unseen into the ozone.

Abrams also went on to produce several other shows with frustrating results. In 2010, he and Josh Reims sent out a spy story, *Undercovers*, the first episode of which Abrams once again directed. The story concerned two sexy ex-spies (married to each other) who open a catering service only to be pulled back into the spy business five years later. Abrams told Brian Ford Sullivan that the idea was to have a show that was energetic but funny, and he decided to direct it because "I just enjoyed the idea of it. I enjoy the script. . . . I enjoyed the chemistry of these two people."[80] It seemed like a property that could not lose.

The premise offers many amusing possibilities, and it was nice to see an action show where the two main characters, Steven and Samantha Bloom, were black, upper middle class, and in a happy, bantering *Hart to Hart*–like marriage. In fact, the common denominator of the three failed shows mentioned thus far was a quirky, humorous take. The United States, however, was facing serious issues: inflation and wars as a consequence of U.S. foreign policy and a banking crisis at home. When the series tanked, Abrams decided the main problem was that he should have played it a bit more dark and serious. In an interview with Christina Radish, he commented,

> The conceit of the show was to do a much more frivolous, fun show, but ultimately, I think it was just too frivolous and too simple, and we didn't go deep enough. We were really desperately trying to stay away from mythology and complexity and intensity and too much serious, dark storytelling and, ultimately, that's not necessarily what I do best. I

Abrams discussing a scene with Lizzy Caplan on the set of *Cloverfield* **(2008).** *Paramount Pictures / Photofest © Paramount Pictures; photographer Sam Emerson*

> think audiences felt that it was a little bit lacking. I see that and completely take responsibility for its failing. [81]

Unfortunately the series got smothered before it had a chance to go anywhere, leaving two of the thirteen episodes unaired. A few years later the series *The Americans* (2013–) would take a less sunny approach to undercover spies. Resembling an earlier pitch—"what if Felicity had been a spy?"—a production completely unrelated to Abrams and Bad Robot would hire Keri Russell to play an undercover spy in a darker series, so dark in fact that she would play a Russian KGB agent undercover in the United States. Abrams is clearly willing to take responsibility for his own misjudgments but through experimentation also seems to have found an idea that was way before its time.

Shelter (2012) and *Alcatraz* (2012) were similarly short-lived Bad Robot productions. *Shelter* did not get beyond pilot stage and has thus become classified as a "made-for-TV movie" about a historic New England resort. Midseason replacement *Alcatraz* did better with thirteen total episodes, but neither had overt connection with Abrams. Both were more serious, and *Alcatraz* at least had a premise that spun out an Abrams-type mystery theme, this time about Alcatraz prison inmates who had disappeared in 1963 at the time of the prison's shutdown mysteriously showing up alive in present-day San Francisco. It was touted by *The Critics Choice Television Awards* as one of the most exciting new series of 2012, which suggests that Abrams and Bad Robot did their job in terms of marketing and early production. [82] It definitely sparked a renewed interest in the prison itself, with people sneaking out of tours in order to go look for the hidden control center that existed only on the television show. The prison had to start posting signs reminding people that the show was a fiction and that tour deserters risked damaging the aging structure and disturbing bird-nesting areas. [83] The show premiered with ten million viewers but lost about half by the end of the season and was thus canceled by the network. [84]

The most successful Bad Robot launch of this time period was Jonathon Nolan's *Person of Interest*, on which Abrams shared the producer credit with Bryan Burk. Although Abrams has no visibly public input on the series, it features Michael Emerson (previously of *Lost*) and contains a mysterious machine that can foretell when someone is going to need help, with a healthy dose of conspiracy theory as icing. This is consistent

with Abrams's past oeuvre, and this one has also sustained public interest. Abrams describes his input on shows like *Alcatraz* and *Person of
Interest* as helping the writers, Liz Sarnoff and Jonah Nolan, take their
works to the next level: "The notes I gave on the scripts were just to help
these people who created these shows realize them to the best of what
they wanted them to be. I feel like I'm there to serve them and help them
do their job."[85] This suggests that Abrams actually does have a significant
hand in the series that Bad Robot produces and his input goes beyond just
viewing the initial scripts. He told Christina Radish of *Collider*,

> I would give notes on outlines, and then the scripts themselves, and
> then cuts of the dailies, and then cuts of the pilots. My involvement in
> the shows will be as much as they need me to be involved, but I'm
> working with people who are awesome and do a great job. I try to help
> them do their thing, and they're trying to help me do mine.[86]

Still, it is hard to know how much of Abrams's involvement is "needed"
or occurs.

No doubt writers with sensibilities similar to Abrams's are more likely
to come to Bad Robot based on their prior productions, but it seems like
Abrams's vision might also be discernible in these works, particularly in
the beginning as the shows struggle to get off the ground. His interest in
drawing the audience in and preserving the mystery while speaking to
warm human values seems apparent in most of the series that Bad Robot
has supported even as he works with the ideas and writing of others.

Abrams's interest in helping others parallels Whedon's political activities and extends beyond encouraging new writers. Abrams spoke with
Tavis Smiley about his Diversity Fellowship Initiative to bring mentorship and opportunities to talented people of color,

> where we pick two directors a year and they make their films, and it's
> at Bad Robot. The idea is to—we set them up with the heads of all the
> departments, the best in the business, and they get to do interviews. . . .
> It is like a crash course in movie-making, and a lot of these people,
> while they may not need it, what you need is relationships. What's
> incredible is you realize how much comes from who you know and
> who you can call and who you're comfortable with.[87]

In 2012 Abrams also received an International Emmy called the Founders
Award, which is given to people whose influence crosses "international

boundaries to touch our common humanity."[88] Steven Spielberg received the same award in 2006.[89] Abrams clearly is covering some of the same ground as the master.

Another Bad Robot production that did not quite make the grade was *Almost Human* (2013–2014), a kind of *Adam-12* remake for the future, where two cops drive around fighting crime, but in this case one of the two was a cyborg and the other had partial amnesia. Like *Alcatraz*, it started strong and then flagged. *Almost Human* started with 9.1 million viewers, which fell to 5.6 million by the end of its thirteen-episode run.[90] Yet another Bad Robot production, *Revolution* (2012–2014) lasted a year longer. It also had a great concept: a postapocalyptic setting without advanced technology, where groups of people attempted to survive in a world dominated by private militias. Fans distraught by the premature cancellation after two seasons have been petitioning networks to pick the series up. By mid-February 2015, they had more than 84,000 signatures.[91] In 2013 Abrams tried again with *Believe*, a series about a girl with supernatural powers. Thirteen episodes were made, of which only twelve were shown before the series was canceled.

There is not a little bit of irony that Abrams did a cameo on a *Family Guy* (1999–) episode called "Ratings Guy."[92] His character was shown pitching a show guaranteed to bring in good Nielsen numbers about an alien that "goes back in time and encounters a koala bear in an Eastern European town." The title character's reaction of not understanding it at all and sending him off to make it might have struck a chord with Abrams, who probably had been doing a lot of much more reasonable pitching to the networks without receiving such encouraging responses.

Abrams also showed creative breadth at this point in his life. He had always been interested in music, having devised musical themes for *Alias*, *Fringe*, and *Lost*. He did a bit for the 2009 MTV Awards in "Cool Guys Don't Look at Explosions," where he played a keyboard solo while Will Ferrell did a glittery Neil Young impersonation and Andy Samberg imitated Bruce Springsteen.[93] The song was intercut with images of macho Hollywood heroes walking boldly away from large explosions without a backward glance. Abrams has also been exploring filmed versions of the video games *Portal* and *Half-Life*.[94] Luke Plunkett of *Kotaku.com* thinks the chances the projects will actually get made are slim: "It's a relationship at the earliest, most tentative stages. A game idea they'd like to work on, a pair of movie projects that Abrams is 'going to be bringing on a writer' for."[95] Nonetheless, the fact that Abrams is looking at unusual media sources is a sign of his creative innovation.

Finally Abrams skipped the comic books and went on to help create the great (though maybe not-so-American) novel *S*. He mentioned to Bill Whittaker of CBS News that he picked up a Robert Ludlum book lying around in an airport and it had an inscription that got his creative juices flowing: "To whomever finds this, please read it, and leave it somewhere for someone else to find it." This notion of a book being used as vessel of communication between two people felt like it was a seed of something potentially exciting and intriguing, he told Whittaker.[96] Joshua Rothman of the *New Yorker* reports that Abrams said,

> It made me smile, this optimistic, romantic idea that you could leave a book with a message for someone. It reminded me of being in college, and seeing the notes that people would leave in the margins of the books they'd checked out of the library. And then, I started to think: what if there were a very cool book that was completely annotated— just covered in marginalia and notes between two people? And what if a conversation, or a relationship, began inside a book? That was the beginning of the process, maybe fifteen years ago.[97]

Abrams then floated a book based on the idea of a romance in the margins to Bad Robot's features head Lindsey Weber. Interviewer Lena Dunham learned at a panel in New York City's Symphony Place that Weber suggested Doug Dorst, a creative writing teacher at Texas State University, as someone who could do the idea justice and then "all we did was find an incredibly talented writer and give him an idea for something, and then you took it and made it completely your own."[98] Abrams stresses in each interview that he did not co-author the book. He got the idea and then Doug Dorst wrote it. Dorst told the panel that when he met with them,

> I was convinced that I was auditioning. . . . I thought, well, there's no way I'll get this gig, so why don't I just go in the most ludicrous direction? What would be most fun for me? . . . They would say, take it as far as you possibly can.[99]

Abrams's story about a grad student, Eric, who meets and falls in love with a college senior, Jen, in the book's margins and their attempt to unearth information about the author for Eric's thesis form the alternate story to that of the actual (fake) 1949 book *The Ship of Theseus* by an author writing under the nom de plume V. M. Straka. It is *The Ship of Theseus* that we get when we remove the volume from its slipcover that is imprinted with the title *S*.

The 1949 tome concerns a man who has lost his memory and washes up on the shore of a gray and unwelcoming unidentified port town. He gets the chance to see the woman of his dreams before being kidnapped and awakening aboard the ultimate in creepy sailing ships. Dorst's addition of a subplot about author V. M. Straka being a false identity used by a famous author to cover his radical activities against a vast corporate conspiracy was right up Abrams's alley. The addition of an editor weighing in with his (or perhaps her) own wild theories about Straka created the recipe for a smashing Abrams mystery.

Dorst deserves the high praise heaped on him by his co-creator. Abrams insists that the library book canvas in whose margins the modern-day love story was to occur must be a literary work that could stand on its own. He explained to Tavis Smiley,

> I've got to tell you, the fun of this is—and the answer will be clear when it is on sale and people buy it or not—but the thing to me that this is, the book itself, just the book, is wildly compelling and a legitimate novel. We knew going into this if the novel didn't work, then all the notes—it's a big gimmick otherwise. [100]

Abrams need not have worried. The book is a literary tour de force that, as wild as it sounds, reads like an existential love story written by Albert Camus in collaboration with Franz Kafka.

The physical volume's title, *The Ship of Theseus*, most likely refers to a conundrum credited by the ancient Greek historian Plutarch to the pre-Socratic philosopher Heraclitus. (Dorst, a three-time winner on *Jeopardy!*, is well versed in all literary matters trivial and not so trivial.) Plutarch poses the paradox as to whether the ship that Theseus left home in is the same one he arrives home in many years later, if every single board and sail has been replaced by new ones piece by piece over the years. [101] The ship in *S.* is indeed destroyed and re-created from other parts, and our main character muses as to whether it can be considered to be the same ship.

The main character, identified only by the initial S., ponders whether the "new" ship is the same one he was captive on. "It is entirely possible, S. realizes, and in fact seems quite likely, that not one plank or hatch or cleat or peg or bolt or nail or rope remains from the night he was first taken aboard."[102] Even more significantly since this is a book about identity and because the main character begins the novel with amnesia and re-creates himself over the course of his adventures aboard the ship, one can also ask if S. is the same person he started out as. This is a particularly poignant question since he has evolved into not only an obsessive writer, one who exhausts himself, literally using himself up in a disturbing be-low-deck ritual, while also having become a skilled assassin on behalf of a rebel group fighting a wealthy corporate syndicate. He has feelings of regret at having missed the chance to spend his life with the woman he calls Sola, whom he saw reading a book in the port town at the novel's start. He wonders thus if he has missed the opportunity of being that other person.

Yet Dorst's and Abrams's answer to the enigma, because of the structure of the story, is definitive: "And yet: this is the ship." It is the same ship because S. has "put his faith in [the] tale of the ship's continuity."[103] Likewise S. holds faith in belief regarding the woman he met in the dreary port town and who, although she appears in various incarnations, represents human relationships that persist and give meaning to life despite the fact that existentially each person lives and dies alone. S.'s epiphany in the final chapter (which is of disputed authorship) is that he does not care about Vevóda, the enemy leader, anymore. "As long as the man lives, S. and others will resist what he brings to the world. When Vevóda dies, someone else will take his place. When S. dies, someone else will take his place. Another S. Another story."[104] And S.'s first reaction is a return to his individualized humanity; he wants to tell Sola about his realization.[105]

The stories in the margin ring with the same messages about love. The two students, represented by different handwriting and different color inks, piece together a story that suggests that V. M. Straka has chosen a life of writing and fomenting political action instead of being with the woman he loves. This gives the students an opportunity to voice their own opinions about these kinds of life choices, although we know that despite a series of obstacles thrown at them from various sides, the two will end up running away to be together in the end. This is, after all, a J. J. Abrams–inspired story and not one created by Joss Whedon.

The words are Dorst's, but the sentiments are consistent with Abrams's faith in the human need to fight for what is right even if the war can never be won. One might question whether Abrams would have that much influence in the work, but his account of his own input makes it clear he could and probably did. Abrams described it as

> not unlike developing a screenplay. There were outlines and pitches at the beginning, then early chapters. Lindsey would often work with Doug, and then show me stuff. It was especially fun, though, because the final product wasn't a script that then needed to be cast and shot and edited. It was the text. And then we worked with a design firm, Melcher Media, who helped make it what it is. [106]

Given Abrams's humility in general, this seems like a fair assessment.

In his interview, Tavis Smiley asked the producer what he wants the J. J. Abrams brand to stand for. Abrams's humility showed anew in his answer, which he prefaced with the remark that "I would hope that whatever we do, and I feel like again, though it may be my name that gets put out there sometimes, it is the company, Bad Robot, that we all work together." [107] His answer to the question invoked the name of Steven Spielberg, how Spielberg's work could be scary, mysterious, and dangerous but also have human compassion.

> I hope that what we're all doing is telling stories that have strong values, that have a big heart. It's one of the reasons I loved as a kid Steven Spielberg's films. . . . His movies were made with a deep sense of humanity, and I think that to me is maybe the most important thing. I would hope that people feel like, when they go to see a movie that we do or watch a show that we do, that there is a sense of humanity, a sense of humor, and a sense ultimately of optimism. [108]

Jen and Eric, Filomela and Straka, and even S. and Sola—the couples of *S.*—will all have to recognize that no battle is definitive, but they get to experience those human victories that can be tough and a little scary but show optimism, mystery, and heart.

Although Dorst may have done the literary heavy lifting, Abrams and Bad Robot marketed the book and worked with Melcher Media and a Chinese printer to create a facsimile of a 1940s book that was filled with library ownership markings, underlining, notes in the margin, and all manner of inserts such as postcards, a map written on a napkin, a code wheel, and a newspaper obituary among other things. [109] A website was set up to offer a wealth of information for those intent on solving all the mysteries of the book and is accompanied by busy musings by fans about the meanings and codes within the novel and its margins. Jen and Eric, the student characters who scribbled in the margins, both have Twitter accounts that also feed fan interest, and Dorst indicates that there are plenty of things remaining to be solved that can keep the Internet fans busy for a very long time. The most notable marketing was J. J. Abrams's August 19 video teaser for the novel released on YouTube. Shot in high-key black and white, the trailer had the feel of a 1950s noir film and showed fragmented shots of waves and the main character coming out of the sea to a voice-over explaining, "He arrived knowing nothing of himself. Who is he? Soon he will know. Because what begins at the water shall end there. And what ends there shall once more begin. This is what happens: men become lost, men vanish, men are erased—and reborn."[110] The trailer created a storm of web inquiries, tweets, and blogs on the Internet with speculations about what it meant and what it was about.[111] At the video's end, we get a mysterious close-up of the character, his mouth sewn shut with black thread. Abrams deserves credit for a marketing coup and producing an eerie and compelling trailer that had massive Internet buzz.

Both creators had a string of scripts and shows that they pitched but that somehow failed to get made or never quite got off the ground. Whedon also had his share of never-rans: the films *Suspension*, *Afterlife*, and *Goners*; an *Empire Strikes Back* remake; and a TV show, *Buffy the Animated Series*, which had a trailer with a dragon and cool library set. There was a much awaited Buffy spin-off, featuring Rupert Giles, that never saw light of day. Whedon also came to loggerheads with the producer of a *Wonder Woman* (2007) film and was unable to bring to life a web series called *Wastelanders*.[112] These frustrations must have driven home the need for persistence and control of all aspects of the creative process from marketing to production.

Abrams has talked about a variety of projects and even bought the rights to make a film revolving around the "Mystery on Fifth Avenue Apartment" featured in the *New York Times*. The apartment was real: a multi-room space fitted out with a series of clues by noted designers and artists in order to create a giant scavenger hunt, which according to reporter Penelope Green, led to a finale involving (in part) removing decorative door knockers from two hallway panels . . . to make a crank, which in turn opened hidden panels in a credenza in the dining room, which displayed multiple keys and keyholes, which, when the correct ones were used, yielded drawers containing acrylic letters and a table-size cloth imprinted with the beginnings of a cross-word puzzle, . . . which led to [a] concealed . . . cham[b]ered magnetic cube, which could be used to open the 24 remaining panels, revealing, in large type . . . [a] poem.[113]

The new owners of the dwelling inherited the mystery and eventually solved it.

Obviously both creators learned from having to keep pitching and keep trying. In an interview, Abrams explained, "I don't know. Pitching is always a weird, difficult thing. I think the key is at the very beginning you just need to make sure that you have a handle on the characters and the potential of those characters. If you know that you want to do some really, really weird stuff, keep it to yourself."[114] In this respect Abrams may have learned better how to sneak the weird stuff by the networks. With *Firefly* and later *Dollhouse*, perhaps Whedon started off a bit too far from network sensibilities and thus Abrams gets the point for "working the business."

Abrams highlights another aspect common to both men's success: paying careful attention to the writing.

What it all comes down to, what matters more and most of all is the idea and the writing and the execution of that. For that, I usually write longhand at first. There's something about it, the tactile, tangible nature of it, that just feels like I'm feeling the stuff more than I am. You know, when there's a deadline and it's crazy, of course, the MacBook Pro is the key. But it's something that I think ultimately just comes down to what is that idea you're scribbling with that pencil.[115]

Whedon is known for working on an antiquated Brother typewriter and on plain pads of paper.[116] Doubtless he would agree both with the importance of the tactile and of the writing itself.

Both men, during this period of erratic successes and failures, learned a lot about humility and working with good teams and that it pays to concentrate on areas that play on one's own strengths. Both creators showed their flexibility and were soon looking ahead to bigger projects. In terms of the competition for this chapter, Whedon is way ahead. He takes the points for fan popularity, for profitability, and for writing by continuing his franchises in comic books. Abrams already has his win for working the business. The two men tie in terms of the challenges of adversity/personal growth and in creative innovation: Abrams for exploring novels, puzzles, and music, Whedon for his political creativity, his comics, and his Internet serial. They also tie for visual creativity: Whedon for his comic-book work and Internet blog and Abrams for his incredible Internet video teaser for his novel *S*. Abrams also gets a wild card point award for his Founder's Award for international influence that touches on our common humanity. The score is Whedon 4.5, Abrams 3.5. In this chapter we have watched Abrams and Whedon approach the cusp of tremendous breakthroughs in the industry, and Hollywood was finally about to validate all those years of paying their dues. Abrams and Whedon were going back to the movies!

6

OH, THE HORROR

Cabin in the Woods and *Super 8*

If you're going through hell, keep going.—Winston Churchill

Whedon and Abrams are no strangers to horror. After all, they had cut their teeth on monsters. On the small screen, Whedon crafted *Buffy* and *Angel*, with their ever-present vampires, werewolves, and other children of the night, while Abrams gave us more esoteric beasts like the genetically modified creatures in *Fringe* and the eerie smoke monster from *Lost*. Abrams confesses: "Take genre, add monster . . . equals my favorite movie of all time."[1] Still, neither had yet done horror on the large screen. Well, yes, there was that *Alien: Resurrection* debacle for Whedon, but he and the director had had monstrous creative differences resulting in horrific failure. By 2010 the two TV monster magnates decided to attack the large screen, one with monster quantity and one with size. Whedon cowrote and produced *The Cabin in the Woods* (2012), which featured a slew of imaginative horribles, and Abrams penned and directed *Super 8* (2011) with its destructive behemoth.

Both Abrams and Whedon, as seen in earlier chapters, are renowned for their genre blending and bending. *Buffy* blended horror with comedy and coming-of-age drama, while *Angel* mashed up the horror and film noir detective genres. *Fringe* and *Lost* were science fiction, mystery thriller, horror, and just about anything else someone might throw in there. Not too surprisingly, though, given Hollywood's penchant for the absurdly convoluted "high concept" yet easily categorized cross-genre pitch, we all still find the notion of genre meaningful.

Genre is a strange thing because it is constantly negotiated between filmmakers and those that love watching films. This means its parameters are continually shifting. Whedon had created his own set of rules for his small-screen vampires, which included such things as turning to dust when staked, special "game faces," and the inability to fly, but he stands in a long line of vampire innovators. Bloodsuckers of the 1930s and 1940s, like Tod Browning's Dracula, feared garlic, had to stay out of the sun, and tended to be foreigners, but vampires in Anthony Hickox's *SunDown: The Vampire in Retreat* (1989) wore sunscreen and sombreros and went on very American retreats. In *Blade* (1998) we learn that it is actually UV light that harms the undead and that there are "Daywalkers," like the eponymous hero, who can withstand its effects. Of course, any knowledgeable teen can tell you today's vampires no longer burn in the sun; they just sparkle. These kinds of changes may seem amusing or even matter-of-fact, but they allow genres to speak to new generations with their own particular issues and also allow us to understand what is important to each new set of media consumers. Changes in genres also create space for creativity on the part of the auteur, giving them rules to bump up against and even break.

Horror, unlike other film genres, tends to be defined in terms of intent. Horror movies aim to scare, and although there are numerous rules and conventions for such films—amusingly outlined in the *Scream* franchise—monsters and the desire to frighten are probably the most important. But are *The Cabin* or *Super 8* really horror films by this standard? Both depend on mad scientists, laboratories, and science run amok, suggesting that they are more akin to science fiction.[2] The role of social structures is particularly important to resolving this question.[3] Most sci-fi films look at the effects of imaginary scientific and technological breakthroughs on societies in the near or distant future. Horror, on the other hand, tends to deal with present-day individuals feeling fears that are primal and a part of being human. Sci-fi often asks sweeping, abstract questions. Horror feels more personal. It is along this spectrum of science fiction/horror that primary differences between Abrams and Whedon as people and creators can be seen.

The Cabin and *Super 8* have obvious elements of both the horror and science-fiction genres. They inject speculative scientific effects into the story of a fictional world, but more importantly they focus on the individual characters affected by the events and on monsters that awaken fears in both the characters and the audience. Each filmmaker insists that, when push comes to shove, these films are all about the characters and their personal experience. Abrams, in his 2007 TED Talk, underscores that the characters are "the stuff that matters."[4] Whedon agrees: "I'm never interested in movies where you don't care about the people you're watching, and that's my biggest quibble about horror, that kids have gotten stupider and stupider."[5] Both *Super 8* and *Cabin* reflect this, offering interesting and believable characters that audiences genuinely care about and fear for.

It makes sense that Abrams and Whedon both confirm their commitment to their films as horror. For Abrams, it is about producing fear: "There's this underlying fear that we all have, every day, that something else might happen at any moment. To me the idea of a monster movie, it allows people to experience that kind of fear safely."[6] Whedon commented in publicizing *The Cabin*, that "I love horror. I love terrible, scary situations and you know, people getting into terrible trouble."[7] His summation of the film: "It's a classical horror movie, until it explodes in your face."[8] But more on this later.

A decision about who deserves the "Horror Geek Crown" is a bit problematic because we have to compare pomegranates to cherry pie. Whereas Abrams both wrote and directed *Super 8*, Whedon only co-wrote and produced *The Cabin in the Woods*. *Super 8*, on the other hand, was produced by (wait for it . . .) none other than Steven Spielberg. The difficulty of assessing credit on TV and film projects because of the multiple contributors and numerous production phases has already been discussed, but it is especially tricky here. Plainly Abrams should get full credit for both writing and directing *Super 8*, but does the fact that Spielberg produced and visited the set and gave advice mean subtracting points on the assumption that some of the ideas are Spielberg's? Or should Abrams get bonus points for landing one of the most recognized and talented producers in Hollywood? Does Whedon get half credit for co-writing but lose points for not directing, or possibly merit added credit for giving his friend Drew Goddard the chance to direct his first film? Should writing and producing equal writing and directing?

There is a further complication. A few years earlier in 2007, Abrams had an idea for a horror film, which he then farmed out to a little-known but prolific television writer who had worked with him on *Alias* and *Lost*. Abrams ended up producing the project: a monster film known as *Cloverfield* (2008), which became the talk of the town. The writer was Drew Goddard, the same person who co-wrote and directed *The Cabin in the Woods* with Whedon. And, if that was not incestuous enough, Goddard had not only written for Abrams's Bad Robot Productions, but also for Whedon's Mutant Enemy! Goddard, it turns out, started with Whedon and wrote five episodes each for *Buffy* and *Angel*. He also wrote five episodes of *Alias* and then went on to write nine episodes of *Lost*, before becoming Abram's choice to write *Cloverfield*.

All three films deserve careful consideration and will be useful in establishing the legitimacy of the title "Heir to the Horror Geek Filmmaking Throne." Although it is impossible to tease the Goddard out of the "Whed-dard" film *The Cabin in the Woods*, it is likewise unfeasible to extract him from "Abra-dard" of *Cloverfield* or Spielberg from *Super 8*. Because each film is a joint venture, Whed-dard and Abra-dard will accrue points as chiefs of their amalgamated film teams.

Certain aspects of *Cloverfield* can be directly credited to Abrams. The first is the idea for the film as a horror/monster film. Abrams explains that while in Japan promoting *Mission: Impossible III*, he visited toy stores with his son only to notice Gojira (Godzilla) toys everywhere he looked. This set him to thinking about the fact that Godzilla had become an enduring national character—a Kaiju (strange creature) tied up with the Japanese psyche—and he wondered what a version of an American national monster might look like.[9] It seems he wanted us to wonder too!

One of the most salient properties of *Cloverfield*, and the one for which Abrams deserves credit, is the relative invisibility of the monster. The basic premise is that the film we see in the theater is video camera footage supposedly found in the ruins of Central Park. The amateurish material records the lives of young upper-middle-class urban adults and the effects of a Godzilla-like monster's rampage in Manhattan. The first twenty minutes of the film consist of a good-bye party caught by our reluctant cameraman, Hud, who has been pressed into doing a commemorative tape for a friend relocating to a new job in Japan. We see explosions and destruction, but there is no clear sign of the monster until thirty-odd minutes into the eighty-five-minute film, when we see a tail. Even then, the monster is spotted rarely and only with obstructed views, being glimpsed close up in a single, brief final sequence when it attacks our cameraman Hud. This withholding of the spectacle is consistent with Abrams's theory of mystery as the key to making great films.

Abrams is well known for his near obsession with adding mystery to his stories. In his 2007 TED Talk, Abrams explains, "What I realize I sort of do in whatever it is that I do, is I find myself drawn to infinite possibility, that sense of potential. And I realize that mystery is the catalyst for imagination."[10] So the monster becomes the mystery that the producer hopes will keep the audience engaged. He continues his talk by reminding us that Spielberg's shark from *Jaws* (1975) had malfunctioned and that, apocryphally, this resulted in a monster that was almost never seen in the first half of the film. To Abrams this made it much more scary, suggesting "the withholding of information" creates a "mystery in terms of imagination . . . [and] doing that intentionally is much more engaging."[11] As we have seen, this is pretty much the central principle of *Cloverfield*.

Scott Henderson compares this tactic to the use of a MacGuffin, Hitchcock's famous object that captures audience interest at the beginning of a film but turns out to be unimportant in the larger scheme of things.[12] While Hitchcock, according to interviews with famous French filmmaker François Truffaut, thought of his MacGuffin as "nothing," as a ruse to occupy the audience, it seems clear that Abrams is actually formulating something else that shows more reverence for his audience and for the idea of the mystery.[13] He revisits the idea continually in interview after interview, noting he values the efforts that viewers and fans put into trying to understand in a way that is different from Hitchcock. In an editorial for *Wired*, he tells readers how important it is to "dig" instead of trying to find an easy way out. Informing oneself with spoilers not only ruins the mystery but is cheating per Abrams: "Skipping ahead . . . lessens the experience. Diminishes the joy. Makes the accomplishment that much duller. Perhaps that's why mystery, now more than ever, has special meaning."[14] Throughout most of *Cloverfield*, both the characters and the viewers are eagerly asking the question "What is going on?"

There is a secondary reason that Abrams feels mystery is so significant for today's audience and that relates to the way the Internet and computers have changed our lives and made any information available at the push of a button. The filmmaker concludes that we need the mystery because of the surfeit of information in our daily lives, "because it's the anomaly, the glaring affirmation that the Age of Immediacy has a meaningful downside. Mystery demands that you stop and consider—or, at the very least, slow down and discover. It's a challenge to get there yourself, on its terms, not yours."[15] For film scholar Daniel North, it is precisely this "overabundance of available information" that *Cloverfield* subverts. It withholds the view of the monster and makes the viewer wait for it, "staging a game of 'hide and seek' between audiences and the monster it promises to deliver."[16] And Matt Reeves, the director, ultimately does deliver, perhaps against the better interests of the film.

This "hide and seek" game extended even to the marketing of *Cloverfield*. It can be found in spurious websites created by the production team to send out hints about the movie, like an obscure campaign to promote the drink Slusho that has a minor reference in the film and a website on the Taguruatu drilling company that may have been responsible for awakening the monster from sleep in the depths of the ocean. At one point Abrams gleefully notified Harry Knowles of *Aint It Cool News* that fans had been missing most of the planted websites: "For what it's worth, the only site of ours that people have even FOUND is the 1-18-08.com site."[17] Trailers released during the opening of *Transformers* show scenes and a date that led to the website mentioned above without even naming the film.[18] On sites such as Dreamindemon.com[19] and Gamespot.com,[20] there was predictably huge fan speculation about the film and what the monster would look like. As producer, this has Abrams's fingerprints all over it.

So Abrams's style revolves around two particular focal points: there must be mystery and there must be good characters. He recaps his own ability this way: "I know the idea of mystery and the idea of asking compelling questions" and reiterates this point when promoting his *Star Trek* film: "The key to any of that is having characters you believe and care about."[21] Thus Abrams's mystery must be a personal challenge for the viewer, but films also depend on characters that seem real and about whom we care enough to be concerned and curious with regard to what will happen to them.

Cloverfield's characters, unfortunately, did not have this effect on a significant number of the fans. While the movie was celebrated for its plotline and daring techniques, comments on various gaming and film websites indicate that *Cloverfield* may not have lived up to these principles, to the detriment of the film's quality. While some raved about the monster, many others complained. The fans who love Abrams clearly do so because of his principles and thus despite the fact that Matt Reeves promised to deliver the monster (and did), and for some the film can be faulted for giving in and showing too much, while others could not get enough.

Abrams deserves more credit for the film he wrote and directed himself. *Super 8* has better success because we get characters we can care about. It is not Reeves's fault that the kids of *Cloverfield* seem so superficial. It is likely a result of the found footage conceit. Setting up characters via the amateur filming of a party is simply not conducive to giving the audience a favorable impression. The close-ups, framing, and lighting techniques usually used to indicate sincerity and help us see character depth and nuance cannot be used without jeopardizing the sense that we are viewing amateur video camera footage. It is not that the actors do a bad job; it is that they have no means of seeming like anything but superficial people at a frivolous party.

Super 8 tells the story of five children making a zombie movie who happen to encounter a mystery. While filming near a rail yard, they see a pickup truck drive onto the tracks and derail a train that carries an enigmatic cargo. The main character, Joe, picks up a mysterious white metallic cube, but the focus of the story is the personal issues and human qualities of the characters. The film opens with an initial shot of an accident board at a chemical plant as it is being reset to announce that it has been one day since the last accident. The next sequence begins with a beautiful long shot of a house in the Midwest with a swing set behind it in the distance. The colors are muted, and as we gaze at the shot, we glimpse a child sitting motionless on one of the swings. The shot shows the grief and isolation of the fourteen-year-old protagonist, who has just returned from his mother's funeral. It is she who has died in the accident referenced in the opening shot, and her absence will be a crucial influence in the film.

At his TED Talk, Abrams reminded us that *Jaws* isn't about a shark and that *E.T.* isn't about an alien that meets a kid. "*E.T.* is about divorce. *E.T.* is about a heartbroken, divorce-crippled family and ultimately, this kid who can't find his way."[22] This story may sound familiar. In *Super 8*, the issue is not a divorce—it is a tragic accident—but the family is maimed and the child is alienated and thus there are strong similarities with *E.T.* (1982). The main difference is that Joe Lamb is left without a mother, while Elliott in *E.T.* is missing his father. For several reasons, however, a better film to compare with *Super 8* is not *E.T.* but a different Spielberg film: *Close Encounters of the Third Kind* (1977).

Visually *Super 8* bears a strong resemblance to *Close Encounters*. The film uses blue overtones in its ample night shots along with copious lens flares to remind the viewer of the Spielberg classic. The establishing shot of Joe Lamb's home in *Super 8* angles the house so as to focus on the distant boy on the swing. In *Close Encounters* there is also an early shot of a house angled the same way. This is the home of little Barry, the toddler who runs gleefully off into the woods after strange electrical surges occur. The angled shot of Barry's home forces the viewer to focus on virtually the same spot on the screen, right and middle, where we have seen Joe Lamb on the swing. In Spielberg's film, however, that same spot is occupied by a cloud on the horizon under an impossibly bright starry night. Both shots place a white area in the spot that attracts the eye and emphasizes distance. We don't really think consciously about the clouds in the *Close Encounters* shot but will later learn to associate roiling clouds with the arrival of alien spacecraft that produce billowing cloud banks before appearing dramatically from their midst.

A comparison of the shot framing of homes in *Super 8* (2011) and in *Close Encounters of the Third Kind* (1977).

Abrams is obviously indebted to Spielberg, and he acknowledged this repeatedly in both interviews and in the *Super 8* DVD commentary. Early shots of family members at the mother's wake in *Super 8* resemble early shots of a bank of scientists in *Close Encounters*. Both shots angle characters so as to emphasize the depth of the shot. Abrams was effusive about Spielberg's help during the production, and it is clear that the way Abrams shot films changed drastically between *Mission: Impossible 3* (*M:I-3*) and his second film. *M:I-3*, despite being an action film, is full of straight-on shots centering on the main character, executed by Dan Mindel's very mobile camera. It is easy to see the difference in the two filming styles in still photos taken from each film. *M:I-3*'s first shot of the house that establishes where the engagement party is taking place shows a group of people arriving directly in front of the drive. The actors are centered on the screen. This framing tends to flatten the distance, and the shot feels less dynamic than the angled shots of houses shown before. *M:I-3* often clamps the focal depth down, centering characters in front of blurry backgrounds. This serves to keep the characters as the focus of the shots and reduce distraction but can also make the shots duller in terms of composition.

A comparison of shots of social occasions in these films reveals important differences in cinematographic style. Abrams shows people attending a wake near the start of *Super 8* and opens with people attending an engagement party in *M:I-3*. People at the wake tend to be placed carefully. These shots are generally angled and thoughtfully framed to give a dynamic image that breaks up horizontal lines and enhances the impression of depth. *M:I-3*'s party frequently places people more randomly. Comparing shots with approximately equal numbers of people shows this style difference vividly. A sample frame of the fiancée and her friends from *M:I-3* presents a flatter image of people mostly in rectilinear planes. Background and foreground are slightly blurred, with attention being drawn to the two characters centered in the shot. In the scene from *Super 8*, the heads form a broken line across the screen in contrast to the straight line of the heads from the *M:I-3* party. The angles of the boys' arms vary greatly, while the women's arms form two double sets of parallel lines, both of which frame the center of the screen and restrict our eyes to the focal point. In short, there is a vibrancy and dynamism to the shot of the juvenile filmmakers at the wake that is missing in the more casual-looking party shots of *Mission: Impossible 3*.

Super 8 does not look like any of Abrams's earlier work. The director chose to use cinematographer Larry Fong, whom he met at a film festival at the age of twelve, to shoot his second film. They had made actual Super 8 films together and worked jointly to give the film a subjective feel of the 1970s, which seemed to them like the glory days of film. Fong's camera style in previous productions like *Watchmen* was quite active but tended to center the focal point and produce straight-on shots with shorter focal lengths so that backgrounds became fuzzy and unclear. In *Super 8* he moved abruptly away from this style. Fong still keeps the camera moving, but rather than obscuring backgrounds and incidental objects through focus, he forces our attention away from the center through shot composition and carefully obstructed views. Abrams has him shoot through crowds and swing sets, for example, a technique that produces dynamic angles and much more composed but interesting shots. Whether Abrams learned this lesson from *Cloverfield* or Spielberg or both, *Super 8* marks a change in the visual style.

In a *Time* magazine interview, Abrams noted, "Steven helped at every stage including editorial."[23] Even at the idea stage, Abrams credited

J. J. Abrams coaching Tom Cruise as Ethan Hunt in *Mission: Impossible 3* (2006).
Paramount / Photofest © Paramount Pictures

Spielberg with inspiration, mentioning they had "countless meetings" before Spielberg pushed him to go off and write on his own.[24] In the *Super 8* extras, Abrams also tells of Spielberg's visits to the set and how he encouraged him to shoot scenes in particular ways. One example was his advice that Abrams hint at the monster by showing its reflection in a gas puddle during a gas station scene in which the sheriff disappears. Spielberg also suggested having a pack of dogs run through the scene, an event that strengthens the story by becoming a tie-in to the mysterious absence of the town's dogs later in the film.[25]

The connection between *Super 8* and *Close Encounters* involves more than a plot about contact between people and aliens. Abrams confesses, in one of the featurettes included on the DVD, that the clutter and chaos of the Neary family from *Close Encounters* influenced the way he chose to portray the family of Joe's best friend, Charles Kaznyk.[26] Scenes in the Kaznyk home are shot by Fong's active camera, but the backgrounds are sharp and deep. In one set-up, Fong shoots across the dining room table and room to focus on the relatively static Joe and Charles watching TV. Spielberg suggested shooting through the family, who are in the midst of lively parental discussions and sibling squabbles.

Both *Super 8* and *Close Encounters* are also structured to connect two dynamically different story halves, but the connection is handled in two different ways. Abrams's film focuses its first section on the personal stories of the characters and how they get pulled into the mystery. He cleaves closely to his own advice about making the characters people we care about. We get to know the now motherless Joe Lamb and his zombie-movie-obsessed friend Charles fairly well before the train wreck introduces the supernatural element. We have already begun to care about Joe when we see the chaos of his home during his mother's wake, but when Charles brings Alice literally into "the picture" because he needs a wife for the detective hero in his amateurish *Super 8* zombie film, he also brings stress to his bond with Joe and a love interest into the larger film.

Abrams uses the premise that Joe doesn't understand why Charles wants a wife in his film, in order to insert a scene in which Charles can school Joe on creating motivation and human interest in film. The budding young director begins telling his friend, "The scene we're filming tonight where the wife is telling the detective that she's scared for him and she loves him . . . ," but Joe interrupts distractedly to exclaim, "I can't believe you talked to Alice Dardain." Here, Joe telegraphs to the viewer his interest in Alice in a particularly sweet and innocent boyish way. Charles pushes on with his explanation, "So when he investigates the zombie stuff you feel something; you don't want him to die because they love each other." Abrams points out he is "doing the very thing in the scene that the scene's talking about."[27] Having Charles explain to his best friend that a film's audience needs to see the human side of his characters in order to care about them makes us, the real audience, care about their friendship and the impending tension over the fact that they both secretly like the same girl.

The second parts of *Close Encounters* and *Super 8* concentrate more on the creatures of the film and feel a bit different from the films' initial halves. In this respect *Cloverfield* does a better job of merging the human stories with the monster/action parts of the film. The transition is seamless, only because there are so many other visible seams in *Cloverfield*, such that the narrative switch from party to monster movie goes unnoticed. Because the footage dissolves into prior footage on the tape that is being recorded over or stops and starts, loses focus, or pixelates, we are less liable to notice the film's story structures. In fact, it seems like random footage without a coherent story, so we simply do not notice the narrative change because of all the other interruptions in the action that slow our ability to put together a coherent story.

Close Encounters takes a different approach from *Super 8*. Rather than opening with our main character, it sets the hero Roy Neary's story between scenes of scientists trying to solve the outer space mystery. The film begins with French scientist Claude Lacombe's investigation into the reappearance of planes that had gone missing decades earlier and ends with his and our discovery of where they had been and why. Neary's quest to discover what happened when he saw the strange lights in the sky gets far more coverage than the scenes in the desert with UFOlogist Lacombe, so by starting with Lacombe, Spielberg solves the problem of narrative imbalance and strengthens the film's structure, making it feel more coherent as it proceeds to slowly reveal how the two stories are related before finally merging them together.

Abrams chooses not to do this with *Super 8*, starting instead with the establishment of the character with whom he wants us to identify. This enhances sympathy for Joe and his friends. Part of the problem with *Close Encounters* is that it spends too much time on Neary's obsession and not enough on establishing who he was before his encounter. This is important given the way we will see him treat his family. As Christopher Lloyd points out on his *Film Yap* review,

> Consider this movie told from the perspective of Roy's wife Ronnie, played by Teri Garr. In that sense, it's the story of a guy who abandons his wife and kids to go wandering after lights in the sky, even making out with some other alien-chasing hussy before fleeing to a black hole in space from whence no child support payments ever returned. [28]

That's pretty tough behavior to defend without some intense character build-up.

Spielberg tries to establish Neary's love of his family with shots of him and his children. He also injects the theme of Pinocchio, who must travel the world in order to become a real boy, but the Pinocchio motif is a symbolic one that is referenced through music cues and imagery and it does not result in a visceral connection to the character. The harshness of Neary's action is even acknowledged by the director himself, who indicated in an interview with Ethan Aames on his *War of the Worlds* (2005) remake that he had no children when he did *Close Encounters*. "Today, I would never have the guy leaving his family and going on the mother ship," Spielberg said. "I would have the guy doing everything he could to protect his children." [29] Thus Neary's fairly rapid descent into monomania makes the character less compelling, whereas Abrams avoids diluting interest in the main character by spending more time in the beginning of *Super 8* showing Joe's sorrow and building the relationship between Charles and Joe.

Both films deal with geeky main characters who get a chance to become heroes, but the distinction between science-fiction film and horror film also plays a role in how we perceive the characters. *Close Encounters* falls squarely into the science-fiction genre. Despite the effort to focus on Roy Neary's psychological state after his encounter with the alien spaceship, the film tends to be less personal and more concentrated on explaining narrative situations. It is not a monster movie per se. Instead it takes a common-knowledge mythology about aliens and weaves it into a story that essentially brings E.T.'s parents to earth for a somewhat believable intercultural powwow. Much of what we see in Spielberg's film involves the effects on townspeople, governmental/military reactions to the presence, and the role of science in our times. The film embraces the science-fiction aspect of the creature and not the horror side.

Super 8 just barely stays on the other side of the horror line. Even though both films have scientists and misunderstood creatures, to a large extent the middle section of *Super 8* depends on fear and the threat that the alien being poses to the characters we care about. The horror component makes it feel more personal. The film inverts the structure of *Close Encounters* by inserting the story of scientific research into the middle section of the larger story about Joe and Charles. It also changes the relationship of scientist to government and makes the former less political. There are no scientists at all visible in *Cloverfield*, and authority is visible only in the form of a well-intentioned but incompetent military trying both to help people and to defeat a basically invincible foe. *Close Encounters*, on the other hand, depicts an uneasy relationship between science and the government, presenting a sympathetic scientist in Lacombe, who works in a troubled affiliation with a militarized government bent on secrecy. The military, as an active arm of the government, is not above lying to the public or gassing helpless animals so they lie about unconscious and simulate the effects of a nerve gas accident (the government's pretext for cordoning off the aliens' landing site). The government has no problem with terrifying the public. Arguments between Lacombe and military advisers lead the viewer to separate scientific curiosity from government interests and lend sympathy to the side of "neutral" science. This is validated by Lacombe's insistence to the military that Neary and the others were invited to the landing site and have more right to be there than the authorities. It can only be intentionally disconcerting, therefore, when a Jewish director uses images of the military loading civilians onto transport vehicles to evacuate them to supposed camps of refuge.

J. J. Abrams also follows Spielberg by using shots reminiscent of Holocaust imagery in *Super 8*. Once again the military, as the long arm of government, is depicted negatively. This time it is the air force that sets fires outside of town to persuade residents they are in danger from a potential eruption of the local chemical plant. The armed forces also evacuate the county with buses and trucks. Both films' imagery echoes familiar, disturbing pictures of Jewish citizens handing baggage and belongings through train windows as Nazi soldiers crowd them into trains for transfer to concentration camps. A more negative metaphor is hard to imagine.

These images highlight the military's cruelty and lack of scruples and the contrasting goodness of science. The internment camp is indirectly referenced by our representative good-guy scientist when he argues with military leaders, and it is the scientist, Dr. Woodward, who drives the truck onto the train tracks in order to thwart the air force's transport of the alien being and its belongings to its new internment camp. At this point in the film, the audience has no idea of what is on the train, but our young heroes are warned by the injured scientist that if they are discovered near the wreck, they are risking their lives and the lives of their parents. Dramatically Woodward announces that some unidentified "they" "will kill you." This dramatic warning mechanism serves to locate *Super 8* solidly in the horror film genre and also crystalizes the nature of the monstrous villain. "They," of course, turns out to refer not to aliens but the air force, and they do not hesitate to torment and experiment upon the alien creature, who ultimately, like poor little E.T., simply wants to reassemble his spaceship so he can go home. A vital aspect of the film is thus its transformation in the final section from a monster movie to a human drama, asking us to see with compassion. One man's monster is another man's freedom fighter.

As Richard Corliss of *Time* magazine put it, *Super 8* "plays with genre expectations, then transcends and obliterates them."[30] We, the characters, and humans in general need to learn compassion for the creature, who is maltreated and misunderstood by heartless military personnel, and it is the beginning that prepares us for this message. The film invokes the mythology of parenthood as the source of compassionate and unconditional love by opening on the boy's sadness at his mother's death. Joe Lamb is shown sitting on a swing in the film's initial moments fingering his mom's locket in memory of her loss. One of the first things the viewer hears at the wake is Charles's mom, Mrs. Kaznyk, as she tells her husband about her concern for Joe. Mr. Kaznyk thinks that Joe's dad, Jack Lamb, is a good man who is going to "step up," but the mother worries that he doesn't understand his son and "has never had to be a father before." Jack will have to learn compassion for his son and to accept who Joe is—realizing, for example, that a sports camp is not the right place for his geeky, film-obsessed child to deal with his grief.

Indeed, over the course of the film, the question of compassion is raised repeatedly. Joe's father, Jack—through his experience of suddenly becoming the town's sole police authority—may even learn a little humility. After the sheriff's mysterious disappearance, he finds himself heir to a sheriff's department and all the problems brought on by the train wreck, the military cover-up, and the weird behavior of objects since the escape of the alien creature. This includes electrical disturbances, strange thefts, and the aforementioned disappearance of every dog in town including his own. This experience of helplessness and being kept in the dark by the military, of being unable to do anything officially to help the citizens of Lillian, Ohio, may be what allows him to feel compassion, not only for Joe but also for others. He will begin to feel sorry for Alice's lonely alcoholic father, Louis Dainard—a man whose wife has left him and whom Jack Lamb personally holds responsible for the death of his own wife. Lamb will come to recognize that laying the blame for Elizabeth Lamb's death on the alcoholic Dainard is a waste of time, and in the end he will be able to assure Dainard dispassionately that his wife's death was an accident. They have both, after all, suffered the loss of a beloved spouse.

Dealing with the loss of the mother may seem very pop-psych oedipal, but it works. Freud suggested that children, in order to grow up, must overcome and thus "kill" the control of their parents in order to develop into independent human beings.[31] Of course, the oedipal process is simply the generation conflict clothed in academic jargon. Joe recognizes when he fights with his father about Alice that his dad is not always right. This is a step toward realizing that he must let go literally of his dependence on his dead mother. At the film's climax, when metallic objects are being drawn toward the town's water tower, Abrams includes a scene in which Joe physically lets go of the locket with his mother's picture and it flies off toward the tower. This release can only occur after his epiphany with the alien. Near the end of the film, the monster begins to advance on the children but instead of running, Joe turns and—looking into the alien's eyes—sees something, and he tells it, "*I know* bad things happen, but you can still live" (italics mine). Joe may be telling the alien, but he is also ac*know*ledging this for himself. Standing up to his father over his desire to have a relationship with Alice sets the oedipal process in motion, and when Joe saves her from the creature's lair, he signals the discovery of a replacement for the missing mother and his readiness to take his place in the world of adults.

Abrams makes this coming-of-age story a bit more interesting by showing us that additional but necessary step toward maturity. You can only move forward if you can learn to let go of the past. As the creature rages and threatens to kill them all, Joe, in a very Spielbergian moment, finds compassion for the alien. This plot point has been set up midway through the film in a rather enigmatic scene between Dr. Woodward and the military commander. The scientist is being threatened and will eventually be killed by the ethically challenged Colonel Nelec, when Woodward says something to the effect that an unidentified "he" "is in me as I am in him." The statement seems somewhat out of place, as if the man of science has suddenly switched to speaking in mystical religious terms, but it sets up the basis for empathetic compassion.

Of course, Woodward's words are as another precisely placed clue to the mystery—a keynote of Abrams's style. We learn in a later sequence, from film footage found in Dr. Woodward's trailer behind the school, that the scientist worked previously with the military on top-secret alien-related experiments. When he was touched by the alien creature, the two of them formed an empathic bond that caused Woodward to question the ethics of the air force's actions. In the footage found in the trailer, Woodward decries the military's lack of compassion for, and treatment of, the alien being, blaming them for frightening and torturing it.

At *Super 8*'s climax, in the creature's lair (or perhaps we should call it his workshop), Joe experiences a similar empathic bond. The creature bats Joe out of the way in pursuit of his victims, but Joe, in his desire to save Alice, refuses to flee, and there is a moment when we fear he will be devoured whole. This is the moment when Joe turns and looks up at the creature. Their eyes meet and Joe delivers his knowing line about knowing that bad things happen. Joe, as a creature in pain and grief, connects with the other creature in pain and grief and gives both himself and his alien companion the permission they need to go home. This E.T. uses a vehicle somewhat larger than a bicycle, but he more or less clicks his heels, assembles his ship, and handily demonstrates Joe's growth into adulthood by heading off into space. Perhaps the alien, too, has matured and learned a little compassion as well.

Looking, rather than being the intrusive act of scientific domination, instead here confers mutual recognition. In a scene with Alice, Joe describes his feelings of loss for his mother. "She used to look at me . . . this way, like really look," he says, "and I just knew I was there . . . that I existed." While this is the look of maternal love, it is also a look that suggests mutuality rather than superiority or dominance. It is a shared moment between sentient beings. It is this look that is repeated between Joe and the monster and that gives the alien dignity and permission to leave. Joe's bravery and growth in recognizing the viewpoint of the Other also give him permission to move on into adulthood and with his relationship with Alice. Freud would be very proud.

Abrams manages the scene with marvelous self-possession. He turns the film, in its last section, from a monster movie into a magical but restrained coming-of-age melodrama. In contrast to similar scenes by Spielberg, there is no grandiosely swelling John Williams music to manipulate the tear ducts and no melodramatic good-byes. There is magnetic chaos, the slightly tearful release of the mother's locket to ensure the audience "gets" it, and then the film goes on. The ship assembles itself, and the alien departs in a spectacular but unsentimental fashion.

Abrams thus follows through beautifully on his principles: he sets a contiguous series of mysteries that pull the audience in; he balances the tone of the film carefully and withholds information at crucial moments to keep our interest. He gets accolades for combining the aspects above with his use of highly personable characters we can care about, for respecting his characters, and for giving them believable and worthwhile issues to contend with, especially in terms of the consistent theme of the importance of compassion.

A similar concern about the significance of character in the horror genre is evident in Joss Whedon's *Cabin in the Woods*. When talking about the film, which he co-wrote with director Drew Goddard, numerous interviewers asked Whedon why he wanted to make a horror film in the first place. His response was that he had loved this type of film as a child but also that he wanted to explore why people needed them.[32] Finally, he mentioned that he was disturbed about the way horror films had been trending. Newer films, which tended toward torture porn, turned the characters into "just fodder" for ever-more-faceless villains.[33] He wanted to reverse the trend.

Abrams and Whedon both shared concerns about the development of torture porn, but Whedon was more outspoken about it. In an interview with Michael Leader, Whedon stressed,

> I'm never interested in movies where you don't care about the people you're watching, and that's my biggest quibble about horror, that kids have gotten stupider and stupider. And people say, "Oh, it's horrible! They are all tortured for 90 minutes, but it's okay because they're not

very likable." And it's like, what part of that sentence was supposed to sell me?[34]

Cabin, he told Franklin Oliver of *GQ*, started as "a logical extension of what I think about horror movies" and the fact that they were "becoming this extremely nihilistic and misogynist exercise in just trying to upset you, as opposed to trying to scare you."[35] We will not be scared if we are dumbfounded by the stupidity of the characters.

In the companion book to the movie, Whedon emphasizes how important it is to have sympathetic, well-developed characters in horror: "You look at the other classics and they're good people—they're friends, they care about each other. And the more they do that, the more charming and the more they care, the more you care about them, the scarier it is."[36] Whedon's co-conspirator Drew Goddard also underscores the significance of character to his friend and co-writer. Addressing the wisdom he garnered in working with both Abrams and Whedon, Goddard said: "The important lesson I always learned from Joss is to respect the characters and the most important lesson I learned from JJ is respect the audience."[37] While each writer uses characters for different purposes, they are clearly central to the aims of the films.

The Cabin in the Woods is the story of five college friends who spend a weekend partying in the woods. The opening sequence actually has nothing to do with the students but establishes instead a sterile laboratory control room peopled by a lab-coated female scientist and two "good old boy" codgers with ties and identity badges. Whedon and Goddard ("Whedard") crosscut between this institute and the college kids starting out on their journey. Somewhere about the time the young people pass through a tunnel and an eagle flying nearby hits a weird force field, the audience begins to make the connection. When the young people stop at an eerie, abandoned gas station and hear words of the harbinger of doom, there can be no question that they are the subject of some kind of strange lab experiment engineered by the scientists at the nefarious institution. We watch the students being observed on-screen and see them being chemically and electronically manipulated via a control panel in a large, multiscreened master control room.

The idea of making these characters people, in whom we take general interest, is a good instinct, but it clashes a bit with another of the filmmakers' goals—that of laying bare the tired tropes of contemporary hor-

Scientists Sitterson (Richard Jenkins), Lin (Amy Acker), and Hadley (Bradley Whitford) confer in *The Cabin in the Woods* (2012). *Lionsgate / Photofest © Lionsgate; photographer Diyah Pera*

ror film. By playing on the typical character stereotypes, "Whedard" risks falling right back into the same stale stories being decried and reducing viewer interest in the characters. *Indiewire* maintains that by "successfully analyzing tired formulas, it gives them new life" but concludes that the primary female character, Dana, "has little to offer beyond the batting of her eyes in terror and the occasional blood-curdling scream, but somebody had to do it. Like the cabin, she's hardly more than a prop."[38] Unfortunately this sounds a bit like the torture porn condemned by Whedon in his interviews.

Indeed, the success of the film to a large extent depends on us caring about the last two characters remaining at the end of the film, but because the satire depends on assigning the five students to the iconic horror-movie roles of the virgin, the athlete, the fool, the whore, and the scholar, there is a tendency for the audience to tag them with these general characteristics and not to see them as individuals. The first scene, which takes place before we have consciously identified the archetypes, attempts to mitigate these kinds of stereotypes but doesn't leave us attached in the way we become to Joe Lamb and his friends in the early scenes of *Super 8*. Perhaps the problems of some college kids headed off to a cabin for a party just don't seem as important as the death of a child's mother. At any rate, both *Cloverfield* and *Cabin* give us financially well-off characters who want to party, and it is harder for us to care about them, especially because we are told of their issues rather than empathizing by experiencing them.

Cabin's first scene with the students works a little too hard to get us involved. We see newly blond Jules trying to get her brainy friend Dana out of the dumps. These women stand in for the "virgin" and "whore," but part of the point of the scene is that neither actually fit the bill. Although Jules is looking forward to a weekend of hooking up with her boyfriend, that hardly makes her either a whore or a slut, and as Whedon's fans know all too well from past television series, like *Buffy* and *Angel*, just because Jules has blond hair, it does not mean she is stupid. Except in this case it does because despite the fact that she is pre-med, the scientists in the lab have drugged her hair dye to cause her to act more on impulse. Whedon's tongue is planted firmly in cheek, and while we find this humorous, this kind of irony also serves to distance us from the characters rather than creating sympathy for them.

Likewise, Dana embodies the "virgin," but she is hardly deserving of the designation. Her friend Marty playfully calls her a "home-wrecker," for she has in fact played the other woman in a relationship with one of her married professors. This representative of the established generation (and the academic establishment) has just ended the relationship via e-mail. Dana has been left reeling and in some pain but certainly not a virgin. A third student, Marty, is "the fool" but also the smartest of the group, and as for the other two—the "scholar" and the "athlete"—they are so similar in appearance and intellect that it is difficult to tell which is supposed to be which without a program. The point is, the "brain" is athletic and the "jock" is smart, but this simply leads to confusion, given that stereotypes are being used in the first place.

The character of Marty demonstrates, however, that it is not merely the formulaic structures that inhibit the audience from bonding with the characters. Marty is a lovable, charismatic geek, who is always stoned out his mind. As the designated fool of the group, he—in typical literary form—shows more sense than any of the others. He warns them (and us) at each appropriate moment when members of the group are about to make bad decisions. Fran Kranz, the actor who brings Marty to life, makes the potentially pretentious dialogue lively and amusing, and with his interpretation of the sagacious stoner, he gives us a genuinely genial character.

Whedon likes to work with young, relatively unknown actors, but in the case of those cast as the other college students, the lack of acting experience and nuance shows. With the exception of Kranz, who has appeared in several Whedon projects, the young person side of the film is fairly lackluster in comparison with the shading and humor found in the manipulative laboratory team characters. Longtime Whedonite Amy Acker, along with Bradley Whitford and Richard Jenkins, make the furtive corporation's representatives—Lin, Hadley, and Sitterson—into tangible characters. They play people we have all encountered at some point in life and likely even worked with. Acker, as usual, portrays a scientist with a conscience, while the other two—the likable codgers from the opening shot—highlight the inexplicable suffering imposed by the older generation on the younger in the rigid belief that what they are doing is important.

The film's photography is solid and classically composed. Under the watchful eye of Peter Deming, the shots are balanced, lively, and beautifully framed. Deming is a superb choice for the film, having previously done cinematography for *Evil Dead II* and the *Scream* movies, as well as for the creatively shot *Mulholland Drive* and *Oz, the Great and Powerful*. Either because of direction or on his own, the cinematographer uses angles in framing to keep the shots vibrant and is fairly careful to avoid centering actors in the middle of the screen. In this the photography rivals the excellence of *Super 8*. Our introduction shots of Hadley and Sitterson, for example, place them slightly to left of center, leaving room for chemist Wendy Lin to enter and join them from the right. Shots of Dana and Jules in Dana's bedroom are visually engaging and balanced, with Jules being shot to the left of center amid the cascading chains of a bead curtain pulled up and away from the opening of a closet. The camera moves fluidly but not constantly, and movement within the frame tends to alternate on diagonals to keep the eye attentive. A shot of the camper taking off shows it moving forward on one angle while a crane lifts the camera upward. An additional shot of the vehicle follows, this time from behind depicting it heading off at an opposing angle. Houses and trees along the angled road keep the shot composition alive and asymmetrical. One notable exception to the avoidance of centrally placed characters is the establishing shot of the cabin. Our first view of this eponymous "character" is a static, low-angle shot that centers it ominously, making it loom above us to create suspense and expectant tension.

Like Spielberg, Deming frequently employs obstructed shots by shooting through a variety of foregrounded visual obstacles. This heightens the tension and makes the viewer work a bit to see the subject. In images as simple as the camper driving up to the cabin, branches of trees impinge on our view as the camera cranes upward to focus on the arrival. An earlier sequence at a deserted gas station is filmed through the various detritus and decaying junk lying around the premises, providing a comely deep focus that emphasizes the eeriness of the desolate location and also the accurate feeling that the students are being watched.

The most magnificent use of this type of camera technique occurs in the unlit cellar of the cabin when the students go down to explore the strange objects that apparently have been left behind by the cabin's prior owners. In dark, emotionally charged low-contrast shots, Deming captures strange toy-like mechanisms, an antique bridal gown, old film projectors, and other mysterious objects with a roving light source that stands in for the flashlight used by Dana as she stumbles around the cellar. The combination of the slowly moving camera and the erratic lighting creates a collage of gorgeous and frightening imagery: of doll faces, old portraits, and crumbling family artifacts, all part of the production design of Martin Whist, who also did the design work on *Cloverfield*. When the other students come down to help Dana explore, they are glimpsed in long, dark shots through the stacks of silhouetted junk, a technique that creates the tension of withheld information so important for suspense.

Cabin does not give us a warm, feel-good story connected to happy childhood memories. On the contrary, it speaks to a world that has become complicated for young people to navigate in part due to the traditions and perspectives of the older generation that controls it. The film's young people are not slackers. They are studying serious college subjects, like political economy, medicine, and sociology, and simply want to enjoy a weekend off; still, as in conventional cabin and slasher movies, they will be punished for wanting to have a little socially transgressive fun.

A social component to the film unfolds in the way it compares the students and the team at the mysterious institution. The scientists too work hard, and at the point when the goal of both groups is achieved by the younger people's arrival at the cabin, the same refrain echoes from both sides, "Let's get this party started!" In reference to her colleagues, scientist Lin tells us, "This job isn't easy, however those clowns may behave!" The two groups, through both parallel editing and dialogue, are thus placed side by side for comparison. The party behavior is equally inane on both sides of the monitors. The young people drink and play games, in this case "Truth or Dare." The scientists drink and play games by betting on the outcome of their endeavor in a huge office pool. The primary difference here is age. The lab people are most probably examples of what these young privileged people would have eventually grown up to be.

While *Super 8* gives us the 1970s and the loss of innocence that leads to the world we see in *Cabin*, it touches us sentimentally and gives us hope for the world. God is in heaven, even if all is not quite right with the world. Not so in *The Cabin in the Woods*. Where *Super 8* is warm and fuzzy, *Cabin* is prickly and snide. It is also very funny. *Cabin* confronts us with yet another wry but pessimistically likely Whedon apocalypse. These modes of storytelling accentuate the differences between the two filmmakers. While Abrams reveals a certain sentimental and optimistic hope for humanity, Whedon reveals a more cynical, pessimistic side. This means while Abrams concentrates on heroic personal victories, Whedon is more likely to examine the failures of the system. In an interview with Abbie Bernstein he made this point explicit:

> Ultimately . . . so much of our behavior is socialized and programmed and so much of it is self-destructive and useless and cruel, and so much of our society is more and more in the hands of a few very rich, very corrupt people, or very well-meaning people who have no business controlling the lives of others. It doesn't matter if they're corrupt or well-intentioned—the point is, we are all controlled, we are all experimented upon, and we are all dying from it. And we are all completely unaware of it.[39]

Adulthood, in other words, means being necessarily corrupted by the system.

Whereas Abrams frees his young hero from his oedipal fixation and lets him get on with his life, Whedon reverses the process. He reconceives the oedipal intergenerational conflict as a process in which the father kills (whatever is genuine or unique about) the child, before allowing its morally zombified remains to take a place of power in the parental world order. The world of *Cabin* is one in which adults both destroy and live vicariously through the actions of the young. The director of the institution says as much at the end of the film, when she begs the two last survivors, Dana and Marty, to complete the ritual sacrifice to appease the old, cruel gods that, she claims, without their sacrifice will be awakened and destroy the world. Her message seems altruistic and utilitarian, "Your deaths will avert countless others," but Dana realizes that it is not just a question of killing. A summary execution on an altar is not enough. This is a question of punishment. In response to the question of why, the director admits that they are being punished "for being young." In light of the Whedon quote above, this means they are being punished for being incompletely socially programmed.

Despite its dark nature, the film is at times laugh-out-loud funny. Interviewer Drew Taylor mentions this "double-edged nature" of the film, as both cutting satire and a celebration of the horror, what Whedon has called "a loving hate letter" to the genre.[40] The sequence in which our two codgers Hadley and Sitterson put the curmudgeonly gas station attendant/harbinger (of doom) on speakerphone is absurd, in all senses of the word. It both acknowledges the customary horror film trope (also used in *Super 8*) of a weird messenger delivering the final ominous warning after which characters can no longer turn back to safety but also adds unpredictable humor. Hearing the nineteenth-century rhetoric of damnation stream from a speakerphone is both uncanny and at the same time hilarious. Hadley and Sitterson cannot help but laugh as Mordecai the harbinger tinnily declaims about the students' blind eyes seeing nothing and the need to cleanse the world of ignorance and sin. They laugh, despite the fact that the two company men believe in the religious dimension of what they are doing. We see this when Sitterson piously kisses a medallion with a religious insignia and delivers an invocation after the sacrificial death of Jules.

An equally double-edged humorous moment comes when Curt, the athlete, announces that they should all stay together and then suddenly reverses this wise decision. The audience watches him do so via chemical manipulation from the control room. After inhaling vapors from the duct system, he draws a different conclusion: "This isn't right," he says. "We should split up. We can cover more ground that way." And everyone in the now confused group agrees. Everyone, that is, except for the already extremely intoxicated Marty, who can only respond with an incredulous "Really?" In these examples, we see that "Whedard" manages to both explain the ridiculous actions of the kids, while also self-reflexively ridiculing the stupidity of the characters in the slasher films that *Cabin* parodies, who set themselves up to be picked off one by one.

Whedon skillfully combines satire and horror and deserves recognition for letting Goddard direct! He has created a masterful, at times scary and at others hilarious and absurd film with excellent cinematography along with a funny, tight script. *Cabin* deserves additional praise for presenting a huge panoply of scary monsters, some seventy or eighty in total, and for having been able to create them on a shoestring budget over a very short period of time. Finally the social criticism aspect of the film gives it unusual depth for a horror film.

The story of *Cabin*'s production would make a fabulous film in itself. The two writers followed the *Cloverfield* model of selling the film by prepackaging the proposal as a completed script needing a small (by Hollywood standards) budget. Goddard told Drew Taylor: "We just said, 'This is what it is, this is what it is going to cost—if you want it, great, if you don't, no hard feelings' and sent it to the studios."[41] After a bit of bidding, the script was picked up by MGM, which then went bankrupt around the time the film finished shooting. The studio needed to make money or else start selling off assets, so after considering and shelving a not-so-brilliant plan to convert *Cabin* to 3-D, MGM sold it to Lionsgate, which released *Cabin* in 2012, some three years after it had been written and made.[42] *Cabin* merits credit for getting out to the public at all.

The Cabin in the Woods does not, however, get any credit for subtlety. You do not need a microscope to detect a message. The film attacks just about any authority figure it references, whether commercial, academic, or scientific, male or female. We are all corruptible and you know what they say about absolute power! When the last two survivors, Dana and Marty, decide not to sacrifice themselves for the survival of the world, some might regard this as a selfish act, but Dana voices what is most likely the sentiment of the writers: "Humanity, pfft," she says, exhaling smoke from Marty's joint. "It's time to give someone else a chance." This echoes Marty's earlier rant in the camper about letting the world crumble. "Society is binding," he says. "It's filling in the cracks with concrete. No cracks to slip through. Everything is recorded, filed, blogged, chips in our kids so they don't get lost—society needs to crumble. We're all too chicken-shit to let it." Besides sounding a lot like Whedon's assessment of the world in the *Cabin* interview, this idea also sets up the finale and clarifies Dana and Marty's decision not to sacrifice themselves to the old gods, not as cowardice, but an act of heroism. The rumbling and destruction seem to indicate the beginning of the end, and *Cabin* finishes leaning more toward the science-fiction end of the spectrum with its clear, uncompromising indictment of the system.

People have asked Goddard and Whedon frequently if there is a possibility for a *Cabin in the Woods* sequel. This might seem pretty silly given what has just been described, but amazingly, they do not reject the idea out of hand. Indeed, hands offer what might perhaps be a hint of hope in the otherwise apocalyptically bleak scenario. As the two survivors lament the fact that they will not get the chance to see the "giant evil gods" about to destroy the world, Dana holds out her hand, which Marty takes and squeezes. *Cabin* thus ends on an idea similar to that found at the end of *Cloverfield*: when you cannot do anything about the destruction of the macrocosm, the answer is in the private world and in relationships with those you care about. *Super 8*, too, ends with Joe and Alice clasping hands as they watch the alien blast off in his rebuilt space vehicle. And yet in *Cabin*, the reassuring hand squeeze is not the last hand that we see. The final shot is of a gigantic god's hand thrusting up through the cabin, completely annihilating it. While it is quite possible that this represents exactly what the corporation's director has predicted—the waking of the ancient evil gods to destroy the world—it could conceivably be something else; such as a gigantic, absurd high five to the petty humans who have refused to uphold a mercilessly unfair system built on abuse of the young.[43]

These three films—*Cloverfield*, *Super 8*, and *The Cabin in the Woods*—tell us much about their makers, but they also share commonalities. Each, in its own way, stresses the importance of relationships but does so in a way reflective of the values and personality of its creative team. All recognize the importance of character and mystery and examine the potential formulation of the contemporary horror film showing the common, core values shared by Whedon and Abrams. The films also show genre creativity by blending categories and redefining generic expectations.

Reviewing Abrams's horror film work reveals a dichotomy. *Cloverfield* gives us the most straightforward monster film but one in which the monster is not conquered and in which the status quo is not restored. This ultimately endorses a turning away from political solutions toward personal ones but threatens to encourage us—like the proverbial ostrich—to hide our heads in the remaining rubble. Love doesn't conquer all, but in some cases it is all we have. *Super 8* looks back to a more golden time of our youth, suggesting discontent with the complexity of the current world and a distrust of the government and military as institutions that both hide the truth from the public and show a proclivity to let ends justify the means. There is a modicum of hope in *Super 8*, as empathy brings resolution to a variety of problems. The alien's disruptive presence is removed, and lessons of compassion are learned. Joe becomes an adult and can move on, giving us the hopeful mantra that we can survive the bad things that happen to us.

The Cabin in the Woods reflects the gloomier vision of *Cloverfield* but with a different tone. Whedon's approach is distinctly humorous and cynical. He has a message, and he is not subtle in its projection. As mentioned by Michael Leader, Whedon intones, "Well, you know, I don't like to create something that doesn't say anything."[44] His pronouncements, made through the character of Marty, tell of a corrupt world that gives little hope for the future without major change. It is depressing and yet he says it in such a funny fashion.

This is not to say that either *Super 8* or *Cloverfield* lack humor. Quite the contrary. *Cloverfield*'s audience is highly entertained and charmed by Hud's wandering eye and lens and by his human curiosity about subjects and conversations he simply should not be filming. *Super 8*, too, is full of warm, fuzzy humor such as Charles, the boy-director, obsessing over "production value." It is a reflexive humor that lovingly pokes fun at itself. Riley Griffiths, who plays Charles, is reported to have based his performance on the way Abrams acted on the set.[45] Another example is the amusing quirkiness of a young convenience store clerk who bobs his head to the music of Blondie on his new Walkman while, unbeknownst to him, disaster happens all around. This is the gentle humor of human foibles and perceptions. We see and feel through the eyes of our characters. The train wreck is huge and lasts forever, not for the sake of realism, but because the boys perceive it to be so. Both *Cloverfield* and *Super 8* share an intriguingly subjective view of their worlds.

Cabin's humor is drier and more sardonic, and the viewer is held at arm's length. It is the sadly wise humor of clever writing and ironic critique. It is the seemingly real humor of a stoner who locks his car door and then, by reaching through the open window, tests the handle to be sure it is locked. It is the quibbling over the pseudo-scientific distinction between a basic zombie versus a zombie redneck torture family. There are also elements of broader humor, such as a merman who blows blood through his blowhole. Then there is the director of the institution commenting on the fact that Dana—their would-be virgin sacrifice—is far from a virgin, sighing, "We work with what we have." This humor tells us about those characters rather than ourselves but leads us to think critically about why they behave as they do. This ironic distance, while leaving us less involved with the characters, also makes a moral of the story easier to see.

Abrams deftly maintains a balance between telling an emotional tale and keeping the story from becoming overly sentimental. Whedon, on the other hand, creates stingingly clever lines and situations that make the viewer question the social structures that would allow such disturbing events to happen. There is no risk of even the slightest trace of sentimentality in Whedon's fictional universe, even when the end of the world is at hand. Both filmmakers relay messages through their productions, and both structure their stories with perfection. While Whedon satirizes the hackneyed tropes of prior genres, Abrams melds them into something new, and both find ways of reinventing themselves with each new project.

J. J. Abrams undeniably deserves the Spielberg personal growth point for creating such a technically novel story as *Cloverfield* and for running a publicity campaign that had the world talking. He loses ground, however, for showing too much of the monster. He gets this ground back for tonal balance in *Super 8* for avoiding excessive sentimentality. Both *Super 8* and *The Cabin in the Woods* are well-structured mysteries that withhold information to maintain suspense, so Abrams and Whedon split the writing point. Both respect their audience and give us believable and worthwhile issues, and both tie again for producing visually striking images: Abrams with complex, Spielbergian shots of his characters and Whedon/Goddard for managing to include such an imaginative and wide variety of scary monsters, for the magnificent set dressing of the *Cabin*'s basement, and for the visual effects complexity of the cube home that holds the monsters.

Whedon once again gets the innovation credit for skillfully combining the genres of satire and horror as well as melding the techniques of humor and fear. He also deserves recognition (but no extra point) for stepping aside and letting Goddard direct *Cabin*. The working the business award is harder to assess. In many respects, Whedon deserves the point for managing to get *Cabin* out to the public after three years on the shelf, along with a lot of credit for opposing the release of the film in 3-D, as proposed midway by the financially ailing MGM—of course, it is hard to imagine any aesthetically conscious filmmaker would do anything else. Whedon nonetheless splits the working the business point with Abrams because producing involves not only bringing forth a great product but also making money with it through marketing. Abrams receives the profitability award for grossing just over $80 million on *Cloverfield*, a film that cost a mere $25 million to make. Whedon, on the other hand, must be credited with amazing special effects on his shoestring budget of $30 million, but since Hollywood is all about the money, and *Cabin* grossed far less (just over $42 million), Abrams keeps the point. Spielberg's production of *Super 8* grossed over $35 million on its opening weekend alone, but of course this is not surprising as he is the uncontested master.

The final point is for popularity. Although *Cloverfield* got great press and *Super 8* was beloved by families and children, they received *Rottentomatoes.com* critics ratings of 6.8/10 for *Cloverfield* and 7.4/10 for *Super 8*. *Cabin* came in at 7.9/10. The public agreed, giving *Cloverfield* a 3.4/5 and *Super 8* 3.7/5, but *Cabin* overtook them at 3.8/5.[46] So the popularity point goes to Whedon. The final score ends up a tie with 3.5 points each. The contest is far from over. *Star Trek* and *Star Wars* versus the two *Avengers* films in chapter 7 provides an opportunity to decide to what extent these popular blockbuster films represent a hit or a miss.

7

HIT AND MYTH!

Defenders of the Franchise

I hate corporations and I'm not happy that they have taken over the film business but on the same hand I find myself being the head of a corporation. There's a certain irony there.—George Lucas

In his interview with Tavis Smiley for PBS, J. J. Abrams noted that he dislikes the term "franchise" and prefers to think of his work in terms of character and story:

> It just feels like it becomes a product, and it's no longer about character or stories or things that move you. It's about a machine. There's no question that I'm working with companies and studios for whom shareholders and the bottom line are hugely important. . . . But the truth is that it really is show business, I understand and I respect it. That's why we make our movies on schedule and on budget and everything.[1]

Yet both Whedon and Abrams have made their money on franchise films, on films that are so big and successful that the studios can make money on additional products sold on the basis of the films' popularity. The hardcore fans were there because of the creators' early creative work, but the money and recognition in the business of Hollywood came with the franchise.

Abrams was the first to succeed at a major franchise by taking the reins of *Mission: Impossible 3* (2006). The film had been mired in delays, and Abrams took over as the third director after David Fincher and then Joe Carnahan each left the project.[2] *M:I-3* was the first Hollywood film Abrams ever directed. Primary star Tom Cruise evidently became enthused with the idea of Abrams directing after binge watching two seasons of *Alias* and, as both co-producer and star, was very supportive of the first-time director.[3] Abrams brought in Roberto Orci and Alex Kurtzman for script rewrites, and the project subsequently lost heavy-hitting actresses Carrie-Ann Moss and Scarlett Johansson as the characters changed and time dragged on.[4]

M:I-3 incorporates most aspects typical of the opening episode of *Lost* (2004). The story begins in the middle at a fast clip with exciting camera work and the pace never lets up. Ethan Hunt, the leader of the Impossible Missions Force, is humanized by his concern for his wife and a kidnapped trainee, but the plot still stays close to the format of the original 1960s TV show. The film splits into two forty-five-minute parts with the first half being like a TV episode in length as well as technique. Hunt and his team go in to kidnap the villain who has blown up one of Hunt's favorite trainees. The mission has unforeseen hitches, but by minute forty-five— with the help of a nifty array of gadgets and the lifelike rubber masks made famous in the TV series and first *Mission: Impossible* film—Hunt and his IMF team are headed home with the villain firmly in hand.

That is, until the villain escapes. The second half of the film begins with the villain being retaken by his own people and quickly escalates with Hunt's wife kidnapped in retaliation and Hunt himself placed in the same position as the trainee he failed to save: free, but with a miniature explosive implanted in his brain by the villain. The second half of the film contains a fast-paced, beautifully choreographed tracking shot of Hunt racing along the crowded river walk in Shanghai and a suspenseful action sequence in which he scales the steeply angled, sheer glass wall of a skyscraper. Critics were pleased, and the film was generally well received.

M:I-3, which was budgeted for $150 million, only pulled in $134 domestically and thus disappointed Paramount, who had hoped for the huge success of the first two films.[5] It nearly tripled its take with foreign markets, however, and then added another $100 million in DVD rentals, so it was far from a failure.[6] Reviews frequently describe it as a great "summer movie," and it enjoys a 66 favorable rating on *Metacritic.com* and did better than both of the two prior *Mission: Impossible* films, garnering a 6.6 out of 10 on *Rotten Tomatoes* with 69 percent of the audience reviewers indicating they liked the film.[7] David Edelstein of *New York Magazine* began his review by referencing ego-bloated, ego-driven star vehicles but continued with

> Abrams is a good director for Cruise. The creator of the TV series *Alias* and *Lost*, he doesn't have much personality of his own to get in the way; he knows how to display—and fetishize—his stars without tipping into Stallone-esque camp; and he's an expert in TV shorthand, in cramming lots of plot into small units of time.[8]

Here Edelstein may be referring to rumors about Cruise that ran rampant because of the so-called Oprah couch incident—when he bounced up and down on the talk-show host's sofa proclaiming his love for Katie Holmes—and because of his scientology-based criticism of Brooke Shields and psychiatry.[9] Edelstein does refer later in his discussion of *M:I-3*'s hospital sex scene to rumors of Cruise's homosexuality and gossip that Cruise had stopped the re-showing of a *South Park* (1997–) episode highly critical of scientology called "Trapped in the Closet."[10] Cruise's off-screen personal antics caused much negative media buzz at the time.

Although rumors suggest it may have been more about disappointing profits from *M:I-3*, Paramount claimed that Cruise's erratic behavior prompted them to revoke his contract.[11] Interestingly enough Cruise was back at Paramount for the fourth installment in the series, *Mission: Impossible—Ghost Protocol* (2011), and again for the fifth, *Mission: Impossible—Rogue Nation*, which was co-produced by Abrams and Bad Robot. If there was bad blood, it must have evaporated under the influence of ample profits. It seems that Abrams does work well with Cruise, but perhaps not because he is lacking personality. Some might consider this rather the talent of collaborating well with others. In the DVD commentary for *M:I-3*, Cruise and Abrams are respectful and highly complimentary of each other, and this deferential and collegial interaction can also be found in the joint *Unscripted* interview about *Mission: Impossible 3*.[12] Abrams and Cruise's continued work together suggests they have a mutually respectful relationship of equals and not one dominated by Cruise.

Abrams's work with screenwriters Roberto Orci and Alex Kurtzman on *Fringe* and *Alias* also gave him access to perhaps the most successful franchise in media history via the rebooted *Star Trek* film. Gail Berman, then president of Paramount Studios, originally hired Kurtzman and Orci for the script and Abrams got involved to produce even though he was not particularly a fan of the original series. When they had asked him to produce, he was uninterested, but Orci and Kurtzman's involvement helped change his mind.[13] Later, he was asked to direct and could not say no, because "Alex and Bob wrote a great script and . . . I felt like I would be so agonizingly envious of whoever stepped in and directed the movie and I just thought, I've got to direct this."[14] Alternatively Abrams credits his wife, Katie McGrath, with convincing him to direct because of the strong female characters.[15] Whatever the real reason, it was a smart move with a proven collaborative team.

Abrams knew he had a fine line to walk because he had not been a "Trekker" and could easily run afoul of hard-core fans that guarded the integrity of the series or he could alienate the larger audience that did not have intimate inside knowledge of the series. Fans, however, are not consistent in their own visions of the show, and opinions about having Abrams helm the franchise were, not surprisingly, mixed. Film critics too weighed in on both sides but were generally positive. *L.A. Weekly* lamented that "this Trek feels like it was made by a committee of logic-minded Vulcans (or franchise-protective studio executives) rather than a filmmaker."[16] Likewise, film critic Roger Ebert gave the film only 2.5 stars, arguing,

> The Gene Roddenberry years, when stories might play with questions of science, ideals or philosophy, have been replaced by stories reduced to loud and colorful action. Like so many franchises, it's more concerned with repeating a successful formula than going boldly where no "Star Trek" has gone before.[17]

Ebert notes the reduction in age of the characters, saying, "There are times when the command deck looks like Bring Your Child to School Day, with the kid sitting in daddy's chair."[18] The *New York Times*, however, made it a critic's pick, calling it a "nuanced interpretation" that "is fundamentally about two men engaged in a continuing conversation about civilizations and their discontents."[19] *Metacritic*'s list of professional reviewers' opinions shows no negative reviews, thirty-five positive reviews, and only two mixed reviews, with Ebert and *L.A. Weekly* thus in the minority.

Fan reaction, too, ran the gamut from feeling that Abrams had single-handedly ruined *Star Trek* to praising his ability to stay true to the original characters. "Nightbringer AT" at *Rotten Tomatoes* called it "The film that killed *Star Trek*," fuming about "unlogical Vulcans, [and] oddly size changing ships (from 320m to 700m, DVD extras)." Similarly "Work In Progress" on Amazon, a self-professed fan, who "can't begin to say how much I loathe this film," cited some significant holes in the plot.

> The timeline has been altered by the dumbest set of Romulans in galactic history. These idiots have a time machine, which they hijack after a failed attempt to HELP them. Rather than going back in time 30 years to SAVE THEIR PEOPLE they go back to revenge the deaths of their families (which wouldn't happen if they had 2 brain cells to rub together).[20]

Indeed the story contains quite a few science and plot holes big enough to drive a 320-meter (or even a 700-meter) spaceship through.

Not all fans were on the same page. Many liked the first reboot film and its focus on the origins of the characters but were not as crazy about the second. At the 2013 Star Trek Con, fans rated Abrams's *Star Trek* as number 6 (thus right in the middle of the group) and *Star Trek: Into Darkness* dead last at number 13.[21] Of 1,239 total nonprofessional reviews on *Metacritic.com*, 1,066 (86 percent) were positive, and generally the opinions of us regular Joes and Josephines fell on the positive side, with a 95 percent audience approval rating by *RottenTomatoes.com*.[22] Amazon reviews are also overwhelmingly favorable with 3,461 (85.6 percent) of a total 4,043 giving the film four or five stars and only 347 (8.5 percent) giving it one or two stars.[23] On *Trekweb.com*, a more fan-oriented website, the results were less clear-cut but still favorable, with 64 percent of 4,331 voters giving *Star Trek* five stars out of a possible five, with only 5.6 percent giving it one star.[24] Abrams's team recognized the challenge before them and seems to have met it well. *Star Trek* ended up the top-grossing film domestically of the entire franchise, pulling in $257,730,019 (with a $150,000,000 budget).[25]

Abrams and team acknowledged two primary goals for their production, finding the characters and producing a story with a heart. He told Sheila Roberts that he wanted

a story that we all embraced, . . . knowing that *Star Trek* inherently
was an optimistic story. It told a future that was about collaboration,
about survival, about working together across cultural, political, racial
lines and spec-ial (species) lines . . . and the idea to go back to Kirk
and Spock and tell their origins story, create an emotional way in,
which would give people like myself a way to love these characters,
was an exciting one, and to tell a story that was ultimately optimistic
with a big heart.[26]

Since one of the things that the Trekkers loved about the original series
was the characters, this was a wise focal point and clearly one consistent
with Bad Robot themes and objectives.

One of Abrams's goals was to allow new people and Trekkers alike to
enjoy the film. He described this balancing act to a self-identified "huge
fan" of the series:

Obviously, you are savvy enough to know that if we were *just* to make
the movie for fans of *Star Trek* we would be limiting the audience
enormously. And the truth is, because we love this, because we are
beholden to you, because the fans of *Star Trek* are what allow us to
make a version of *Star Trek* at all, I can assure you that we [are]
making this movie for you. It goes without saying, although it is important that we say it. I have taken some flack for saying in the press
"we are making this for *future* fans of *Star Trek*" as if we don't care
about the existing fans. That could not be farther from the truth.[27]

Working on the film made Abrams a fan. He told the Wondercon 2009
audience, "As someone who was not a fan to begin with, I've come to
appreciate and understand and actually feel jealous I didn't get hooked
earlier because I can understand how amazing the show was."[28] Abrams
showed the ability to walk that very fine line between the Trekkers and
the newbies.

Elements from Abrams's earlier work pop up along with references to
older *Star Trek* canon, like a tribble on Scotty's desk, a mention of Nurse
Chapel from the original series, and Admiral Jonathan Archer's beagle
from *Star Trek: Enterprise* (2001–2005). From earlier Abrams works, we
have the voice of the ever-present Greg Grunberg as Kirk's stepfather and
the gigantic red Mueller Device ball, one of the Rambaldi inventions
from *Alias* that contains the time-altering red matter. Spock banishes Kirk
from the ship to a deserted planet reminiscent of the island from *Lost*,

Some of the iconic characters of the original *Star Trek* series rebooted for the big screen in 2009: Chekov (Anton Yelchin), Kirk (Chris Pine), "Scotty" (Simon Pegg), "Bones" (Karl Urban), Sulu (John Cho), and Uhura (Zoë Saldana). *Paramount / Photofest © Paramount Pictures*

where there is a gigantic reptilian beast reminiscent of *Cloverfield*. There is also the focus on a love triangle with two men (a reliable, nerdy one and a popular, handsome one) and one woman as in *Felicity*. In the *Star Trek* movie, however, it is the geek (the local equivalent of Noel, not Ben) who gets the girl, and the viewer gets to be gleeful over rebuffed playboy Kirk watching Uhura kiss Spock.

Like the original *Star Trek* TV series, the film drives home the importance of both the brain and the heart. Abrams remarks on the Freudian component of the original:

> The genius of what Roddenberry created is that paradigm of all of these characters. You've got the id, the ego, the superego. The group obviously beyond just Kirk and Spock and Bones, with this film especially the end of the movie, you realize they wouldn't be there if all of them hadn't done their job, meaning that each one of them contributed in a critical way and each one of them has put their lives in the other's hands.[29]

At times, however, the film seems to support the heart over the brain in rather foolish ways. Near the film's end, Spock encounters an older version of himself who has time-traveled to the future, and this older Spock (known as Spock Prime) tells the younger one that he will need to learn to gamble at times (perhaps even lie as an act of faith).[30]

Kirk's mutinous insubordination in disagreeing with his commanding officer, Spock, may be right within the context of the situation, but as someone who is shown to be hot-headed and insolent (and who, as in the bar scene near the beginning of the film, gets into fights he cannot win), it is hard not to consider the possibility of Kirk being wrong here and thus heedlessly jeopardizing the lives of the entire crew. If McCoy's role is to provide humanistic moral input, then perhaps he is underutilized in the Bad Robot film. Instead Captain Christopher Pike, a man who served under Kirk's father in Starfleet, functions as the sort of replacement fatherly super-ego, who tries to help the angry youth, Kirk, channel his energy. Pike is tortured for his nobility and must be rescued by that same insolent, rule-breaking, ersatz son. Perhaps this is a metaphor for what the Bad Robot team feels needs to be done to the franchise, but eventually the film justifies ends over means in a large way. Despite Kirk not following protocol, both he and Pike will be promoted because of Kirk's success based on guts and emotions without even the usual wrist slap that the original Kirk would have received for not following the prime directive.[31]

Abrams emphasized the upbeat about *Star Trek* when making the first reboot, but the tone changed dramatically when it came to the second film, *Star Trek: Into Darkness* (2013). He told Sheila Roberts of *Moviesonline*,

> There were many films in recent years, many of which we have all loved, that have depicted a very dark, dismal, cynical, grim future and that's not what Roddenberry created and that's not what we were interested in doing.[32]

In the second film, however, it suddenly *was* what they were interested in doing. The film is a revamp of *Star Trek II: The Wrath of Khan* (1982) but occurs in a much darker world where military commanders foment war and evil super-races strive to conquer humanity. The advantage of the second film is that the primary characters are now defined and in place, but the film falters by not sticking with the dictum that it is all about the characters and instead gets involved in excessive action heroics.

Criticisms of the first film for having failed to include the philosophical aspects of the original series are taken on directly in the second film. It starts with Kirk facing the thorny issue of whether to uphold the prime directive not to interfere with primitive life or to rescue Spock from an erupting volcano, thus revealing the *Enterprise* to the primitive inhabitants of the planet below. It will surprise no one, except perhaps Spock, that Kirk decides to rescue his friend and risk the wrath of Starfleet Command. Friendship and the safety of crew thus become, at the outset, primary themes of the film. In fact, the film even creates momentary sympathy for the villain, when he shows deep concern about the safety of his own cryogenically frozen crew. It is a moment that humanizes him and confuses us as to who the bad guy really is—he or the person assailing him. The film's darkness suggests that the answer is both.

Into Darkness continued to work hard to bring in a new, younger audience, but it also succeeded better at satisfying the die-hard fans. A *Trek.web* poll of more than three thousand genuine Trek fans revealed that 50.1 percent preferred *Into Darkness* to Abrams's first *Star Trek* film, with another 17.2 percent feeling it was a "draw."[33] Abrams and team achieved success with fans by making the film a revisioning of the second franchise film, while still making it interesting to potential new fans. The Bad Robot version, however, reverses the basic scenario of the original film by exchanging some of the roles of Spock and Kirk. In the original, an intellectually and physically superior being named Khan blames Kirk for the death of his wife and seeks his revenge on Kirk. Near the film's climax, the *Enterprise* is severely damaged in battle and Captain Spock enters an area flooded with lethal levels of radiation in order to repair the warp-drive and save the vessel. Famous lines from the original film reflect the philosophical approach praised by fans as Spock, dying of radiation poisoning, says good-bye to his old friend through a transparent partition:

> **Spock:** Don't grieve, Admiral—it is logical: the needs of the many outweigh—
> [*He almost keels over. Kirk has tears streaming down his face.*]
> **Kirk:** . . . the needs of the few . . .
> **Spock:** Or the one.
> [*He props a hand on the glass to support himself. Kirk's hand reflexively goes to match Spock's on the other side of the glass.*][34]

Their hands meet, separated by glass, as Spock proffers the Vulcan benediction, saying, "I have been—and always shall be—your friend. Live. Long. And Prosper."[35] Spock then dies (and must be resurrected in the next film in order for the franchise to continue).

The revised version is not as elegant but still retains the pathos and reveals slightly different priorities in comparison. It is Kirk who chooses to sacrifice himself for the resurrection of the *Enterprise*. The dialogue is simplified and is now personal rather than philosophical:

> **Kirk:** How do you choose not to feel?
> **Spock:** I do not know. Right now I am failing.
> **Kirk:** I want you to know why I couldn't let you die. Why I went back for you.
> **Spock:** Because you are my friend. [*A tear falls from Spock's eye.*]

Kirk places his hand on the glass and Spock follows suit with the Vulcan benediction. Kirk dies, and the scream of rage and pain that Kirk utters after being marooned by Khan in the original film—"KHAN!"—is now shouted instead by Spock.

This echo from the original is satisfying but also jarring. While we are accustomed to Kirk's outbursts compounded by William Shatner's emo-

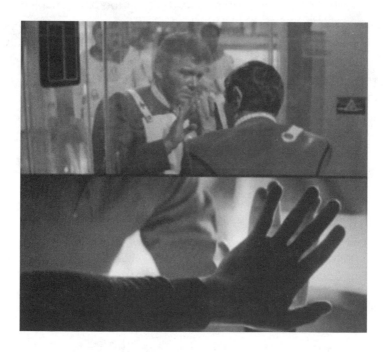

A comparison of the radiation sacrifice scene in *Star Trek II: The Wrath of Khan* (1982; top)—featuring Kirk (William Shatner) and Spock (Leonard Nimoy)—with that of *Star Trek: Into Darkness* (2013).

tive acting style, to see the rational Spock engage in such behavior is jarring to someone familiar with the original series. In the original *Wrath of Khan*, Spock dies stoically, leaving the emotional spectacle to Kirk. Abrams's Spock, however, goes on to engage in a frenzied and passionate battle with Khan atop a flying garbage scow. The explanation for the emotional Spock who strives to batter the arrogant and biologically superior Khan seems inconsistent with the original character and inappropriate, especially since in both versions he tells Dr. McCoy that the doctor needs to learn self-control: "to govern his passions" (*Star Trek II: The Wrath of Khan*) and " Perhaps you, too, should learn to govern your emotions, Doctor."[36] The difference in the way Spock handles his emotions is indicative of the changes that Orci, Kurtzman, and Abrams made, and it seems to relate to the age of their audience.

The original *Wrath of Khan* has Kirk respond to Spock's death with the opening lines of *A Tale of Two Cities*, an antique book that Spock had given Kirk for his birthday near the opening of the film. When asked how he feels, Kirk replies in contrast to his earlier comment that he felt old, "Young. I feel young." This theme echoes through the film because Kirk is, in fact, showing his age, learning that he is the father of a grown son and being retired from commanding a starship. By the time *Wrath of Khan* came out, the youthful fans of the original series would have aged sixteen years since the series' first episode and would most likely also be facing the effects of parenthood and aging, if not grown children. Thus the fans and characters could share the experiences of middle adulthood. Abrams turns this relationship on its head in an effort to appeal to younger prospective fans.

In both Abrams films, Kirk and Spock deal not with their own children but with relationships to their parents. Dr. Carol Marcus in the older film is Kirk's ex-lover and the mother of his son. In the updated version, she is an accomplished physicist, and like the others embodies a more youthful, potentially available member of the younger generation rather than a conservative parental one. Spock tries to understand his parents' relationship and how his mixed heritage affects who he is, and Kirk struggles with a rebellious streak and an oedipal complex that prevent him from obeying his surrogate father, Commander Pike. Such themes would tend to resonate more strongly with the eighteen- to twenty-four-year-old males who were targeted by filmmakers in 2009.[37]

Into Darkness does offer more complex issues to consider than the first *Star Trek* reboot. By removing the story of Kirk's reconciliation with his lover and son and moving the emphasis to concern for his friends and crew, the film also touches on larger political issues. Fathers in the film can be good or bad. Pike, as the good-guy dad, tries to steer the headstrong Kirk in the right direction. On the other hand, authority cannot always be trusted. Carol Marcus's father, Admiral Marcus, decides to take independent action to incite a war with the Klingons because he dislikes the diplomatic peace that has been struck with the Federation and views war between the two as inevitable. He thus feels no compunction about hurrying it along by stirring up an artificial locus of controversy (the resurrection of super-being Khan) in order to start the war.

Abrams's claim that his wife encouraged him to take the initial directing job because of the strong female roles might be a bit mystifying at first. There are a few females in *Star Trek* but no strong women characters. While Uhura does stand up for herself, she plays little part in the film except for snubbing Kirk and being in love with Spock—both fairly traditional female roles. The little bit of spine that she shows is offset by her green roommate, who is sexualized in a bedroom scene with Kirk and who seems to enjoy inviting strange men into her bunk.[38] There are few female speaking roles except for Kirk's and Spock's traditionally inscribed mothers.

In *Into Darkness*, Uhura has a more significant role, particularly in interacting with the Klingons. As it turns out, the Klingons were supposed to show up in the first *Star Trek* film but had to be cut along with Uhura's main show of strength. In the second film, she exhibits more gumption, putting Kirk in his place and using her knowledge of Klingon language and culture to stand up to the Klingons on their own terms. Once again, however, the film undercuts women by making them objects of spectacle. While the inclusion of the two catlike women Kirk beds (Caitian, perhaps, from the animated series) might be excused as allusions to Kirk's womanizing, other aspects of the film have little excuse, like showing science officer Carol Marcus clad in underwear midway through the film simply so she can change in order to open a torpedo casing.

Sadly, in *Star Trek* (2009) less than one-third (twenty-six of eighty-eight) of major cast members listed by IMDb are women with less than one-fourth (twenty-three of ninety-one) of minor "rest of cast" members being female. *Into Darkness* fares slightly better with four (a little more than one-fourth) of the top-billed fifteen actors being women. This is hardly surprising as research suggests that for the past fifteen years the percentage of women characters in films has remained stable at roughly 28 percent.[39] The other significant female role is Carol Marcus, who tells Spock she has a degree in applied physics and a specialty in advanced weaponry and is shown slapping her father, a very powerful admiral.

Marcus's role has become arguably more independent here than the role she had as Kirk's ex-lover and mother of his son in *The Wrath of Khan*. This is not to say that Carol Marcus from the earlier film was helpless. She is shown as determined and standing up for her very difficult research, but we never see her with power. Her transmission calls of outrage at apparent Starfleet interference in her work are interrupted and ineffectual, and Khan uses the effect of her distress on Kirk in his attempt to avenge himself. As the film reaches its conclusion, in a low-cut blouse, she references her maternal role in creating a new world (she giving birth to it while Kirk plays the role of protective father) as knowing how to cook. In *Into Darkness*, Marcus is also frequently shown in a dress, and she comments on Kirk's negative effects on Nurse Chapel (a recurring character in the series who does not appear in either film). As previously mentioned, she is undressed and thus made less imposing before going in to defuse a torpedo. Her efforts to save the *Enterprise* are based on her pleas as Daddy's little girl for her dad to take the moral high ground. Her final function is to be wounded and shoved aside before emitting the traditional female scream when her father is killed. She will have to be saved and carried to sickbay by Scotty and Kirk. The themes of relationships with fathers hold, but women, because of antiquated visions of female familial roles, have no position of strength in comparison to the men who ultimately come to terms with their fathers.

Likewise there is little place for other women on the *Enterprise* except as perfunctory crewmembers. In *Into Darkness*, twenty-five women (five of whom are merely "additional voices") out of ninety-three characters are credited as "cast." In IMDb's "rest of cast" section, fourteen (about 27 percent) of fifty-two are women.[40] This may be better than most Hollywood adventure/science-fiction films, but researcher Stacey L. Smith specifically blames films such as Abrams's *Star Trek*, Whedon's *The Avengers*, and Jackson's *The Hobbit* for bringing down the year's average for female characters to a range of 20 to 23 percent.[41] This calls into question claims of "strong" female roles in the films, made evidently because one of the two films has women who show occasional strength.

So which was the better film? That depends on who is talking. In a *Trek.web*'s survey, roughly a quarter of 4,386 respondents agreed that *Star Trek* was "a great reimagining and I have no complaints," and roughly another quarter found it "different, but no less valid." Only 28.32 percent felt it did not remain true to the franchise.[42] Still, in May 2013, *Into Darkness*'s re-visioning of *The Wrath of Khan* was more popular among fans.[43] In August of the same year, Devin Faraci's previously mentioned convention fans felt the opposite, listing *Star Trek* as number 6 on their list of favorite films and *Into Darkness* as number 13 behind *Star Trek: Nemesis* (2002), *Star Trek: Insurrection* (1998), and *Star Trek V: Final Frontier* (1989) and behind *Galaxy Quest* (1999), which was a fan favorite although not technically a *Star Trek* film.[44] It seems likely that the use of the Khan material might resonate with older fans and make the film generally more popular with them than the first reboot, especially given the initial extreme negativity of some fans.

In general, *Into Darkness* made more total money than *Star Trek* (2009). The former pulled in $277,381,584 after subtracting its $190,000,000 budget, while the latter came in a close second with a profit $235,680,446 after subtracting its $150,000,000 budget.[45] Yet even this does not tell the whole story, for this included the foreign profits for each film. On domestic income alone *Into Darkness* barely covered its $190,000,000 budget costs taking in only $228,778,661, while *Star Trek* (2009) brought in $257,730,019 with a lower budget of $150,000,000. The fans were split: the foreign market loved the darker Khan remake and Americans liked the action-packed, less-political, and less-philosophical first film. According to Box Office Mojo *Star Trek* (2009) was the most financially successful of the entire franchise domestically.[46] In terms of unadjusted world gross, of course, that spot is taken by *Star Trek: Into Darkness*.[47] Bad Robot managed to split the difference and make a film for everyone, by making two different films.

Whichever film you prefer, Abrams should be given credit for his committed pursuit of technical excellence in terms of the visual feel of the *Star Trek* films. In fact he has been! In 2014 he was awarded the thirteenth annual "Visionary Award" by the Visual Effects Society. The purpose of the award was to recognize in Abrams someone who "uniquely and consistently employed the art and science of visual effects to foster imagination and ignite future discoveries by way of artistry, invention and groundbreaking work."[48] Abrams was chosen for the award, according to the Visionary Effects Society's chair Jeffrey A. Okun, because he has

> consistently elevated not just the technical aspect of visual effects, but also the emotional. . . . He has redefined the relationship between the viewer and the story—you can easily see this from the epic cult followings of his highly engaging work, a testament to his expert blending of visual effects, evocative characters and a remarkable imagination.[49]

Abrams was modest to a fault, telling interviewers before the ceremony it was "clearly a clerical error. But mostly, I just work with a whole lot of incredible VFX artists. This is what made me want to get involved in movies."[50] His speech included nods to technical people but also his parents, "who let me blow s*it up," and his sister, "who let me blow her up."[51] Abrams's humility and family values (although not family-friendly vocabulary) shone through.

Meanwhile, Whedon was also working on another franchise, most notably *The Avengers* (2012), but took time out between filming and editing to work on franchise material of a whole other type, at least if you can consider Shakespeare a franchise and his *Much Ado about Nothing* (2012) a franchise film. He decided to film a little black-and-white home movie in his backyard, and it became an award-winning and even money-making film project.[52] Noting Whedon's references to DIY and "miniature paycheques" in his press release about the film, the *Guardian*'s Ben Child elaborates that micro-budget films tend to cost about $10,000 to $27,000.[53] At an Academy of Motion Picture Arts and Science's Q and A session, he told a questioner about the budget, "Whatever you're thinking, it's less."[54] What Whedon learned by doing *Dr. Horrible* was plainly useful in his *Much Ado* production both in terms of financial acuity and production. For one thing he ended up writing the hauntingly beautiful music and music themes for the film himself. There is no doubt that he and his actors have been now fully compensated for their twelve days of filming. *Much Ado* ended up bringing in more than $4 million.[55]

Of course Shakespeare is not exactly a franchise. There are no corporately held rights to product licensing across a variety of media, yet as might be expected there were videos, sound tracks, and even a screenplay book available, so it is not exactly not a franchise either. One could argue that Shakespeare's plays are composed of similar material. They use larger-than-life characters that have cultural capital because of their long tradition of being loved and performed, and they have a following, even though Beatrice and Benedick may not be the most famous of Shakespeare's characters. Also, as someone on the *Guinness Book of World Records*–winning commentary notes, a large number of Whedon fans turn out also to be Shakespeare fans, so there was a dedicated audience to play to.[56] He spoke with David Fear about his use of characters.

> Someone came up to me . . . and said, Wow, this is so different from *The Avengers*! And I thought, actually, it really isn't. You have to make each of those superheroes shine, and get the audience to feel like they know where each of those people are coming from before they collectively save the world. I had to know why they were willing to risk everything. My interpretation of this text was coming from the same place: Who are all of these people? Why, exactly, does Borachio do what he does in the play? At what point does he become the most noble person, and why?[57]

Abrams and Whedon stress two similar elements in the reworking of their franchises. The first is that it is about character and the second is that a film should be made for everyone and not just the zealous fans. "What it all boils down to, though" he told Fear, "with whatever I do—whether it's big or small—is to try to make something for everybody. My aim is to make something that's personal but not the least bit exclusionary at all."

Whedon struggled with figuring out what the play was about, since it was about "nothing." He knew it was funny and that he loved it and that he wanted to do it, but he could not figure out why. Shakespeare plays generally develop a theme and then explore the theme in a variety of different character pairings, what *Slate.com* in its review of the film calls "a canny catalogue of the varieties of human romantic folly."[58] There is no question that the characters other than Beatrice and Benedick play a significant role in this exploration and that this was an idea that Whedon grasped. When Whedon's wife, Kai Cole, told him to look at the text again, he says "I got it . . . the understanding that everything in the play is an important part of the play, that all of the relationships and all of the schemes and all of the plot devices have equal weight."[59] For Whedon the topic of how characters lie to each other about relationships became one of the driving issues, but recognition of the importance of the full spectrum of characters was more important to the success not only of this film, but also to all those to come.

Besides being about female virginity or lack of it (the lack of an "O thing"), the play has much to say about leaders, politics, and the nature of love, beyond the entertainment it offers as a dramatic comedy.[60] Whedon begins the action with a parade of limousines indicative of wealth and power. The story is framed by interactions between a prince and a governor and plays with the ideas of spying, surveillance, and overheard and miscomprehended conversation. "Marking" and "noting"/(nothing) are common themes in the Shakespeare wordings, which have been adopted and adapted by Whedon; thus the film hints at ideas of recognizing, seeing, and having characters think that they know things, even though they all get things wrong through eavesdropping and their willingness to pay attention to only portions of the story.[61]

Those with ill intent (Don John, Conrade, and Borachio) use the mechanism of eavesdropping to mislead those in power (Claudio, Leonato, and Don Pedro). Hence the prince, Don Pedro, and his governor, Leonato, come to believe that Leonato's young, innocent daughter Hero is sexually disloyal. These mostly sympathetic authority figures, out of sheer glee in their own power, also manipulate others, contriving Benedick and Beatrice to overhear staged messages so as to bring together and exert influence on two people who believe they hate each other. The film thus speaks to the prevalence of manipulation by the empowered without dealing with the technology of manipulation so much as with those who are willing to believe in it unwisely. This was a natural theme at a time when U.S. officials had become obsessed with security leaks and the big news was the uproar about Edward Snowden and his whistle-blowing on CIA surveillance and data collection.

Viewers are given further reason to be dubious about the validity of surveillance when we see the ineptitude of the officers of the state in the form of the local constabulary (Dogberry, Verges, and the Watchmen). This intellectually challenged crew overhears the truth of the insidious plot to besmirch Hero's reputation but miscomprehend its meaning and thus almost miss their opportunity to prevent disaster from happening. Luckily this is a Shakespeare comedy so all's well that ends well. In Whedon's capable hands, the viewer recognizes that the greater the claims being made on the basis of surveillance, the greater the danger if they are not properly substantiated. Nothing is never really nothing. For the ingénue, death is the possible (but luckily only simulated) result of the belief in surveillance over trust and good character, and the recognition of this error means characters will be more realistic and careful in their approach to relationships and love.

With *The Avengers* (only the second film he ever directed), Whedon landed in the midst of a giant and important franchise, and—despite others' concerns about his inexperience—he ended up creating the third-highest-grossing film in Hollywood history. He managed to construct a film that returns to Marvel Comics creator Stan Lee's original idea for the characters and that simultaneously asks Americans to consider what makes us what we are. Whedon's ambivalent portrayals of characters and the political systems around them made him the perfect person to deal with a contemporary reconfiguration of the Marvel universe; one that would both stay true to the original characters (some of whom had come onto the scene in the late 1930s) but would also handle the complexity of ethical actions in our present-day world.

When hired, Whedon was given what he describes as "a basic skeleton of three acts that I knew I had to hang on."[62] The Avengers had to be assembled, had to have a big fight that tore them apart, and had to reunite for a finale. The roles were pre-cast and thus predetermined. Only the Hulk and Hawkeye were chosen after Whedon joined the project.[63] What Whedon brought to the table was nuance in characterization and the words of the characters, their interactions and opinions, and the choice of which aspects of their historic personae would get represented.

Using two scenes in particular, Whedon—in a film overfilled with action and spectacle—magnificently shows how the defining traits of two of his characters (traits that also define the American character) can be both major strengths and major weaknesses. The primary conflict occurs between Tony Stark (Iron Man) and Steve Rogers (Captain America). Stark is a wealthy engineer-entrepreneur—spoiled, individualistic, and cocky. Like America itself, he has derived wealth and power from the development of high-tech armaments but also has idealistic visions of helping people and being esteemed for his contributions. He has, in fact, built a monument to his own accomplishments, a huge office tower bearing his name. Stark is working on clean energy production and, like his deceased father, represents the best of visionary American scientific and technological ingenuity and the worst of controlling egotism, a trait that ultimately allows him to understand and thus fight the self-centered villain Loki on his own terms.

Rogers, on the other hand, is the boyish, self-abasing ideal of polite American can-do spirit: the soldier who gave bubble gum to kids after the war, the cheery icon of the guy who will not let a comrade down. He is also decisive and a natural leader but has to be careful about naïvely trusting and following those above him. Whedon plays the egotistical Stark and altruistic Rogers against each other as two sides of the American character that have made the country great. Added to the mix are Dr. Bruce Banner's humanitarian medical efforts in foreign lands, Thor's concern for family and tradition, Hawkeye's technical expertise and training, and Black Widow's fierce independence, resilience, and commitment to repaying debts. Finally Nick Fury embodies faith in authority and care for safety or security.

In a stroke of brilliance, Whedon brings the characters together so that, under the spell of Loki's nefarious scepter, they can—in Aristotelian fashion—have these virtues transform into their opposing vices. Tony Stark is quick to attack Rogers, the obedient soldier who had been lost in the ocean and frozen in ice for decades after the Second World War. Stark criticizes the newly thawed-out Rogers for being old-fashioned and thus useless in today's technologically advanced world. Stark is right. When he asks Rogers to find which circuits on their aircraft are overloaded, upon inspection, Rogers can reply only that it looks like they run on some kind of electricity. Whedon hints that America (both Rogers and the country) does not fathom the world as it now is: a world where American power and importance have waned. We delight in Rogers's joy when after a conversation full of contemporary cultural nods, the man from the 1940s finally understands a reference to "not being somebody's flying monkey." He does not command the electronic wizardry of today, but at least he recognizes the reference to blind obedience from the *Wizard of Oz*, an attribute embodying the potential failing of the idealistic American. Abrams and Whedon find different footings in their work. *Star Trek* shows us a world that does not question the validity of the Federation despite occasional corruption in individuals such as Admiral Marcus. Whedon suggests that it is power itself that corrupts.

The political motives visible in *Much Ado about Nothing* also surface here. While Rogers recognizes that the villain Loki is trying to manipulate them (and, as leader, announces this to the group), he must also recognize the possibility that his own side is equally controlling. Stark acknowledges and intentionally aggravates the Captain by underscoring that it can also be a weakness to be an obedient soldier with a boyish desire to believe that those at the top are honest and transparent. Captain America in *The Avengers* thus comes to represent the loss of American innocence both personally and on a political level. As Loki says, "you lie and kill in the service of liars and killers," and ultimately Loki perceives himself to be simply one step farther ahead of our heroes in terms of making the ends justify the means.

This theme is renewed in the second *Avengers* film, *Avengers: Age of Ultron* (2015). Stark is again the representative of unquestioned militaristic response, a man who wants to build military programs in secret without interference from people who will lecture him with the "Man's not meant to meddle medley." He is again played against Rogers, the sadder but wiser soldier, who tries to remind Tony: "Every time someone tries to win a war before it starts, people die." Loki's viewpoint from the first film is voiced here by the new villain, Ultron. He reminds Captain America of the purpose of soldiers and that he should not pretend he "can live without a war." As in the first *Avengers*, the audience sympathizes with the Captain, although in this case (as with much military scientific research), Stark's creation will be two-sided, producing both an annihilating monster and a visionary defender of humanity.

The first *Avengers* film comments on the sad decline of American culture. Whedon indicates he had to cut certain scenes with Captain America due to time and editing rhythm, but noted, "I really do feel a sense of loss about what's happening in our culture, loss of the idea of community, loss of health care and welfare and all sorts of things. I was spending a lot of time having him say it."[64] Indeed Rogers's obedience and faith in his superiors is something that he must give up in order to be able to lead in our present-day society.

Nick Fury, another of the heroes and head of the secret organization S.H.I.E.L.D. (the Strategic Homeland Intervention, Enforcement and Logistics Division), is obsessed with keeping his people and country safe—a virtue of course, but one that easily tips into ends justifying the means. Not only does Cap have to discover for himself that S.H.I.E.L.D.'s research on a mysterious object called a tesseract is all about developing superweapons, he learns that the government's tinkering with this energy source (a thinly veiled analog for nuclear power) simply raises the stakes and brings greater potential for disaster than it does possible benefit. The tesseract research draws warriors from other planets, who, as Thor explains, now believe Earth is capable and willing to wage war on a higher level.

Despite Thor's origin as Norse god, he displays another typically American virtue—pride in one's civilization and culture—a virtue that can result in excessive adherence to tradition and family values. When members of the Avengers disparage Loki for killing numerous innocent people, Thor bristles at criticism of his brother, before recognizing this as true and demurring that, well, his stepbrother "was adopted." Under the negative influence of the scepter, Thor will soon show what happens when this virtue is taken too far. Excessive cultural pride becomes bigotry. He later sneers, "I thought humans were more evolved than this." Banner, the humanitarian as representative of American foreign aid, also has an alter ego that shows virtue made excess. As the Hulk, he is wrathful and uncontrollably destructive. This echoes the fact that a large amount of American foreign aid is not medical but the sale and donation of arms. ($14 billion of our $23 billion foreign aid budget, for example, went to military aid in 2013.)[65]

Rogers emphasizes this ambivalence, starting the crucial argument scene by asking Stark: "Remind me how you made your fortune?" Stark disavows responsibility for the damage caused by weapons invented and sold by his company saying, "How is this about me?" which gives Rogers the chance to stress Stark's and America's (the country's) weakness, retorting: "I'm sorry, isn't everything about you?" This also sets up the final sequence because Rogers correctly notes Stark is not the kind to lie down on a (barbed) wire (barrier) to let team members crawl across (as soldiers had to do in World War II). Stark is, as Rogers states tersely, "not the guy to make the sacrifice play," and in the end, this is what the film is all about—learning to be a team.

Whedon emphasizes the dissolution of the group under the influence of Loki's scepter by literally turning the image upside down in the same way that the heroes' values have been turned into their reverse components. It is not that the scepter turns them bad; rather it simply enhances the qualities that are prone to tear them apart. Under its influence, Banner (the Hulk's alter ego) emphasizes the significance of the idea of team: "What are we, a team?" he demands of Fury sarcastically. "We're a chemical mixture that makes chaos!" Unquestionably they are both.

Thor (Chris Hemsworth) and Captain America (Chris Evans) fight to keep the Chitauri army from destroying New York City in *The Avengers* (2012). *Walt Disney Studios Motion Pictures / Photofest © Walt Disney Studios Motion Pictures*

Phil Coulson, Fury's trusted sidekick, emphasizes the importance of team to the Avengers, who face the almost unbeatable god, Thor's half-brother, Loki, and his army of alien shape shifters called the Chitauri. "This was never going to work, Boss," he says to S.H.I.E.L.D. head Nick Fury, "unless they had something to . . . " Although the sentiment remains unfinished, Fury knows that, beyond needing something to avenge, the Avengers must have a common goal. Coulson sees what is going on, and his apparent death prompts Fury, who wears an eye patch, to remark he has lost his one good eye. He dishonestly uses Coulson's bloodied Captain America trading cards to try and rekindle unity in the heroes by referencing idealistic American kids collecting cards of their stalwart hero. This idealism ties into old-fashioned American values of teamwork and selflessness, and it is what will ultimately bring the group together and convince Stark there is something to what Captain America has said about being willing to sacrifice oneself for the good of others. It also sets up the film's climax, in which Stark offers to sacrifice himself to prevent a nuclear bomb from destroying New York. Rocketing to the edge of space with a soon-to-detonate bomb, he calls his lover and business partner, Pepper Potts, in order to say good-bye but cannot reach her—thus doing penance for his prior arrogance. In the end, however, he narrowly escapes death and is rewarded for his virtue with survival, reunion with his lover, and renewed heroic status.

Whedon shows this unification of purpose with a second moving camera shot, this time doing a 360-degree shot around the heroes as they are united on the streets of Manhattan to fight the common menace. Each hero is then allowed to use his or her special talents in concert with others to help defeat Loki and his Chitauri army. Black Widow's ability to manipulate her own body and the actions of others allows her to save Hawkeye, who has been turned traitor by the brainwashing effects of Loki's scepter. She physically knocks the foreign invader from his head. Under the direction of Captain America, they reunite and coordinate joint efforts to foil the invasion. Iron Man has his opportunity to save Earth with a sacrifice play and Widow's acrobatic skills allow the tesseract to be disarmed while the Hulk smashes Loki into the ground, which permits his defeat and capture. American virtues of solidarity, belief in tradition, determination, technological ingenuity, teamwork, and justice shine through and create a portrait of America at its best. That such disparate values cannot be permanently melded together is then underscored by the fact that the individual Avengers are shown going their separate ways. The film suggests that the greatest attribute of America is being able to bring such a divergent group together for a short time but that, with so much difference, the melting pot is not cohesive. The center cannot hold and all things fall apart, but there is always hope for reunion in the future.

The ending feels authentic because the Avengers are fractious characters that, when grouped together as a family, tell us something about the importance of difference and cooperation especially with regard to themes of responsibility, duty, individuality, and caring. Simply put, Whedon's *Avengers* achieves all the amazing feats of Abrams's *Star Trek* but adds the structural superiority that he recognized in Shakespeare's plays. Whedon produced a work that has no superfluous scenes and that succeeds in reinforcing the importance of each character—not just the two or three primary ones that some might have wanted to be the film's focus. In this, he knew better than the producers who wanted him to cut out Black Widow in order to focus more on the "important heroes." They are all important heroes.

Whedon's return to TV in producing *Agents of S.H.I.E.L.D.* was also a likely next step after directing *The Avengers* as it took place in the same universe. The purpose was to do a show about "the peripheral people . . . on the edges of the grand adventures."[66] The point, he said,

> is that even with all these big things, the little things matter. . . . It's about people who don't have super powers. There will be some people with powers, there will be FX, and there will be the spectacle of science-fiction storytelling—but all played on a very human, small level. That's the appeal of the thing.[67]

As it turns out, the little people have powers of their own. Whedon sheepishly admitted at the Humanist Award Q and A, "I try to write everyday Joes and end up with X-Men every time."[68] *Agents of S.H.I.E.L.D.* got off to a slow start. The show was created by Whedon, his brother Jed, and Jed's wife, Maurissa Tancharoen; Joss, who had been actively involved in the other Marvel franchise films behind the scenes, both wrote and directed the first episode.[69] Viewership started high but declined consistently, raising questions about the show's longevity.

> Despite the episode's overall quality, and growing interest in the team of characters, the series lost another 400,000 viewers (7.03 to 6.63 million) before airing "The Hub" [the first season's seventh episode]. To put those numbers in perspective, ABC's prior superhero ensemble show *No Ordinary Family*—cancelled after one season—had 6.9 million viewers in its seventh episode (300,000 more than *Agents of S.H.I.E.L.D.*).[70]

The show has had ups and downs but has never regained the 12 million viewers that tuned in for the first episode. It did have a respectable 7.5 million viewer showing for the season 3 opener, putting it in the number one spot for viewers eighteen to forty-nine.[71] It still needs to find its stride but seems to be getting closer, having settled in at roughly 3 million viewers per episode in the third season.[72]

S.H.I.E.L.D.'s first season deals with typical 1970s comic-book fare. It introduces characters and shows the mythical government organization S.H.I.E.L.D. as it tries to deal with issues arising out of the existence of mutant-type beings, mad science, alien powers, and a Nazi-inspired supervillain organization. The topics are completely in keeping with Whedon's Harvard Humanities speech, in which he indicated "there are two things that interest me and both are power. One is not having it and one is abusing it."[73] Elements of power were central, but somehow not compelling, in *S.H.I.E.L.D.*'s first season.

The second season improved, as characters' interactions became more nuanced and thus more interesting. The politics also heated up and a schism developed within S.H.I.E.L.D.'s ranks about who should have power and why, with recognizable Marvel comics characters falling on either side of the split. Whedon also earned the enmity of fans by, once again, killing off a significant character and by turning a much-loved character into a double agent for the bad guys.[74] Others were more forgiving, but considering *Firefly* was canceled with viewership of 4.7 million, the series may need to be more accommodating of fans.[75] The series has the darker feel of *Dollhouse*'s flash-forward "epilogue" episodes, on which Tancharoen and Jed Whedon also worked, rather than the cynical lightness of *Firefly*.

Prior chapters compare what Abrams and Whedon could do with innovation and limited budgets and that is telling in itself, but looking at the franchise films shows us their abilities without the restriction of narrow budgets. Both directors have always insisted that with the new technology there is greater access to filmmaking for almost everyone. As Steven Spielberg said in an interview with *La Journal du Dimanche*, "Il ne faut pas rêver son film, il faut le réaliser!" (One shouldn't dream one's film, one should make it real.)[76] *Much Ado about Nothing* shows that with limited resources one can indeed make a beautiful work of art. With almost unlimited resources, the works may be more popular but scarcely better. They may, however, be more spectacular.

Both Abrams and Whedon do magnificent jobs with special effects and spectacle. Both also recognize that everything revolves around character. Abrams may have had a harder job in *Star Trek* because Kirk, Spock, and the other members of the original *Enterprise* crew have prior, beloved filmic incarnations. Abrams succeeded, however, in bravely reinventing them according to his own values system. On the other hand, Whedon has had to compete with comic-book readers' imaginations of characters, but his path was smoothed by earlier films featuring Thor, Captain America, Iron Man, and the Hulk that already established the major Avengers' movie personae. This lessened Whedon's chance of being held responsible for changes from the originals, but of course he script-doctored the characters and was responsible for character continuity in many of those earlier films, so he would not actually be completely blameless.

His second *Avengers* film was possibly a bit tougher as he worked to establish film versions of Scarlet Witch (Wanda Maximoff) and her brother, Quicksilver. Whedon has remarked,

> I enter upon *Avengers 2* with a different mindset than I did the first one. I feel like I know so well what it is that I want to accomplish, and like *Much Ado*, I now have a real sense of the troop I'm working with and the strictures and the opportunities. [77]

In the case of *The Avengers: Age of Ultron*, however, Whedon may have sought to go for the everyday Joe, but he has still ended up with X-Men. Well, not X-Men—the legal rights to them are owned by Fox—but he has ended up with a gigantic spectacle that makes focusing on character in the television format an even harder task.

The Avengers: Age of Ultron offers spectacle on the level of a Michael Bay *Transformers* film. [78] But more is not necessarily better and simply having infinite financial resources does not equate with superior quality. In fact, it is possible that limitations stimulate greater creative thinking and more resourceful art. The film did well at the box office, although probably not as well as Marvel had hoped. Projected at a $210–230 million opener, *Ultron*'s opening only pulled in roughly $187.6 million, less than its record-breaking progenitor, which raked in an unexpected $207.4 million. [79] The second film brought in a two-week total of $478 million abroad as opposed to $425 million for *Avengers*, but additional weeks' viewings and markets have ultimately given *Avengers* the edge. The first *Avengers* film pulled in $1,519,557,910 as opposed to $1,405,035,767 for *Ultron*. [80] No doubt, Whedon made a very good, very big film that will continue to bring in financial profits for a long time to come.

Age of Ultron is quite complex and reportedly ran for three hours before being pruned to 141 minutes in the released version. Although some fans may not care, the sheer quantity of explosions and battle scenes overwhelms the character pieces that are central to *The Avengers* and Whedon's hallmark. Still, the character material is there if you look and may, in fact, be some of Whedon's finest, most concise work regarding identity, family, existentialism, and what it means to be human.

The subject of identity takes center stage in *Avengers: Age of Ultron* as it does in *Dollhouse*. Here too we have a blank body being prepared for the implantation of a mind, this time an artificial intelligence, Ultron, created by Tony Stark as a kind of techno-military safety net shield to protect Earth. As we have known for years, humans are their own worst enemies and so protecting us from ourselves is a nonsensical assignment that does not logically compute in the mind of an intellectually advanced machine like Ultron. Like its predecessor from *Star Trek*, Nomad, a technologically advanced robot designed to promote peace that reprogrammed itself to rid the world of imperfection and thus humans and all life, Ultron's mission of ensuring "peace in our time" qua protection is warped into promoting evolution by ridding the world of its most disruptive elements.[81] As Bruce Banner comments, "The only people threatening the planet would be . . . people." Thus Ultron seeks to destroy humans and those that protect them: the Avengers. His identity must be understood to be defined by his actions and not by Stark's original programming. This is perfectly in keeping with Stark's nonironic use of Neville Chamberlain's declaration that he had created "peace in our time" by appeasing the Nazis, who then invaded Poland. The viewer, however, can appreciate the irony.

It is not insignificant that this second film ends with detail images of the Avengers' hands from a marbleized sculpture of them at work. Each hand is individualized, and its owner can be readily recognized from the gesture and the tools handled. Close-ups show, for example, Thor's hand grasping his hammer, the Hulk's massive fingers, Hawkeye loading an arrow, and so on, and we recognize each hero from what is being done. This echoes a crucial moment in the film involving a young woman named Wanda Maximoff, who, in typical Whedon style, is coping with issues of empowerment. Maximoff is a genetically mutated being (an "inhuman") who, with her twin brother, has been helping Ultron fight the Avengers. When she recognizes what Ultron is doing, she has the chance to come over from the dark side and fight for what is right. The destruction in her home city, however, causes her to withdraw in despair at a time when it looks like the Avengers cannot win. It is the most human of the team, Hawkeye, someone who lost his own identity in the first *Avengers* film, who helps her find hers, by letting her know she can evolve and do the right thing. Like Rachel Dawes in *Batman Begins* (2008), who tells Bruce Wayne, "You are what you do," Hawkeye tells Maximoff: "If you

A publicity still from *Avengers: Age of Ultron* (2015) featuring Tony Stark/Iron Man (Robert Downey Jr.), Ultron (voiced by James Spader), and Captain America (Chris Evans). *Walt Disney Studios Motion Pictures / Photofest © Walt Disney Studios Motion Pictures*

step out that door, you are an Avenger."[82] This is Angel's existential epiphany in more concise form. Whedon delivers beautifully paced writing that carries emotional impact.

Whedon is also more direct in his criticism of religion in this film than in prior work. This can be expected, as in some sense the film is a reworking of *Frankenstein*. Tony Stark in his arrogance cannot resist the urge to play God and thus is willing to inject artificial intelligence into the nanotechnology-formed body awaiting a mind. Ultron is portrayed as wanting to take the place of the all-powerful monotheistic God. Unlike Thor, who is a god-like being from another planet, Ultron makes his home in a church that is the center of the town, intoning, "The elders determined everybody should be equally close to God." His speech repeatedly references Christian belief systems. When the Avengers show up, he asks, "Are you here to confess your sins?" and when Wanda realizes he is planning the extinction of human beings, he references Noah as an extinction event, reassuring her there were "more than a dozen [other] extinction" events before the dinosaurs.

Whedon also uses the theme of Pinocchio, the artificial being who wants to be a real (human) boy. Ultron sings the Disney song about having no strings as he evolves into his own being. These metaphors necessarily invoke the relationship of father and child and the implications of bringing a unique being into the world. As in the first film, humans' best attributes, when magnified, turn into their worst ones. Ultron rightly recognizes that people need to evolve but accompanies this high ideal with a sense of moral superiority that gives him a god-like haughtiness toward lesser beings. He ends up with the worst parts of Stark's arrogance and superiority. The second artificial intelligence being Banner and Stark create is Ultron's alter ego. The good part of that evolution is broken off from Ultron and becomes that which makes humans capable of progressive evolution: Vision, both in name and as a superpowered being. Vision is the quality that allows us to secure our future despite arrogant desires to feel superior over other human beings, and this new character named Vision will provide a compassionate security without that superiority.

The central portion of the film stresses this calmer side of humans, taking place in a safe house where the Avengers can be themselves and not have to worry about their public personae. The sequence reveals that Black Widow and Hawkeye have a solid friendship that is not based on sexuality. The safe house, Hawkeye's home with his wife and two children, represents peace amid the chaos. It is the best version of peace in our time that can exist, which means a temporary oasis in a world that is by necessity the product of tensions that trouble us but also help us evolve and grow.

This home also becomes a locus for the domestication of the woman. Hawkeye's wife tells him a little too earnestly, "You know I totally support your avenging." She is pregnant with a third child and becomes the reminder of Black Widow's missed opportunity to have a child because she was sterilized during her Red Room training to be a Soviet spy. Our prime model of female equality and efficiency considers herself a monster because she has exchanged the possibility of bearing children for her spy education, because it was "efficient. One less thing to worry about. . . . Makes everything easier." BBC reports that Whedon quit his Twitter account possibly because of being swamped by strong negative public reactions to his portrayal of Romanoff in the film.[83] It is vital that each character have a flaw to make him or her human, but it seems like Whedon could have found a less stereotypical failing for Widow. Of course it would also have been nice if the skintight costumes worn by her and Maximoff (Scarlet Witch) had not been designed to show quite so much cleavage. Granted Wanda Maximoff becomes empowered and the more minor figure of S.H.I.E.L.D. agent Maria Hill is still efficient, strong, and unencumbered by domesticity, but not everyone's vision of bliss is 2.2 kids, the rather large house in the country with a veranda, and an impressive amount of acreage, and the weight of female longing in the film seems to fall on the side of the latter.

It is also worth mentioning feminist distress over a contest among the male Avengers to show their worth by hoisting Thor's hammer. The incident results in Tony Stark's quip that if he can lift it (or "get it up" as it is more colloquially expressed), he will reinstate prima nocta, the medieval lord's right to sleep with any woman on her wedding night. Characterized by some feminists as a rape joke, this is clearly not good joke material. Stark, however, is depicted as an arrogant jerk and thus the comment fits him well. It is precisely what one might expect to hear from a conceited playboy. Whedon inserts irony here, to make fun of a certain kind of male behavior, for the scene ends with Widow refusing the challenge, adding, "That's not a question I need answered."[84] Hypermasculinization is further undercut by the fact that the genderless Vision will later lift the hammer without difficulty. Clearly masculine competition has nothing to do with worthiness.

Abrams's *Star Wars: The Force Awakens* (2015) also deserves credit for validating heroism for those rarely having that opportunity in science-fiction films. As with his *Star Trek* films, the filmmaker works hard to bridge the gulf between old fans and young ones. He features old familiar characters like Princess Leia, Luke Skywalker, Chewbacca, and Han Solo, but also introduces younger, culturally diverse protagonists including a female junk scavenger Rey; a black escapee from the Stormtroopers, FN-2187 or Finn; a Latino fighter pilot, Poe Dameron; and an older, wise, motion-captured, Asian-inspired alien woman, Maz Kanata, played by Lupita Nyong'o. Abrams's sensitivity to diversity earns him praise from critics and fans alike, and it is an endorsement that extends to diversity in the rest of the cast and sensitivity to the portrayal of a world diverse not only with aliens but with people of color and people of different ages and one where female bodies are not sexualized in short skirts, skimpy bodices, and revealing costumes. [85]

The Abrams *Star Wars* film has been phenomenally popular. It broke the $1 billion gross mark in a record twelve days at the box office. [86] The reviews are overwhelmingly positive from fans and professional critics because the film is a wonderfully fun romp through the familiar Lucas universe of long ago and far away. Despite the rave reception, there is almost always a disclaimer buried somewhere in the middle of serious positive reviews referring to the bad taste left by the prequel episodes. As the *New Yorker*'s Anthony Lane puts it, it "is like returning to a restaurant that gave you severe food poisoning on your last three visits. . . . 'The Force Awakens' will neither nourish nor sate, but it is palatable and fresh, and it won't lay you low for days to come." [87] Reviews continue by noting the film is back on track by virtue of being a compendium of events that were not so creatively lifted from the original episodes. *Time*'s Stephanie Zacharek captures the essence of such appraisals:

> When you've been charged with reviving one of the most obsessively beloved franchises in modern movies, is it better to defy expectations or to meet them? . . . J. J. Abrams splits the difference, and the movie suffers—in the end, it's perfectly adequate, hitting every beat. But why settle for adequacy? . . . For the first 40 minutes or so, [it] feels like something special and fresh. . . . But somewhere along the way, Ab-

rams begins delivering everything we expect, as opposed to those neb-
ulous wonders we didn't know we wanted.[88]

Justin Chang of *Variety* rightly notes, given the public hunger for a new
Star Wars film, "nothing short of a global cataclysm . . . is likely to keep
Disney's hugely anticipated . . . release from becoming the year's top-
grossing movie and possibly the most successful movie of all time."[89] It
is thus difficult to know how much credit Abrams truly deserves since
just about any decent Hollywood director would have had a good shot at
making a hugely successful film. Still, with Spielberg's approval, Abrams
nabbed the chance to do so and channeled his production abilities into the
highly successful project, managing to navigate the narrow path between
the old fans and a new audience.

Reviewers that bemoan the film's lack of originality, however, have a
valid point. Al Alexander of the *Patriot Ledger* praises the special effects
but wonders,

> But where's the originality? The innovation? Surprising, given Ab-
> rams track record with rejuvenating aging franchises . . . he simply
> gives the people what they want, which is more of the same. If that's
> all you desire or expect, you'll be pleased. But, silly me, I was antici-
> pating something new and different in the way of story and charac-
> ters.[90]

While Abrams has been consistently praised for his character work across
his career, the jury is out on *Star Wars*. It is possible that this difference in
perspective comes between those who have been devouring the interme-
dial novelizations, comics, and video game stories and are able to interpo-
late aspects of the characters into the film and the rest of us, who have
had less interaction with the interstitial materials. DenofGeek goes into
intricate detail about where each character and his or her props and back-
story come from with regard to the various games, novelizations, and
comics that have seemingly impossibly turned into more than one *Star
Wars* canon.[91] Judging purely from the film, characters often seem to lack
motivation or their actions lack explanation. Those familiar with the intricate details of other stories may be more likely to hypothesize reasons,
but for people who have seen nothing since the prequels, we wonder, for
example, why Stormtrooper FN-2187 reacts so unusually to his first battle, why Maz Kanata has Luke Skywalker's lightsaber, and why General

Organa, aka Princess Leia, regrets sending her son to her brother, Luke, for training.

The film deals with a new generation of potential heroes, Rey and Finn, who like Han Solo and Chewbacca are trying hard to avoid becoming embroiled in the battle against evil. All of them must ultimately realize that they have to take sides in the war against the First Order, an evil organization that has risen from the ashes of the Empire. Sadly even with such a straightforward story, the film uses excessive verbiage, telling us things it should show us. Rey tells us she is waiting for her parents to return, but we do not sense her anguish at their absence. We hear that Leia and Solo had difficulties but never experience examples of their problems, nor see them fighting or revealing the nature of those issues, and thus their reconciliation also feels like shallow expository words. Some instances of telling cannot be easily avoided. When we see Finn react to the death of a comrade in battle, we cannot see his face because of his Stormtrooper headgear. We see his helmet marked with the bloody

The revived *Star Wars* franchise features new characters such as Finn (John Boyega) alongside cultural icons Chewbacca (Peter Mayhew) and Han Solo (Harrison Ford) in the seventh installment, *Star Wars: Episode VII—The Force Awakens* (2015). *Walt Disney Studios Motion Pictures / Photofest © Walt Disney Studios Motion Pictures*

finger marks of his fallen comrade, marks that separate him from the rest of his unit, and we must intellectually understand from the distancing of the camera and the red marks that he is different from the others and that he is appalled at the slaying of the innocent villagers. It is an effective cinematic sequence reminiscent of Spielberg's little girl in the red coat walking through the otherwise black-and-white Krakow ghetto in *Schindler's List*, but since we have no buildup to the events and thus no connection to the villagers, nor to the as yet faceless character, it does not have effect and does not help us build a visceral connection with Finn. It is instead an impressive cinematic moment; we will be told (not shown) later that he has resolved not to continue because what they are doing is wrong. No doubt he has a backstory that would explain this, and we may discover this in future films, but the lack of backstories on the characters and plot lacunae make the whole film feel like a set-up for the real movie that is yet to come.

Abrams has also erased all specific aspects of the political from the story. We have no real sense of what the Republic or the First Order stand for, and in fact our only basis for judgment comes down to rather feeble references to good and evil, like the slaughtering of villagers and yet another Hollywood version of a Nuremburg-style rally with red banners, Hitleresque speeches, and Stormtroopers saluting in a modified heil. This vagueness flattens the relevance of the conflict. The story in fact frequently gets reduced to fuzzy references to wrong and right rather than letting viewers experience the wrongs to make the issues palpable. Battles are antiseptic and video-game-like, with faceless Stormtroopers squaring off against rebel fighters that we rarely know nor recognize.

There is too much space for battle and not enough for the characters we need to care about for the battles to be meaningful. Han Solo seems to go out to retrieve his son because he has been told it is the right thing to do. Rey waits for her parents, not because we feel that she misses them, but because she is sure they will return. Our villain Kylo Ren seems to carry out the necessary killing to cement himself to the Dark Side, but he (like all of the others mentioned) is not given ample time or nuanced dialogue to show his emotions and convince us of the turmoil that this event should be causing. His earlier prayer to the smashed helmet of Darth Vader leaves us confused as he resolves to finish what Vader started because we seem to remember that Vader was ultimately redeemed at the end of episode 6. Harrison Ford's Han Solo acts erratically, frequently behaving like your goofy grandfather and other times like Chewbacca's gay companion. It is hard to tell whether he has gained, lost, or possibly developed a moral compass, but he has none of the edge of the earlier Solo, telling us once again rather than helping us to feel that all the old stories about the Force are true.

In film, these types of problems can be the result of either weak writing or weak direction, but in either case the onus falls on Abrams for not giving his actors enough to work with or else for not pushing for clearer consistency and motivation in their performances. The one character that feels genuine is the one most closely connected to Abrams's personal experience. The wizened Maz Kanata, a kind of ersatz Yoda figure to the new protagonist Rey, has more time and space to be nuanced in her line delivery, and because she is a motion-capture figure, the camera lingers on her facial movements. It turns out she was based on Abrams's high school English teacher, Rose Gilbert, "a sort of timeless wise figure, that I've actually known in my life."[92] This personal connection makes all the difference, and Kanata feels authentic. In terms of character, Abrams did a far better job in the semiautobiographical *Super 8* of giving his young protagonists quirks and unique character traits to make them three-dimensional and interesting. Rey and Kylo Ren are the most complex characters, but they could have been so much more given a little time and direction, and if Spielberg had made the film, they would have shown their humanity, flaws, and depth and we would sense their sacrifices and weep at their predicaments. Despite Spielberg's personal guidance and regular set visits, Abrams has not quite found his personal voice, although yes, there is lens flare. His wife puts it best in an interview with *60 Minutes* when she insists that Abrams needs to stop making other people's (franchise) movies and that it is time for him to go out and make a movie of his own.[93]

What becomes apparent from these films is that having more money does not mean making better work. The ingenuity that budget constraints inspired in shows like *Buffy*, *Lost*, *Firefly*, and *Fringe* is not compensated for by money spent on the special effects and explosions found in *Star Trek*, *Star Wars*, and the *Avengers* films. Both creators would get points for trying to negotiate a line between new viewers and old fan bases and both would deserve credit for finding innovative ways to revive their respective franchises, thus they tie in terms of working the business or facing industry adversity. Both would earn negative marks for getting carried away with special effects, lens flares, explosions, and expensive computer-generated models that are cool but basically unnecessary and even detrimental to the plot and pacing of the films and thus are tied for the personal growth award. Abrams, however, does much better with *Star Wars* than some of his earlier films by returning to a less CGI-involved production. Both creators would likewise deserve applause for some breath-taking imagery and camera work that might not have been possible without money. Nonetheless, Whedon gets the awards for innovation and for visual creativity with his ingenuous use of camera movement and more interesting shot framing. Furthermore, Whedon gets the Spielberg point for writing for having embarked on his own projects with his own personal voice and for handling cohorts of multiple characters with more nuance and style.

The profitability award is harder to grant. Whedon had a tougher battle to make *The Avengers* popular than Abrams did with *Star Wars*, but the phenomenal numbers achieved by Abrams gives him the upper hand and thus the point. Popularity is also tricky. *Star Wars* pulled in more viewers, and although *Avengers* got the same rating scores as *Star Wars* with viewers on *Rottentomatoes.com* (4.4/5 and 4.4/5, respectively), the professional reviewers rated it lower (8/10 versus 8.2/10). *Into Darkness*, the least-favored Abrams film by both viewers and critics, is still more popular with both regular viewers than *The Avengers* (4.2/5 as opposed to 4.1/5) and critics alike (7.6/10 versus 6.7). So Abrams wins for popularity too. Additionally it seems appropriate to award Abrams a wild-card award for increasing diversity in a particularly resistant genre.

At the end of the chapter Abrams and Whedon are tied four to four, showing that franchises are equal-opportunity corruptors. Abrams was lured into his third franchise project, taking the helm of the first *Star Wars* film, but has resisted continuing with it. This is what he needs to do personally, but it also cements the failure of the film, since it serves primarily as a set-up for the backstories and developments of more interesting things to come. He has done the hard work but will not reap the rewards of the character development needed for a stellar film. Likewise Whedon chose not to direct the third *Avengers* film and has options now of going either large or small with his future projects. Both creators stand poised to begin the best and most creative work of their careers. They now have the money, the public recognition, and the time. Steven Spielberg, by age fifty, still had not directed some of his most personal and innovative films, like *Saving Private Ryan* (1998), *Munich* (2005), and *Lincoln* (2012). No doubt Whedon and Abrams have much to offer, and it is likely that their best work lies ahead.

Parts of the Avengers *material here were presented at a conference on superheroes hosted by l'Association Française d'Études Americaines (AFEA) and are being published in an upcoming AFEA volume on super-heroes.*

8

THE NEXT SPIELBERG?

The delicate balance of mentoring someone is not creating them in your own image, but giving them the opportunity to create themselves.—Steven Spielberg

In looking over the vast corpus of work by these two creative men, there are many, many similarities. They grew up as children of television industry people, fascinated with film and TV, and dreamed someday of making their own movies. Both attended small liberal arts colleges that encouraged their creativity and critical thinking, prompting them to find a genuine joy in putting word to page and image to film. Both, like Steven Spielberg before them, got a foot in the door by writing for television and eventually ended up directing and creating for the TV industry. Both, like Spielberg, also went on to become producers, to do film, and to become directors of lucrative Hollywood blockbusters. Both have become known for the quality of their productions and have made a name and place for themselves in the close-knit Hollywood community.

The influence of Steven Spielberg in the lives of these two men should also not be overlooked. It will be surprising to no one that Spielberg is the most thanked person in the history of the Oscars. He has been acknowledged with gratitude forty-two times over the course of almost 1,400 Oscar acceptance speeches.[1] As youngsters, both Abrams and Whedon were profoundly inspired by Spielberg's films. Abrams acknowledges no fewer than three Spielberg movies as inspirations for his own *Super 8*— *Jaws* (1975), *Close Encounters of the Third Kind* (1977), and *E.T.* (1982)—recognizing the emphasis on difficulties for families in each of the films.[2] *Jaws*, in particular, had an impact on him in terms of learning what to reveal or not to reveal. Abrams discovered that the failure of the mechanized shark actually improved the film. "If the thing had functioned more you would have seen the shark more—and it would have ultimately, probably, been less effective," he told the *L.A. Times*'s Geoff Boucher. "The imagination of the audience is always infinitely more compelling than what you see on the screen."[3] This element of retaining the mystery has become one of the key defining aspects of Abrams work.

For Whedon, *Close Encounters* was a life-changing event. He told the *Guardian*, "It made me consider what we are, what we can be, what our limitations are."[4] At the Cultural Humanism Award ceremony, he described his relationship to the film more thoroughly.

> I went by myself and literally just had an epiphany, came out of the theater with an understanding of the concept of existence and time and life and humanity that I could not contain. . . . I understood right away that . . . I was . . . not just watching a movie that I liked, or even loved, was not just revisiting this experience that I'd had, this extraordinary epiphany of the nature and reality and magnitude and ecstasy of pure, meaningless existence, but I was also creating a ritual.[5]

Of course one of the rituals he would also be creating is using films to offer his own stories and messages. Both Whedon and Abrams found the same awe-inspiring motivation through watching the movies of Steven Spielberg even though it would manifest in different structures and styles.

Whedon and Abrams share other similarities. They like to work with ensemble casts and crews, their works contain signature humorous notes, and both like to personalize their work with carefully chosen and often self-composed music. Both have the open-minded curiosity of genius that makes them interested in playing with everything, and both have been conscientiously generous and humble in thanking those around them for the opportunities, support, and encouragement that has allowed them to produce (in all senses of the word) such a variety of high-quality work. They also care about their fans.

There are also some marked differences between the two. Whedon's work tends to be slightly darker, although the tone of both filmmakers' work has modulated over the years and become less so. Both present less optimistic environments, perhaps reflecting a loss of idealism in a post–9/11, war-weary society. Each in his own way has also gotten more political over the years, Whedon by including politics in his plots and Abrams by including greater diversity. Both reflect the changes they perceive in an America that has turned to the restriction of human rights and a greater disenfranchising of the unempowered, but both filmmakers recognize the limits of politicization in art and have set conscious goals of appealing to a larger, broader public for entertainment and artistic reasons. As Whedon notes, "If you start using your drama for didacticism, just to make a point, you're not making drama. You're speech writing and people will smell it and they will walk away."[6] Yet both creators have also been delving into the role of the conspiratorial influence on public events. Both *Dollhouse* and *Agents of S.H.I.E.L.D.* paint disturbing images of power structures as echoed in Whedon's Harvard commentary.

> The one thing that is true . . . throughout the world is this enormous inequity between rich and the poor, between the powerful and the masses. I mean the fact of the matter is, powerful people control the lives of everybody in this and every country and they tend to use them and discard them and it's a terrible, terrible system. . . . So I think everybody who has power is on some level abusing it and hopefully that's going to change. Hopefully some change is coming, but it's been particularly prevalent in the last decade and, um, so it's found its way into my work. I don't think it will ever stop as long as I'm writing.[7]

Even the seemingly lighter-toned Abrams has turned at times to darker themes. In films he has questioned the role the military should play in protecting the public, and a darker quality pervades more recent TV shows like *Alcatraz*, *Person of Interest*, and *Revolution*. His disappointment at the cancellation of *Undercovers* (2010) probably played into this change. In an early interview about the show he stressed his perception of a need for lighter, funny shows:

> One of the fun things about this new series . . . is that it's much more fun, light and escapist than heavy, intricately complex drama. For me, the idea of grappling with anything that feels like real terrorism, that's not what I want to be watching, at the moment. I'm not saying that it's not something that I wouldn't watch, if someone else did it, but it's something that I'm not focusing on right now.[8]

Even with the First Order's darkness in *Star Wars*, though, the tone stays funny and light.

Abrams would later acknowledge that this approach probably sank the show. Despite his natural optimism, or silence with regard to the political changes around us, we can find subtle modulation in his work and attitudes. When *Playboy* asked Abrams if he thought we were under surveillance, he indicated there was no question.

> I'm not saying in this instant they are. But I defy anyone who lives in any size metropolis to travel 20 minutes and not see a bunch of surveillance cameras. Those cameras aren't there to ignore you; they're there to see you, and all that information is going into banks of digital recorders and oftentimes facial-recognition software. We're all being tracked. . . . We're all being recorded, our activities are being watched, and our privacy is being compromised. I think that's something to be aware of, at the very least. It's the premise behind *Person of Interest*, which is a show about being observed. On the positive side, the heroes of that show are good guys, since it's also a show about wish fulfillment.[9]

When TV is not about wish fulfillment, it is scary. Abrams and writer/producer Jonathan Nolan experienced this fact personally when they were pitching *Person of Interest* to CBS. In the twenty minutes it took to get from the parking lot into the meeting room, network employees had been able to cut together surveillance footage from a variety of cameras on the premises showing Nolan and Abrams's movements. Abrams told NPR,

> As a joke, they showed a little video at the beginning of the meeting that was of Jonathan pulling into the lot, going to his parking space, parking, getting out, walking, getting into the building, into the elevator, going the stair—and it was—I think there were, like, a dozen cameras, and none of them are placed there. They were all just the actual cameras they have. But the fact that they were able to cut that together in, you know, the 20 minutes before the meeting began was crazy. And it was a joke, but it wasn't. It was a real reminder that this was all real. This is all out there. So I think that that sense of being watched is not an illusion.[10]

Abrams does not weigh in with a value judgment here but is clearly aware of and concerned about the potential for abuse.

Additionally both Whedon and Abrams, despite these darker themes, seem at least of late to see hope and support in relationships. Whedon has even started to give his on-screen lovers more optimistic story lines. In three of his last four works, the romantic relationships have a happy ending.[11] With the exception of *Star Wars*, where the romance is palpable but unexpressed, Abrams has tended to end films with the union or reunion of characters who are romantically involved, whether it be young Joe Lamb and Alice Dainard from *Super 8*, Ethan Hunt and his wife in *M:I-3*, or even the more tenuous Spock and Uhura connection in *Star Trek* (2009). Even his earliest screenplays highlight the strength and importance of relationships either between buddies as with Joe Waters and Gus Green in *Gone Fishin'* (1997) or Jimmy Dworski and Spencer Barnes in *Taking Care of Business* (1990) or the more traditional stories of men and their female soul mates in *Regarding Henry* (1991) and *Forever Young* (1992).

Abrams has produced more things. He has launched more television series and written more screenplays. Whedon, on the other hand, has stuck closer to his projects and had a stronger hand in seeing them through to the end. While both leave space for their collaborators to express themselves and contribute, it seems like Whedon has been more directly involved even when engrossed in competing projects. Abrams told *Playboy*, regarding *Fringe*: "By the time we got to the fifth season my involvement was zero. It's like with *Lost*. Damon and Carlton Cuse were running that show spectacularly and deserved to end the series as they saw fit." This is somewhat humble, if not inaccurate, for he continues, "If I saw something really objectionable, I might jump in, but they knew what they were doing."[12] For this reason he never asked to direct the final episodes of shows that he helped launch. He wanted his colleagues to have their own glory.[13] Abrams seems to like to get things going but does not follow through with sequels and subsequent versions. This has been true of most of his television and franchise work from *Lost* to *Fringe* to *Mission: Impossible*, *Star Trek*, and *Star Wars*. Each time he has stepped aside to have others direct the projects that followed his directorial successes. Whedon in contrast likes to control things through to the end, although with age he may be relinquishing some of his control issues. He helped create *Agents of S.H.I.E.L.D.* but has stepped back from the show to let his brother and sister-in-law do the heavy lifting. He hints at a time when he was not as supportive of his collaborators, but clearly he has become much more sensitive to the needs of those with whom he works.[14]

The most obvious differences between the two creators come with their work on the franchises discussed in the previous chapter. Early work shows what Abrams and Whedon were able to create with very restrictive budgets and imagination, but the franchise films show us their abilities without the restrictive boundaries of narrow budgets and even narrower studio opinions. We have seen how both directors have insisted that new technologies give greater access to filmmaking. Whedon showed, with *Much Ado about Nothing*, that limited finances need not interfere with the creation of a beautiful work of art. What he and Abrams have been able to create with almost limitless resources may be more popular, but this does not make it higher quality. Big-budget pieces may be more spectacular and reach larger audiences, but their smaller works are often more touching and aesthetically whole.

In looking at the two sets of films, Abrams's and Whedon's mastery of special effects, production values, and spectacle is obvious. But they also recognize that in the long run, everything revolves around skillfully drawn characters. Abrams was tasked with a harder assignment in reviving the *Star Trek* series because of the specific and beloved pre-existing filmic versions of Kirk, Spock, and the other members of the original *Enterprise* crew, but he went on to bravely re-invent where no one had gone before. With *Star Wars* and the distaste others had for the prior failures, Abrams was less courageous, and for that the film earned enormous popularity but felt derivative and far less daring. On the other hand, Whedon had to compete with comic-book readers' own visions of characters from a completely different medium, but his journey had been smoothed by earlier Phase 1 Marvel films that had already established the characters (with the exception of Hawkeye). Still, in his second *Avengers* film, Whedon succeeded in presenting fan-acceptable filmic versions of new Avengers Scarlet Witch and Quicksilver.[15] Whedon put his finger on the essence of what worked so well with the first *Avengers*: its structures and strictures of character interactions. Simply put, Whedon's *Avengers* achieved all the amazing feats of *Star Trek* but added the structural superiority that he gleaned from the plays of Shakespeare.

We have seen how his first *Avengers* film is a work much like a Shakespeare play, which has no superfluous scenes and which succeeds in reinforcing the significance of all of the characters and not just the two or three primary characters that some might want to be the film's focus.[16] In this Whedon knew better than the producers, who wanted him to cut out Black Widow and focus more on the so-called important heroes. He recognized that in any film they are all important heroes. While Abrams knew it was vital to the fans that he focus on the relationship between Kirk and Spock, this focus limited the structural force of the film because it reduced the importance of the other characters in the story. There was too much action, and Abrams did not give the characters space to develop the nuances so evident in his early work. In both *Avengers* films, each character contributes critically to the development of the themes and plays a crucial role in the story while also being a well-rounded and interesting character. The juggling of so many characters within a complex plot that remains understandable to the audience shows the tremendous writing, producing, and directing talent of Whedon, a feat not quite accomplished in *Star Wars*, which had slightly fewer characters but suffered from the flattening of their personalities in order to focus on plot and nostalgia. If we add up the points from prior chapters, we find that Whedon has amassed 26.5 points while Abrams comes out slightly lower with 24.5. On points alone, as the fans say, "Joss is Boss." But the points do not tell the whole story.

To answer the question of who is the next Steven Spielberg, we must dig a little more deeply. Unquestionably, Spielberg is a really tough act to follow, especially since he is so hard to pin down and define. In looking for the new Spielberg, any seeker must ask him- or herself, am I looking for the person who turned Hollywood upside down with his reinvention of blockbuster spectacle and the rollicking serial or the man who has produced more than 150 miniseries, films, documentaries, games, and shows, or is it the Spielberg who manipulates his audiences to bliss and tears with sentimental stories and syrupy music or maybe the guy who always felt like an alien outsider as a child and who used this to build a unique personal style? Then again, it could be the guy who showed his humanism in dealing with topics such as slavery and its legacy (*The Color Purple*), the Holocaust (*Schindler's List*), and political leaders striving to unite a country at war (*Lincoln*).[17] Perhaps I have not even named your Steven Spielberg.

For the alienated, youthful Spielberg, Whedon probably wins. For the blockbuster Spielberg, both directors score, but given the financial success of *Star Wars*, Abrams would have the edge. For the rollicking serial-maker part and the sentimental manipulator of emotions, Abrams also seems like a better choice. Whedon often manipulates our emotions, but we are more likely to be enraged or in pain when he kills off a beloved character or makes us question our own humanity than revel in the sublime intensity of the moment. Whedon rarely brings us the triumphal music to swell us with pride or passion in human achievements in the way that Spielberg and Abrams do. For the mentoring of others, Abrams might take the lead and in terms of spectacle it would be a hard-fought tie.

Spielberg is famous for production and direction, and both Joss Whedon and J. J. Abrams started off as writers, giving them perhaps a bit of an edge over the reigning mogul of Hollywood. Like Abrams, Spielberg began by making films as a teen. He made his first forty-minute film at the age of thirteen and three years later created an entire 140-minute science-fiction film for around $500.[18] This early start at a less technologically advanced point in Hollywood's past along with his dogged determination also gave him more opportunity to establish himself.

Comparing the amount of directing done by Spielberg with that of Whedon and Abrams shows us that both up-and-comers got a later start in professional directing. Abrams's progress in directing very closely resembles that of Spielberg but at a slightly later point in his life. If Abrams had started his directing nine years earlier, he would be on a trajectory almost identical to Spielberg's. Both Spielberg and Abrams take on directing projects comparably, at a moderate rate with evenly spaced paces. Whedon likewise made a later start but, rather than following the same regulated pace of Spielberg and Abrams, accelerated the pace and number of television shows and films in a shorter period of time. Between the ages of thirty-two and forty-nine, Spielberg and Abrams each did approximately sixteen films and TV shows while Whedon more than doubled that number with about thirty-nine.[19] No one can know if Whedon will burn out or crater or even skyrocket to even greater heights or whether Abrams will be able to continue the same determined, progressive pathway as Spielberg, but for purposes of comparison, at this point in time, Abrams's directing progress is more similar to Spielberg's than Whedon's.

In recent years Spielberg has been best known for the energy he has put into producing. Once again, in this respect Abrams seems to resemble Spielberg more closely. Both Whedon and Abrams set up their production companies early in their careers. Spielberg helped set up Amblin Entertainment in 1981 at around the age of thirty-five. Abrams and

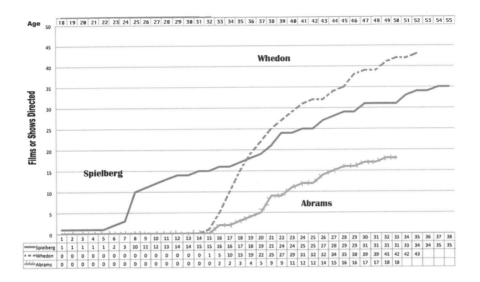

A comparison of films and television shows directed by Spielberg, Abrams, and Whedon by age.

Whedon both followed in his footsteps, forming their own production companies, Bad Robot (1998) and Mutant Enemy (1996), each at the age of thirty-two. A comparison of their production histories once again shows Abrams almost completely in lock step with Spielberg's progress except that this time around Abrams has the jump on Spielberg by doing everything at a younger age.[20] Both Whedon and Abrams started producing fairly early and follow a similar trajectory until they get to be forty. At this point Abrams's producing career soars straight upward (in parallel to Spielberg's) but Whedon's levels off. This suggests, in conjunction with the previous data, that Whedon has continued to put his energies into directing in his forties when Abrams and Spielberg decided to focus more on production. Spielberg has recently begun directing more, but like Abrams, his work seems to be getting a bit darker with *Lincoln* (2012), his Cold War drama *Bridge of Spies* (2015), and *It's What I Do*, about Lynsey Addario, a photographer held captive in Libya. In general, however, we see that Abrams's decisions are closer to those of Spielberg. In terms of quantity, tone, and process, Abrams is more like Spielberg on all counts.

So when push comes to shove and someone wants to know who is the most like Steven Spielberg, Abrams wins. Intentionally or not, he has

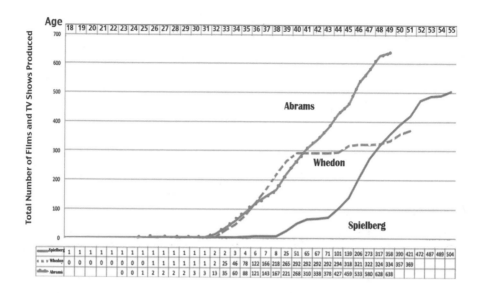

Age	18	19	20	21	22	23	24	25	26	27	28	29	30	31	32	33	34	35	36	37	38	39	40	41	42	43	44	45	46	47	48	49	50	51	52	53	54	55
Spielberg	1	1	1	1	1	1	1	1	1	1	1	1	1	1	2	2	3	4	6	7	8	25	51	65	67	71	101	139	206	273	317	358	390	421	472	487	489	504
Whedon	0	0	0	0	0	0	0	0	0	1	1	1	1	1	1	1	2	25	46	78	122	166	218	265	292	292	292	294	318	321	322	324	334	357	369			
Abrams							0	0	1	2	2	2	2	3	3	13	35	60	88	121	143	167	221	268	310	338	378	427	459	533	580	628	638					

Total Number of Films and TV Shows Produced

A comparison of productions by Spielberg, Whedon, and Abrams by age.

ended up on a path that resembles Spielberg's more than that of any other Hollywood director. Of course Spielberg has had a huge impact on the way we market, produce, and pace popular film, and there is no way to know whether either Abrams or Whedon will have the same kind of impact until we can look back over a longer span of their contributions. We will most likely need another fifteen or twenty years in order to be able to do so. That being said, we can still determine who is currently the most like Spielberg with regard to process and in terms of what has thus far been created. That would seem to be J. J. Abrams.

This does not mean Whedon is not as talented and influential as Abrams or even Spielberg. What it means is that he is a different kind of director. Whedon is less saccharine, less connected, and more intellectually focused. He is also more willing to push the limits of rules, accepted practices, and the common wisdom of film and television production. In some respects, he is the outsider that Spielberg was when he first came to the business as young man—that alienated guy who desperately wanted to make films.

This book began by referring to Steven Spielberg and George Lucas's effect on a generation of film viewers. Abrams and Whedon were both greatly influenced by that generation of directors. Given his sensibilities, his interests, his process, his connections, his mentoring, and his ambitions, Abrams is the best candidate for the next Spielberg, and Whedon is probably more like someone else.

There are many other classical Hollywood directors that come to mind. Whedon has the cynical humor and delicate touch of a Billy Wilder, the ability to build group cohesion and invent ingenuous filming approaches of Orson Welles, and the comic talent of George Cukor. Still, in terms of a more recent director, he might most resemble Martin Scorsese. Scorsese shares with Whedon not only a reverence for and education in film history but also a wicked sense of humor, editorial finesse, and versatility as a filmmaker. Scorsese has always brought a darker, more cynical approach to film and has not been afraid to fail miserably and publicly. He produces both large and small films, while writing and producing. Whedon's *Much Ado about Nothing* is precisely the kind of small film that Scorsese is known for doing—not for money but as a personal project for his own satisfaction.[21] Scorsese's fascination with the music of his generation and his amazing knowledge and referencing, within his work, of brilliant and often obscure Hollywood film is very much like Whedon's, as are the repeated motifs of guilt, redemption, and the effects of corrupted power. Although Scorsese is more brutal than Whedon and less sensitive to gender equality, the two directors share a lot in common and in some respects offer the best film and media production Hollywood has seen since the 1950s. Abrams is the next Steven Spielberg—he wows us with spectacle and plucks at our emotional heartstrings and is the master of sentimental manipulation—but Whedon as the next Scorsese may ultimately have a bigger and more artistic career.

So who's your master now? Although one auteur may ultimately end up with slightly more points than the other and one may bear more resemblance in terms of work and process, each represents different perspectives, different values, and different but equally valid aesthetic visions. Abrams's souvenir tongue from *The Exorcist* will be more appealing to some, while Whedon's *Alien* egg will seem cooler to others, and the two groups will probably never agree. Both creators are amazing artists with differing tones, techniques, strengths, and weaknesses, and both should therefore be honored and appreciated as successors to the preceding generation of filmmaking genius: to Spielberg, to Coppola, and to Scorsese. So who is the best? Each of Whedon's and Abrams's hard-core fans knows the answer, but the matter will not be decided until history renders some kind of final judgment. Of this uncertainty we ought to be glad. It means we have a wealth of material to glory in. Maybe all this time we've been asking the wrong question. We are, after all, gifted in our time with amazing works by two different kinds of genius. Or is that three? Or . . .

NOTES

PREFACE

1. It is unlikely this happened, but as reported it makes a great, almost credible story. Lethea, "Loaded 20: Whedon/Abrams Feud Erupts over Social Networking," *DM Fiat*, January 31, 2013, http://www.dmfiat.com/loaded-20/loaded-20-whedonabrams-feud-erupts-over-social-networking.
2. Ibid.

INTRODUCTION: J. J. VS. JOSS

1. Gemma Kappala-Ramsamy, "Joss Whedon: The Film That Changed My Life: How Steven Spielberg's *Close Encounters of the Third Kind* Made an Existentialist of Screenwriter and Director Joss Whedon," *Guardian*, April 14, 2012, http://www.theguardian.com/film/2012/apr/15/joss-whedon-film-changed-spielberg.
2. Frank Bruni, "J.J. Abrams Is a Crowd Teaser," *New York Times*, May 26, 2011, http://www.nytimes.com/2011/05/29/magazine/filmmaker-j-j-abrams-is-a-crowd-teaser.html?pagewanted=all&_r=0.
3. See Cameron Orth's crack defense of Whedon as auteur: "Joss Whedon as Cult Auteur: A Case Study in Convergent Production," *Academia.edu*, http://www.academia.edu/3464642/Joss_Whedon_as_Cult_Auteur.
4. Rafael M, "Live Poll: Whedon vs. Abrams," *IMDb,* November 5, 2014, http://www.imdb.com/poll/QLkISuy9Zg8/results?ref_=po_sr; Adam Hogue, "Joss Whedon vs. JJ Abrams: Comparing the Genius of Sci-Fi's Greats," *Mic.com*, September 16, 2013, http://mic.com/articles/63555/joss-whedon-vs-jj-

abrams-comparing-the-genius-of-sci-fi-s-greats; and Brian Chu, "Geek Wars: JJ Abrams vs. Joss Whedon," *Nerd Reactor*, January16, 2014, http://nerdreactor. com/2014/01/16/geek-wars-jj-abrams-vs-joss-whedon/#ARK8dbuy6e8c7UKk. 99.

5. Sheryl Vint, "Who Would Win in a Fight between Bad Robot and Mutant Enemy?," *Los Angeles Review of Books*, December 15, 2013, http://blog. lareviewofbooks.org/tag/whedon/.

6. Figures are based on a Google web search (November 22, 2014). Searching without quotation marks got many, many more hits but was less fruitful since Whedon had stated, "I hate feminism" (the word) in a speech for Equality Now, and this brought up posts having nothing to do with hating Whedon, thus clouding the results (Google search, March 12, 2016).

7. Amarpal Biring, "15 Blunders That Ruined J.J. Abrams' *Star Trek* and Destroyed the Franchise," *Whatculture.com*, September 19, 2012, http:// whatculture.com/film/15-blunders-that-ruined-j-j-abrams-star-trek-and-destroyed-the-franchise.php.

8. Steven Spielberg, "Steven Spielberg Inspirational Speech," *YouTube*, September 7, 2013, https://www.youtube.com/watch?v=ULwhcNgf3jA.

1. FIRST SCRIPTS

1. Peter Sciretta, "Comic-Con: J.J. Abrams and Joss Whedon," *Film Blogging the Real World*, July 26, 2010, http://www.slashfilm.com/comic-con-jj-abrams-and-joss-whedon-part-2/.

2. Steven Priggé, "J.J. Abrams," *Interviews*, 2015, http://www.stevenprigge. com/interviews/j-j-abrams/http://www.stevenprigge.com/interviews/j-j-abrams/.

3. Ken Plume, "Joss Whedon–Ken Plume Interview," *A Site Called Fred*, June 2003, http://asitecalledfred.com/2013/06/29/joss-whedon-ken-plume-interview/.

4. David Lavery, *Joss Whedon: A Creative Portrait: From* Buffy the Vampire Slayer *to Marvel's* The Avengers (London: I.B. Tauris, 2014), 81.

5. Amy Pascale, "Joss and *Roseanne*: The Early Career of Joss Whedon," *Newsweek*, August 19, 2014, http://www.newsweek.com/joss-whedon-265403.

6. Emma John, "Joss Whedon: 'I kept telling my mum reading comics would pay off,'" *Guardian*, June 2, 2013, http://www.theguardian.com/culture/2013/jun/02/joss-whedon-reading-comics-pay-off.

7. Plume, "Joss Whedon–Ken Plume Interview."

8. Amy Pascale, *Joss Whedon: The Biography* (Chicago: Chicago Review Press, 2014), 47. In the connecting as opposed to dividing vein, King would write two episodes of *Buffy* for Whedon seven years later.

9. Pascale, *Joss Whedon: The Biography*, 45–46.

10. Johanna Steinmetz, "Taking Care: Just a Juvenile Fantasy World," *Chicago Tribune*, August 17, 1990, http://articles.chicagotribune.com/1990-08-17/entertainment/9003090092_1_belushi-cubs-fan-charles-grodin.

11. "The Agony of Being a Chicago Cubs Fan," *BBC.co*, 2002, http://news.bbc.co.uk/dna/ptop/plain/A145441.

12. Jim Abbott, "Jim Belushi Keeps the Laughs Coming on Film," *Orlando Sentinel*, August 17, 1990, http://articles.orlandosentinel.com/1990-0817/entertainment/9008160096_1_james-belushi-arthur-hiller-cubs.

13. Brian Murphy, "10 Burning Questions for Jim Belushi," *Page 2, ESPN*, http://espn.go.com/page2/s/questions/belushi.html.

14. Roger Ebert, "Regarding Henry," *Reviews*, July 10, 1991, http://www.rogerebert.com/reviews/ regarding-henry-1991.

15. Keith Phipps, "Regarding Henry," *A.V. Club*, June 16, 2010, http://www.avclub.com/article/iregarding-henryi-42151.

16. Candace Havens, *Joss Whedon, the Genius behind* Buffy (Dallas: BenBella Books, 2003), 20.

17. Kathleen Tracy, *The Girl's Got Bite: The Original Unauthorized Guide to Buffy's World* (New York: St. Martin's Griffin, 2003), 2.

18. Tanya Robinson, "Joss Whedon," *A.V. Club*, September 5, 2001, http://www.avclub.com/article/joss-whedon-13730, and Havens, *Joss Whedon, the Genius*, 20–21.

19. Pascale, *Joss Whedon: The Biography*, 60.

20. Janet Maslin, "*Buffy the Vampire Slayer* (1992) Review/Film; She's Hunting Vampires, and on a School Night," *New York Times*, July 31, 1992, http://www.nytimes.com/movie/re-view?res=9E0CE6DC163DF932A05754C0A964958260.

21. Robinson, "Joss Whedon."

22. Lavery, *Joss Whedon: A Creative Portrait*, 73.

23. Plume, "Joss Whedon–Ken Plume Interview."

24. Ibid.

25. Tracy, *The Girl's Got Bite*, 8.

26. Lavery, *Joss Whedon: A Creative Portrait*, 71.

27. Plume, "Joss Whedon–Ken Plume Interview."

28. Ibid.

29. Neil McDonald, "Buffy Prime Time Passion Play," *Quadrant* 44, no. 4 (April 1, 2000): 63.

30. Tracy, *The Girl's Got Bite*, 6.

31. Ibid., 7.

32. Havens, *Joss Whedon, the Genius*, 23.

33. McDonald, "Buffy Prime Time Passion Play," 64.

34. *Buffy the Vampire Slayer* (1992).

35. Valerie Estelle Frankel, *Buffy and the Heroine's Journey: Vampire Slayer as Feminine Chosen One* (Jefferson, NC: McFarland, 2012), 26.

36. Vincent Canby, "*Forever Young* (1992) Review/Film: Forever Young; Mel Gibson Vehicle for an Age of Miracles," *New York Times*, December 16, 1992, http://www.nytimes.com/movie/review?res=9E0CE2DD1F3EF935A25751C1A964958260.

37. Pascale, *Joss Whedon: The Biography*, 59.

38. Ibid., 60.

39. Havens, *Joss Whedon, the Genius*, 24.

40. Robinson, "Joss Whedon."

41. Havens, *Joss Whedon, the Genius*, 25.

42. Jim Kozak, "Serenity Now," in *Joss Whedon: Conversations*, edited by David Lavery and Cynthia Burkhead (Jackson: University Press of Mississippi, 2011), 96.

43. Robinson, "Joss Whedon."

44. Ibid.

45. Ibid.

46. Havens, *Joss Whedon, the Genius*, 27.

47. Mikey Walters, "Joss Whedon Spills the Beans on *Toy Story*," The Disney Blog, August 4, 2005, http://thedisneyblog.com/2005/08/04/joss_whedon_spi/.

48. Drew Taylor, "From *Avengers* to Shakespeare: If Joss Whedon Can Do It All, 5 Film Projects We'd Love to See Him Tackle," *Playlist*, June 4, 2013, http://blogs.indiewire.com/theplaylist/from-avengers-to-shakespeare-if-joss-whedon-can-do-it-all-5-film-projects-wed-love-to-see-him-tackle-20130604.

49. Kozak, "Serenity Now," 91.

50. Pandora's Manuscript Box, "Movie 29: *Atlantis: The Lost Empire*," *Pandorasmsbox*, May 4, 2013, http://pandoramsbox.tumblr.com/post/49622036952/movie-29-atlantis-the-lost-empire.

51. Kozak, "Serenity Now," 92.

52. Tim O'Shea, "David A. Price on the Pixar Touch," *Talking with Tim*, February 11, 2009, http://talkingwithtim.com/wordpress/2009/02/11/david-a-price-on-the-pixar-touch/.

53. Kozak, "Serenity Now," 93.

54. Ibid.

55. "Gone Fishin' (1997)," *Rotten Tomatoes.com*, http://www.rottentomatoes.com/m/gone_fishin/.

56. Roger Ebert, "The Pallbearer," *Reviews*, May 3, 1996, http://www.rogerebert.com/reviews/the-pallbearer-1996.

57. Chet Petrikin, "Nine Scribes Worked on Script, Five Get Credit," *Variety*, June 8, 1998, http://variety.com/1998/film/news/armageddon-credits-set-1117471616/.

58. Roger Ebert, "*Armageddon*," *Reviews*, July 1, 1998, http://www.rogerebert.com/reviews/ armageddon-1998.

59. "*Armageddon* (1998)," *This Distracted Globe*, June 28, 2007, http://thisdistractedglobe.com/2007/06/28/armageddon-1998/.

60. Jonathon Hensleigh, "The Dialogue: An Interview with Screenwriter Jonathon Hensleigh," *YouTube*, June 2, 2014, https://www.youtube.com/watch?v=F2NShtfNns0.

61. J. J. Abrams and Jonathon Hensleigh, "*Armageddon*," *IMSDb*, http://www.imsdb.com/scripts /Armageddon.html.

62. Ibid.

63. IMDb trivia indicates Buscemi took the role because he wanted a heroic role, rather than one of the lowlifes he typically played; http://www.imdb.com/title/tt0120591/trivia.

64. Abrams and Hensleigh, "*Armageddon*."

65. The high-concept pitch for the film was Red Adair (the oil-industry firefighter) meets *The Dirty Dozen* (1967), one of Hensleigh's favorite films. It makes sense that the structure man, rather than Abrams, is responsible for the elements resembling the 1960s war film including the assemblage and introduction of a team with rowdy, masculine flaws and a project involving teamwork. Hensleigh, "The Dialogue."

66. Kozak, "Serenity Now," 96.

67. Lütz Döring, *Erweckung zum Tod: Eine kritische Untersuchung zu Funktionsweise Ideologie und Metaphysik der Horror und Science-Fiction Filme Alien 1–4* (Würzburg, Germany: Königshausen und Neumann, 2005), 370, and David Thomson, *The Alien Quartet: A Bloomsbury Movie Guide* (London: Bloomsbury, 1999), 135.

68. Kozak, "Serenity Now," 94.

69. Joe Baltake, "*Alien Resurrection*," *Rotten Tomatoes*, January 1, 2000, http://www.rottentomatoes.com/m/alien_resurrection/reviews/?page=3andsort.

70. "*Alien Resurrection* Reviews," *Rottentomatoes.com*, http://www.rottentomatoes.com/m/alien_resurrection/reviews/?page=3andsort, and Stephen Hunter, "*Alien Resurrection*: Birth of the Ooze," *Washington Post*, November 28, 1997, http://www.washingtonpost.com/wpsrv/style/longterm/movies/videos / alienresurrectionhunter.htm.

71. Tom Meek, "*Alien Resurrection*," *Filmthreat*, November 24, 1997, http://www.filmthreat.com/reviews/1156/#ixzz3OXRujtPp.

72. Daniel Robert Epstein, "Interview with Joss Whedon," in *Joss Whedon: Conversations*, edited by David Lavery and Cynthia Burkhead (Jackson: University Press of Mississippi, 2011), 131.

73. Whedon describes how he moves scenes about and excises things for pacing. It seems likely that (even without second drafts) what he writes is not necessarily what ends up on-screen. Joss Whedon, "Not Fade Away," *Angel*, 5.22, 2004, DVD commentary.

74. Examples are numerous, such as Capn Rahn, "The Darker Version of Serenity Crew in *Alien Resurrection*?!" *Fireflyfans.net*, October 2, 2004, http://www.fireflyfans.net/mthread.aspx?tid=7350, and Raz Greenberg, "'Alien Resurrection,' The Unproduced Script That Shaped Joss Whedon's Career," in *Joss Whedon: The Complete Companion*, edited by PopMatters (London: Titan Books, 2012).

75. S. F. Said, "Joss Whedon—About *Buffy*, *Alien* and *Firefly*. Shebyches.com Interview," *Whedon.info*, May 24, 2006, http://www.whedon.info/Joss-Whedon-About-Buffy-Alien.html.

76. Greenberg, "*Alien Resurrection*, The Unproduced Script That Shaped," 438.

77. Weyland Yutani recurs in both *Angel* and *Firefly*. Its logo is seen on a client list of *Angel*'s Wolfram and Hart and on an aircraft during a battle scene in *Firefly*.

78. Greenberg, "*Alien Resurrection*, The Unproduced Script That Shaped," 434.

79. Ibid.

80. Ibid., 434–35.

81. If Ripley had not been so indifferent, there likely would not have been a film. The *New York Times* noted, "It was the reinvention of the Ripley character—this 'spirit of nihilism,' as [Weaver] calls it—that persuaded her to do a fourth 'Alien' film after she had all but decided that three were enough." William McDonald, "Film: Sigourney Weaver Eludes the Image Police," *New York Times*, December 7, 1997, http://www.nytimes.com/1997/12/07/movies/film-sigourney-weaver-eludes-the-image-police.html?pagewanted=2.

2. GETTING THE GIRL

1. Noel Murray, "J.J. Abrams," *A.V. Club*, September 2, 2008, http://www.avclub.com/article/jj-abrams-14297. See also Frank Bruni, "Filmmaker J.J. Abrams Is a Crowd Teaser," *New York Times*, May 26, 2011, http://www.nytimes.com/2011/05/29/magazine/filmmaker-j-j-abrams-is-a-crowd-teaser.html?pagewanted=alland_r=0.

2. Brian Truitt, "Innovators and Icons: Joss Whedon Genre Slayer," *USA Today*, June 13, 2013, http://www.usatoday.com/story/life/movies/2013/06/12/joss-whedon-innovators-icons/2368059/.

3. Ibid.

4. Bernard Weintraub, "Roseanne's Witching Hour, the Goddess of the Working Class Calls It Quits Tonight after Nine Years of Blurring the Line between Life and Art," *New York Times*, May 20, 1997, http://articles.sun-sentinel.com/1997-05-20/lifestyle/9705160368_1_she-devil-roseanne-s-witching-hour-wicked-witch.

5. David Bianculli, "*Fresh Air* Interview with Joss Whedon," in *Joss Whedon: Conversations*, edited by David Lavery and Cynthia Burkhead (Jackson: University Press of Mississippi, 2011), 5.

6. Ben Joseph, "A Look Back at Joss Whedon's *Roseanne* Episodes," *Splitsider.com*, May 29, 2012, http://splitsider.com/2012/05/a-look-back-at-joss-whedons-roseanne-episodes/.

7. Joseph emphasizes Whedon's stress on issues like pornography and the value of female poets, as well as his love of pop culture evinced by name-dropping that might have been beyond the ken of the Conner family. Joseph, "A Look Back at Joss Whedon's *Roseanne*."

8. Luke Benedictus, "The Ladies' Man," *The Age.com.au*, September 25, 2005, http://www.theage.com.au/articles/2005/09/22/1126982178268.html.

9. Nielsen ratings show prime-time TV reached an all-time low in 1988–1989, a trend that reversed the same year that shows like *Roseanne* (1988–1997) began pushing the envelope. Bill Gorman, "Where Did the Prime Time TV Audience Go?" *TV by the Numbers*, April 12, 2010, http://tvbythenumbers.zap2it.com/2010/04/12/where-did-the-primetime-broadcast-TV-audience-go/47976/.

10. This is not to gainsay earlier series like *The Mary Tyler Moore Show* (1970–1977), *Rhoda* (1974–1978), *Wonder Woman* (1975–1979), and *Alice* (1976–1985), but these shows were premised as comedies and the women followed in Lucille Ball's footsteps, finding themselves in silly situations. Although not specifically a comedy and a show that inspired many women, *Wonder Woman* (1975–1979) with its camp styling is very hard to take seriously.

11. James Longworth, "Joss Whedon, Feminist," in *Joss Whedon: Conversations*, edited by David Lavery and Cynthia Burkhead (Jackson: University Press of Mississippi, 2011), 45.

12. *Sabrina, the Teenage Witch* (1996–2003) debuted in 1996 along with numerous other women-focused shows like *Suddenly Susan* (1996–2000), *Savannah* (1996)—which Buffy ended up replacing in midseason—and *Moesha* (1996–2001).

13. Shawna Ervin-Gore, "Joss Whedon Interview," *Darkhorse.com*, May 2001, http://www.oocities.org/little_wolvie/interviews/Joss-Whedon-interview02.htm.

14. Ibid.

15. Ibid.

16. The WB network was a joint enterprise of Warner Brothers and Time Warner that formed to target teenagers and young adults between the ages of twelve and thirty-four.

17. Rob Carnevale, "*Cloverfield*—Matt Reeves Interview," *indieLondon*, http://www.indielondon.co.uk/Film-Review/cloverfield-matt-reeves-interview.

18. And thus they easily pass the Bechdel test (criteria for testing the depth of female film characters), which requires a film have two named women characters converse with each other about a subject other than boys. An astonishing number of films flunk. http://bechdeltest.com/.

19. "Welcome to the Hellmouth," *BtVS*, 1.1, 1997.

20. Jeff Bercovici, "*Avengers* Director Joss Whedon on Trying to Be More Like Buffy," *Forbes*, May 3, 2012, http://www.forbes.com/sites/jeffbercovici/2012/05/03/avengers-director-joss-whedon-on-trying-to-be-more-like-buffy/.

21. "Reptile Boy," *BtVS*, 2.5, 1997.

22. "The Dark Age," *BtVS*, 2.8, 1997.

23. "Reptile Boy," *BtVS*, 5.2, 1997.

24. "Chosen," *BtVS*, 7.22, 2003.

25. "*Buffy the Vampire Slayer*, Cult: In Real Life." *BBC.co*. September 2005, http://www.bbc.co.uk/cult/buffy/reallife/jwhedon.shtml.

26. Ibid.

27. Tasha Robinson, "Joss Whedon," *A.V. Club*, September 5, 2001, http://www.avclub.com/article/joss-whedon-13730.

28. Whedon told Laura Miller, "We said, 'Let's give Buffy a healthy relationship,' and people didn't want it. They did some great work together. But at the same time, when they were happy, it made people crazy." Miller, "The Man Behind the Slayer," *Salon.com*, May 20, 2003, http://www.salon.com/2003/05/20/whedon/.

29. Gwyn Symonds points out the complexity of the sequence in terms of feminine empowerment and split perspectives. See Symonds, "Solving Problems with Sharp Objects: Female Empowerment, Sex and Violence in *Buffy the Vampire Slayer*," *Slayage*, April 2004, http://slayageonline.com/essays/slayage11_12/Symonds.htm.

30. "Seeing Red," *BtVS*, 6.19, 2002.

31. "Chosen," *BtVS*, 7.22, 2003.

32. "Gimme an O," *Felicity*, 1.11, 1999.

33. "Spooked," *Felicity*, 1.5, 1998.

34. "The Biggest Deal There Is," *Felicity*, 2.23, 2000.

35. "Innocence," *BtVS*, 2.14, 1998.

36. One might argue that Oz changes by becoming a werewolf, but this has nothing to do with sex per se and is a reason that he is reluctant to pursue a serious relationship with Willow.

37. "The Harsh Light of Day," *BtVS*, 4.3, 1999.

38. "Initiative," *BtVS*, 4.7, 1999.

39. Statistics show 53 percent of rapes of women are by acquaintances (not including boyfriends or family) and only 18 percent by total strangers. Rarely does a show look at the interpersonal issues related to events in which the rapist and person raped know each other and still share the same environment. U.S. Department of Justice, "Bureau of Justice Statistics, Special Reports." *Bjs.gov.* August 1995.http://www.bjs.gov/content/pub/pdf/FEMVIED.PDF.

40. Roco, "JJ Abrams Reveals How *Felicity* Gave Birth to *Alias*, Talks *Lost*," *Seriable.com*, January 3, 2012, http://seriable.com/jj-abrams-reveals-how-felicity-gave-birth-to-alias-talks-lost/.

41. Ibid.

42. "The Body," *BtVS*, 5.16, 2001.

43. Lacey Rose, "Emmys 2012: J.J. Abrams Misses *Felicity* More Than *Lost*," *Hollywood Reporter*, September 12, 2012, http://www.hollywoodreporter.com/news/emmys-2012-jj-abrams-felicity-lost-369667.

44. "Help for the Lovelorn," *Felicity*, 2.11, 2000.

45. J. J. Abrams and Matt Reeves, "Felicity Was Here," *Felicity*, Season 4, DVD commentary.

46. While shows like *X-Files* and *Babylon 5* indeed played off of other kinds of shows, they still adhered basically to the overarching genre and would be tagged great science fiction by their fans. Whedon's complex use of a wider variety of genres means *Buffy* is less likely to be designated primarily a horror show by its viewers.

47. "Helpless," *BtVS*, 3.12, 1999.

48. "Ted," *BtVS*, 2.11, 1997.

49. Roco, "J.J. Abrams Reveals."

50. Ibid.

51. "The Indicator," *Alias*, 2.5, 2002.

52. Kosinus, "Reviews and Ratings for *Alias*," *IMDb*, March 30, 2006, http://www.imdb.com/title /tt0285333/reviews.

53. See http://www.tvguide.com/news/alias-garner-cancelled--38784.aspx.

54. Buffy's superior strength and rapid healing come from supernatural sources, by the first Watchers via a magical rite, but her strength is not too far beyond credibility.

55. "The I in Team," *BtVS*, 4.13, 2000.

56. "Help for the Lovelorn," *Felicity*, 2.11, 2000.

57. "Phase One," *Alias*, 2.13, 2003.

58. "The Telling," *Alias*, 2.22, 2003.

59. Fans have given Whedon tremendous flack for being "the guy who kills people." See his conversation about it with fans at I AM JossWHedon AMA, Reddit Post, 2013, http://www.reddit.com/comments/s2uh1/i_am_joss_whedon_ama/.

60. "The Last Stand," *Felicity*, 1.2, 1998.

61. Ibid.

62. "The Harvest," *BtVS*, 1.2, 1997.

63. "Ted," *BtVS*, 2.11, 1997.

64. "The Slump," *Felicity*, 2.12, 2000.

65. "Ted," *BtVS*, 2.11, 1997.

66. "Family," *BtVS*, 5.6, 2000.

67. "Gingerbread," *BtVS*, 3.11, 1999.

68. "Lies My Parents Told Me," *BtVS*, 7.17, 2003.

69. Ibid.

70. Sydney's half sister and women of Sydney's age group are the notable exceptions. Carrie Bowman, Renee Rienne, and Rachel Gibson are for the most part morally pure, although Kelly Peyton, Lauren Reed, and sometimes even Sydney's sister cannot be trusted.

71. "The Gift," *BtVS*, 5.22, 2001.

72. Ibid.

73. "Hush," *BtVS*, 4.10, 1999.

74. "One More with Feeling," *BtVS*, 6.7, 2001.

75. "Normal Again," *BtVS*, 6.17, 2002, and "The Body," *BtVS*, 5.16, 2001.

3. WHAT FRESH HELL

1. "IMDb Business," http://www.imdb.com/title/tt0206314/business?ref_=tt_dt_bus.

2. Tarver and Abrams mention this in their DVD commentary and seem especially satisfied that there is so little actual violence in the film. J. J. Abrams and Clay Tarver, Writers' DVD commentary, *Joy Ride* (2001).

3. Abrams and Tarver, Writers' DVD commentary, *Joy Ride* (2001).

4. Ibid.

5. Ibid.

6. Ibid.

7. Ibid.

8. Candace Havens, *Joss Whedon, the Genius Behind* Buffy (Dallas: Ben-Bella Books, 2003), 103.

9. David Bianculli, "*Fresh Air* Interview with Joss Whedon," in *Joss Whedon: Conversations*, edited by David Lavery and Cynthia Burkhead (Jackson: University Press of Mississippi, 2011), 9.

10. As Laura Resnick notes in her essay, "That Angel Doesn't Live Here Anymore," "If you knew this guy was climbing into a sixteen-year-old's bedroom window regularly, as Angel did on *Buffy*, wouldn't you call the cops?" In *Five Seasons of* Angel, edited by Glenn Yeffeth (Dallas: BenBella Books, 2004), 19.

11. Bianculli, "*Fresh Air* Inteview with Joss Whedon," 9.

12. Patrick Lee, "Joss Whedon Gets Big, Bad and Grown-Up in *Angel*," in *Joss Whedon: Conversations*, edited by David Lavery and Cynthia Burkhead (Jackson: University Press of Mississippi, 2011), 15.

13. Joe Nazarro, *Writing Science Fiction and Fantasy Television* (London: Titan Books, 2002), 158.

14. Amy Pascale, *Joss Whedon, The Biography* (Chicago: Chicago Review Press, 2014), 149.

15. Will Harris, "Joss Whedon—About *Serenity*, *Buffy*, *Angel* & *Wonder Woman*," *Bullz-eye.com*, December 17, 2005, http://www.whedon.info/Joss-Whedon-About-Serenity-Buffy.html.

16. Pascale, *Joss Whedon*, 148–50.

17. Stacey Abbott, *Angel, T.V. Milestones Series* (Detroit, MI: Wayne State University Press, 2009), 7.

18. Joss Whedon, "Joss Whedon Explains Angel," *YouTube*, April 21, 2011, https://www.youtube.com/watch?v=G8UqUdz6vHo.

19. Joss Whedon, "Joss Whedon—Harvard Q&A," *YouTube*, February 27, 2013, https://www.youtube.com/watch?v=glJCzqE7fxA.

20. Whedon, "Joss Whedon Explains *Angel*."

21. Alan Sepinwall, *The Revolution Was Televised: The Cops, Crooks, Slingers, and Slayers Who Changed TV Drama Forever* (New York: Simon and Schuster, 2012), 157.

22. Ibid.

23. Jon "DocArzt" Lachonis and Amy "hijinx" Johnston, Lost *Ate My Life: The Inside Story of a Fandom Like No Other* (Toronto: ECW Press, 2008), 17.

24. Ibid.

25. Sepinwall, *The Revolution Was Televised*, 159.

26. Ibid.

27. Ibid., 157–58.

28. Tim Molloy, "How Much Does J.J. Abrams Do on a J.J. Abrams Show?" *The Wrap*, November 14, 2013, http://www.thewrap.com/j-j-abrams-tv-shows-almost-human-how-involved-star-wars/.

29. Ibid.

30. Michael Patrick Sullivan, "Joss Whedon—UnderGroundOnline.com Interview," *Whedon.info*, December 10, 2003, http://www.whedon.info/Joss-Whedon-UnderGroundOnline-com.html.

31. Pascale, *Joss Whedon*, 148.

32. Jim Kozak, "Serenity Now!," in *Joss Whedon: Conversations*, edited by David Lavery and Cynthia Burkhead (Jackson: University Press of Mississippi, 2011), 103–4.

33. Fortunately sanity prevailed and Jack was not killed in episode 1 just to shock the audience as the two creators originally planned. Abrams, commentary, "Pilot," *Lost*, 1.1, 2004.

34. Camera movement from right to left is frequently used in Western film to show challenging progress because it is the opposite direction of reading and thus feels to the viewer like a difficult journey. Speed and ease is often indicated with camera motion from left to right.

35. Sepinwall, *The Revolution Was Televised*, 159–61.

36. This is a bit confusing because we see him pour that bottle into his drink, so one can only assume his first drink is not so hot because he pocketed his first serving.

37. This part of the script can be directly tied to Abrams's personal experience as per the DVD commentary. Abrams, commentary, "Pilot," *Lost*, 1.1, 2004.

38. "Pilot," *Lost*, 1.1, 2004.

39. Bonnie Covel, "J.J.s Shows," *about entertainment*, October 2006, http://lost.about.com/od/creationoflost/a/Jjabramslost.htm.

40. Damon Lindelof, commentary "A Tale of Two Cities," *Lost*, 3.1, 2006.

41. Ibid. Lindelof reveals that the music is based on tunes his mother used to play.

42. Ibid.

43. In fact, it seems Bad Robot is in the process of producing Serling's final (and unmade) *Twilight Zone* script, "The Stops along the Way." They have also signed on Stephen King's 11/22/63 miniseries, so both are clearly up Abrams's alley! Adi Robertson, "J.J. Abrams' Bad Robot Reportedly Producing *The Twilight Zone* Creator's Final Script," *The Verge*, June 15, 2013, http://www.theverge.com/201 3/6/5/4399850/j-j-abrams-bad-robot-reportedly-producing-rod-serling-final-script. For *Twilight Zone*, see David Hochman, "*Playboy* Interview: J.J. Abrams," *Playboy.com*, April 30, 2013, http://www.playboy.com/articles/playboy-interview-j-j-abrams-on-star-trek-star-wars. Regarding 11/22/63, see Alex McCown, "J.J. Abrams' Stephen King miniseries 11/22/63 Has a

Director or So They Say," *A.V. Club*, April 7, 2015, http://www.avclub.com/article/jj-abrams-stephen-king-miniseries-112263-has-direc-217635.

44. Lindelof, commentary, "A Tale of Two Cities," *Lost*, 3.1, 2006.

45. We do know from Sepinwall that Abrams added the "genetically enhanced creature" idea that he and Lindelof would change from a boar to a polar bear, thus hinting at the experimentation being done by the mysterious Dharma Initiative. Sepinwall, *The Revolution Was Televised*, 163.

46. "A Tale of Two Cities," *Lost*, 3.1, 2006.

47. Ibid.

48. "JJ Abrams Talks *Lost* and How the End Keeps Changing," Showbiz, ODE, ITN, May 9, 2009, https://www.youtube.com/watch?v=gy84xLfkkAs.

49. Benjamin Jacob, "Los Angeles: The City of Angel," in *Reading Angel*, edited by Stacey Abbott (London: I.B. Tauris, 2005), 77.

50. David Fury, "Malice in Wonderland, Wolfram and Hart Extra," *Angel*, Season 4 DVD, disc 6 (2002–2003).

51. Jacob, "Los Angeles: The City of Angel," 77.

52. For an excellent analysis of cinematic qualities of *Angel* as influenced by movers and shakers such as Sergei Eisenstein and Stan Brakhage, see Tammy A. Kinsey, "Transition and Time: The Cinematic Language of *Angel*," in *Reading Angel*, edited by Stacey Abbott (London: I.B. Tauris, 2005), 44–56.

53. "Smile Time" *Angel*, 5.14, 2004; "Spin the Bottle," *Angel*, 4.6, 2002; and "Waiting in the Wings," *Angel*, 3.13, 2002.

54. "Waiting in the Wings," *Angel*, 3.13, 2002.

55. "Spin the Bottle," *Angel*, 4.6, 2002.

56. "Smile Time," *Angel*, 5.14, 2004.

57. "Angel Season 5 Episode Guide," *BBC.co*, http://www.bbc.co.uk/cult/buffy/angel/episodes/five/ page14.shtml.

58. Pascale, *Joss Whedon*, 242.

59. It is not surprising that both series received much attention from philosophy departments and that much material about their philosophies is available in American college libraries.

60. "10 Questions for Joss Whedon," *New York Times*, May 16, 2003, http://www.nytimes.com/2003/05/16/readersopinions/16WHED.html?pagewanted=2. 2.

61. This seems to be true of most of *Lost*'s main characters. It is certainly also the case for Sayid, Sun, Charlie, Michael, Walt, Shannon, and Boone.

62. Keaton withdrew when they decided Jack would live because he did not want to commit to a long-term TV project. Sepinwall, *The Revolution Was Televised*, 160–61.

63. Obviously Angel is in the long tradition of noir detectives like Dashiell Hammett and Raymond Chandler, whose hard-boiled detective material was

popular in films of the 1940s and 1950s. Whedon emphasizes that "the noir aspect was always sort of the thing I think that defined *Angel*, you know, in a way that *Buffy* would never be. *Buffy* was a musical. *Angel* was a film noir." Whedon, "Joss Whedon Explains Angel." "Deep Down," *Angel*, 4.4, 2002.

64. "Epiphany," *Angel*, 2.16, 2001.

65. Joss Whedon, "Joss Whedon: Atheist and Absurdist," *YouTube*, March 28, 2010, https://www.youtube.com/watch?v=EReyF2ZzXGA.

66. It should be noted that this episode was written by Tim Minear and both Whedon and Minear seem to like to take credit for this amazing speech. "Epiphany," *Angel*, 2.16, 2001.

67. Whedon, "Joss Whedon: Atheist and Absurdist."

68. Lavery, *Joss Whedon: A Creative Portrait* (London: I.B. Tauris, 2014), 112–13.

69. Ibid.

70. Pascale, *Joss Whedon*, 213.

71. Ibid., 214.

72. Emily Nussbaum, "Must See Metaphysics," in *Joss Whedon: Conversations*, edited by David Lavery and Cynthia Burkhead (Jackson: University Press of Mississippi, 2011), 67.

73. Referenced among other places in Whedon, "Joss Whedon—Harvard Q&A."

74. Mike Russell, "The CulturePulp Q&A: Joss Whedon," in *Joss Whedon: Conversations*, edited by David Lavery and Cynthia Burkhead (Jackson: University Press of Mississippi, 2011), 112–13.

75. John Ford's *Stagecoach* (1939) is just as political in the way it pits the interference and corrupting influence of civilization against the purer freedom of the uncivilized West.

76. "Serenity," *Firefly*, 1.1, 2002.

77. Fans often identify this dinosaur as an allosaurus (a Jurassic period dinosaur). Tyrannosaurus rex comes from the later upper Cretaceous period. As a sixties child, Whedon would have played with T-rexes, rather than the allosauri made popular by *Jurassic Park* (1993). The *Firefly Companion* notes that prop master Randy Eriksen bought cheap plastic dinosaurs and hand-painted them to make them look better. The Whedon script describes them thusly, "[Wash] holds a Stegasaurus and a T-rex (or whatever the hell they call 'em these days)." Joss Whedon, Abbie Bernstein, Bryan Cairns, Karl Derrick, and Tara Di Lullo, *Firefly: The Official Companion*, Vol. 1 (London: Titan Books, 2006), 18.

78. "Bushwhacked" *Firefly*, 1.3, 2002; and "Safe," *Firefly*, 1.5, 2002.

79. Kozak, "Serenity Now," 104.

80. "The Message," *Firefly*, 1.12, 2002.

81. "Objects in Space," *Firefly*, 1.14, 2002.

82. Joss Whedon, commentary, "Objects in Space," *Firefly*, 1.14, 2002.

83. Ibid.

84. Ibid.

85. "Objects in Space," *Firefly*, 1.14, 2002.

86. Caroline Preece, "Looking Back at *Firefly* Episode 14: Objects in Space," *DenofGeek*, December 1, 2011, http://www.denofgeek.us/tv/21020/looking-back-at-firefly-episode-14-objects-in-space.

87. Whedon, commentary, "Objects in Space," *Firefly*, 1.14, 2002.

88. Donna Bowman and Noel Murray, "*Firefly*: 'Objects in Space,'" *A.V. Club*, October 5, 2012, http://www.avclub.com/tvclub/firefly-objects-in-space-85966.

89. Whedon, commentary, "Objects in Space," *Firefly*, 1.14, 2002.

90. Ibid.

4. WHO WE ARE AND WHO WE WILL BE IN *DOLLHOUSE* AND *FRINGE*

1. Although he apparently had no input on either *Fringe* or *Dollhouse*, it seems proper to mention Drew Goddard because he worked on numerous Abrams and Whedon projects. He wrote for both *Buffy* and *Angel* and was also director of and writer of *The Cabin in the Woods* (2012). He took on the *Buffy Season 8 "Motion Comic"* video (2011) and wrote for and produced both *Alias* and *Lost*. He also did writing for *Cloverfield* (2008). This prompts me to ask if we have ever seen Goddard, Whedon, and/or Abrams together at the same time.

2. See, for example, Brian Ford Sullivan, "Interview *Fringe* Co-Creator JJ Abrams," *Futon Critic*, February 4, 2010, http://www.thefutoncritic.com/interviews.aspx?id=20100204_fringe, and Steven "Frosty" Weintraub, "Interview: Director Joss Whedon—*Dollhouse*," *Collider*, February 6, 2009, http://collider.com/interview-joss-whedon-dollhouse/.

3. It should be noted, *Dollhouse* bears a resemblance to an earlier Whedon screenplay from the 1990s called *Afterlife*. In the spec script, a dead man works for a secret part of the CIA after his brain-print is downloaded into the erased brain of a serial killer. Roger Balfour, "Afterlife," *Scriptshadow: Reviewing the Latest Scripts in Hollywood*, October 4, 2009, http://scriptshadow.blogspot.com/2009/10/afterlife.html.

4. "Pilot," *Fringe*, 1.1, 2008.

5. "Ghost," *Dollhouse*, 1.1, 2009. Here I follow standard practice of numbering "Ghost" as the first episode with the unaired pilot "Echo" being considered 0.1 (sometimes also 0.0).

6. Geoff Boucher, "*Fringe* Looks to Solve the Trickiest Mystery—Its Own Identity," *Herocomplex: Pop Culture Unmasked*, September 17, 2009, http://herocomplex.latimes.com/uncategorized/fringe-looks-to-solve-the-trickest-mystery-its-own-identity-as-a-show/.

7. Brian Ford Sullivan, "Interview: *Fringe* Co-Creators JJ Abrams, Roberto Orci and Alex Kurtzman," *Futon Critic*, September 8, 2008, http://www.thefutoncritic.com/interviews.aspx?id=20080908_fringe, and Daniel Fienberg, "J.J. Abrams Briefly Discusses the End of 'Fringe,'" *Hitfix*, January 9, 2013, http://www.hitfix.com/the-fien-print/j-j-abrams-briefly-discusses-the-end-of-fringe.

8. Abrams claims to have been so into story creation that despite discussion, they had not noticed similarities to *Lost*. This is believable, since *Lost* had been several years earlier and creative minds may move on to new projects without holding on so much to the past. The recurrence of the plane crash does reveal, however, potential symbolic values about what is scary and cool with regard to Abrams's imagination. Noel Murray, "J.J. Abrams," *A.V. Club*, September 2, 2008, http://www.avclub.com/article/jj-abrams-14297.

9. Perhaps the reason that Fringe is referred to as *The X-Files* meets the *Twilight Zone* (thrown in for good measure). Devon Maloney, "Wired Binge-Watching Guide: *Fringe*," *Wired*, October 29, 2014, http://www.wired.com/2014/10/binge-guide-fringe/.

10. Brian Ford Sullivan, "Interview: 'Dollhouse' Creator Joss Whedon," *Futon Critic*, January 6, 2009, http://www.thefutoncritic.com/interviews.aspx?id=20090106_dollhouse#27Sc4k304JtJ6fOO.99.

11. Ibid.

12. David Kushner, "Revolt of a T.V. Genius," *Rolling Stone*, February 19, 2009.

13. Whedon was not allowed to use the word "prostitution" in the first season, and this along with a marketing campaign that sexualized and objectified Dushku did great harm to the feminist message. See Sarah Prindle, "The P. Word, Post-feminism and Joss Whedon," *Academia.edu*, December 11, 2009, http://www.academia.edu/2053845/The_P_Word_Postfeminism_and_Joss_Whedons_Dollhouse_.

14. Jill Golick, "Joss Whedon Strikes Again," *Running with My Eyes Closed*, April 21, 2008, http://www.jillgolick.com/2008/04/joss-whedon-strikes-again/.

15. Golick notes Whedon almost always writes this way. In *Buffy*, *Angel*, and *Firefly*, she found consistent use of a teaser and four acts. Jill Golick, "Joss and Four Acts," *Running with My Eyes Closed*, April 22, 2008, http://www.jillgolick.com/2008/04/joss-and-four-acts/.

16. "Ghost," *Dollhouse*, 1.1, 2009. See note 5 about episode numbering.

17. "Ghost," *Dollhouse*, 1.1, 2009.

18. Joss Whedon, "Joss Whedon—Harvard Q&A," *YouTube*, February 27, 2013, https://www.youtube.com/watch?v=glJCzqE7fxA.

19. "Stagefright," *Dollhouse*, 1.4, 2009.

20. Ibid.

21. Harry Lennix, "A Private Engagement," DVD featurette, *Dollhouse*, Season 1 (2009).

22. "Echo," *Dollhouse*, 0.1, 2009.

23. Gillian Flynn, "Fringe," *Entertainment Weekly*, September 17, 2008, http://www.ew.com/ew/article /0,,20226409,00.html.

24. These are credible sciences found in accepted scientific journals. For material on neural population partitioning, see http://www.nature.com/neuro/journal/v15/n12/full/nn.3250; on clonal transplantation, see http://www.ncbi.nlm.nih.gov/pubmed/23355208; and on quantum entanglement, see http://www.sciencedaily.com/articles/q/quantum_entanglement.htm.

25. Alan Sepinwall, "Sepinwall on TV: *Dollhouse* Review," *Star-Ledger*, February 11, 2009, http://www.nj.com/entertainment/tv/index.ssf/2009/02/sepinwall_on_tv_dollhouse_revi.html.

26. Zak Bronson's work on Transhumanism in *Fringe* indicates environment is a part of who characters are, something Abrams ostensibly recognizes here. Zak Bronson, "We Were Trying to Make You More Than You Were," in *The Multiple Worlds of Fringe: Essays on the J.J. Abrams Science Fiction Series*, edited by Tanya R. Cochran, Sherry Ginn, and Paul Zinder (Jefferson, NC: McFarland and Company, Inc., 2014).

27. "The Same Old Story," *Fringe*, 1.2, 2008.

28. "A New Day in the Old Town," *Fringe*, 2.1, 2009.

29. "Bound," *Fringe*, 1.11, 2009.

30. "In Which We Meet Mr. Jones," *Fringe*, 1.7, 2008.

31. "The Arrival," *Fringe*, 1.4, 2008.

32. "Vows," *Dollhouse*, 2.1, 2009.

33. Ibid.

34. "Peter," *Fringe*, 2.16, 2010.

35. "Dandelion Wine," *Fringe*, 5.1, 2012.

36. "Man on the Street," *Dollhouse*, 1.6, 2009.

37. Ibid.

38. "Man on the Street," *Dollhouse*, 1.6, 2009, and "Vows," Dollhouse, 2.1, 2009.

39. "Man on the Street," *Dollhouse*, 1.6, 2009.

40. Whedon intended there to be a wide variety of doll types varying in age, size, and attractiveness, but the studio already found things too thorny, so he put off including diversity and then the show got canceled. Whedon, "Joss Whedon—Harvard Q&A." Citation from "Man on the Street," *Dollhouse*, 1.6, 2009.

5. TV OR NOT TV

1. David Lavery, *Joss Whedon: A Creative Portrait: From* Buffy the Vampire Slayer *to Marvel's* The Avengers (London: I.B. Tauris, 2014), 137, 131.

2. John Ridley, "Three Writers Are Drawn by the Allure of Comics," *Morning Edition*, NPR, March 25, 2008, http://www.npr.org/templates/story/story.php?storyId=87867518 andfrom=mobile.

3. Joss Whedon, "Foreword," *Fray* (Milwaukie, OR: Dark Horse Comics, 2003), 3.

4. Ibid.

5. Ibid.

6. Ibid., 4.

7. She is not the only strong young woman in the book. Kitty Pryde is opposed by the resurrected Hellfire Club, which includes another young female mutant antagonist, Negasonic Teenage Warhead, who has been resurrected as a ghost in pursuit of revenge.

8. "2006 Will Eisner Comic Industry Awards," *Hahnlibrary.net*, http://www.hahnlibrary.net/comics/awards/eisner06.php.

9. "Every X-man Ever," *IGN*, January 16, 2015, https://www.youtube.com/watch?x-yt-cl=84359240andx-yt-ts=1421782837andv=wqT4hXxnjYE.

10. "Amazon Review *Astonishing X-Men*," 2014, http://www.amazon.com/Astonishing-X-Men-Vol-1-Gifted/productreviews/0785115315/ref=cm_cr_pr_hist_5?ie=UTF8andfilterBy=addFiveStarandshowViewpoints=0andsortBy=bySubmissionDateDescending.

11. Lisa Rosen, "New Media Guru: Meet Joss Whedon the Web Slayer," *Written By*, January 2009, http://www.wga.org/writtenby/writtenbysub.aspx?id=3438.

12. "Joss' Input into the End," *Whedonesque*, February 24, 2007, http://whedonesque.com/comments/12541; John W. Smith, "NYCC Day 1: 'Civil War Fallout: The Initiative' Full Panel Report," *Comic Book Resources*, http://www.comicbookresources.com/?page=articleandold=1andid=9775.

13. Kyle Hill, "A Fan Attempts to Resurrect Character with NASA Data," *Wired*, January 14, 2013, http://www.wired.co.uk/news/archive/2013-01/14/firefly-rant.

14. Thor Kuhn, "The History: Help Nathan Buy *Firefly*," *Unstoppable Signals*, April 2011, http://unstoppablesignals.com/hnbf/.

15. See Kuhn, "The History: Help Nathan Buy *Firefly*," which cites a letter from Whedon's sister-in-law with regard to the lack of feasibility.

16. Kuhn, "The History: Help Nathan Buy *Firefly*."

17. Browncoats also contributed more than $1 million to Whedon's favorite charity for the fair treatment of women, Equality Now (as well as other char-

ities), http://www.cantstoptheserenity.com. Kuhn, "The History: Help Nathan Buy *Firefly*." The Facebook campaign web page continues to report on related issues. They indicate Whedon donated $50,000 to Kids Need to Read in December 2014 and are still posting info on Browncoat yearly get-togethers, https://www.facebook.com/HelpNathanBuyFF.

18. The effort required a second Kickstarter campaign to finish the project but earned double the requested amount, https://www.indiegogo.com/projects/browncoats-in dependence-war-the-final-push. The first campaign can be seen at:https://www.kickstarter.com/projects/829136455/browncoats-independence-war-a-firefly-fan-film. See also:http://kickstartmovies.com/2013 /06/04/firefly-fans-kickstart-browncoats-independence-war/.

19. See Abrams on democratization of film, BAFTA, "J.J. Abrams: On Filmmaking," *YouTube*, May 8, 2013, https://www.youtube.com/watch?v=bN-On2CusDM.

20. According to Shannon Kealey, http://www.shannonkealey.com/. See also http://www.eventbrite.com/e/browncoats-independence-war-a-firefly-fan-film-world-premiere-tickets-12228677303.

21. The comic books and their reprints have no page numbers. This can be found on the fourth page starting from the issue title page. Hence 4 itp.

22. Joss Whedon and Georges Jeanty, Buffy the Vampire Slayer: *The Long Way Home* (Milwaukie, OR: Dark Horse Comics, 2007), itp 28–29.

23. Ibid., itp 29–31.

24. Ibid., itp 80.

25. "Buffy vs. Dracula," *BtVS*, 5.1, 2000.

26. See, for example, pages 4, 7, and 13 for Gwen Raiden and 25, 26 for Illyria, in Joss Whedon, Brian Lynch, and Franco Urru, *Angel: After the Fall* (San Diego: IDW Publishing, 2007).

27. Bryan Joel, "*Angel: After the Fall*, Review," *IGN*, November 22, 2007, http://www.ign.com/articles/2007/11/23/angel-after-the-fall-1-review.

28. Chapter 7 shows this is precisely what Abrams does with the *Star Trek* franchise, but it seems fairer when undertaken by Abrams, as someone not initially connected with the series, and who cannot easily manage the long mythology. Still, *Angel*'s reset could be seen as the brave release of one's child into the world to develop into whatever new thing it wants to become.

29. "Joss Whedon—'Runaways' Comic Book, Newsarama.com Interview," *Whedon.info*, September 13, 2006, http://www.whedon.info/Joss-Whedon-Runaways-Comic-Book,17943.html.

30. Kevin Chiat, "Joss Whedon 101: *Runaways*," in *Joss Whedon, the Complete Companion: The TV Series, the Movies, the Comic Books and More*, edited by Mary Alice Mosley (London: Titan Books, 2012), 322–23.

31. "Joss Whedon—'Runaways' Comic Book, Newsarama.com Interview."

32. "Business School," *The Office*, 3.17, 2007.

33. Ibid.

34. Robinson, "Joss Whedon," August 8, 2007.

35. "Branch Wars," *The Office*, 4.10, 2007.

36. "*Total Film* Exclusive: JJ Abrams Directing US Office," *Total Film*, September 15, 2006, http://www.gamercaptain.com/total-film-exclusive-jj-abrams-directing-the-us-office/.

37. Brian Chu, "Geek Wars: JJ Abrams vs. Joss Whedon," *Nerd Reactor*, January 16, 2014, http://nerdreactor.com/2014/01/16/geek-wars-jj-abrams-vs-joss-whedon/#ARK8dbuy6e8c7UKk.99.

38. "Cocktails," *The Office*, 3.18, 2007.

39. "The Office Nielsen Ratings, Seasons 1–4," *Office Tally*, October 10, 2008, http://www.officetally.com/the-office-nielsen-ratings/2.

40. Jeff Bercovici, "'Avengers' Director Joss Whedon on Trying to Be More Like Buffy," *Forbes*, May 3, 2012, http://www.forbes.com/sites/jeffbercovici/2012/05/03/avengers-director-joss-whedon-on-trying-to-be-more-like-buffy/.

41. Rosen, "New Media Guru: Meet Joss Whedon the Web Slayer."

42. Pascale, *Joss Whedon*, 307.

43. Bercovici, "*Avengers* Director Joss Whedon on Trying," 3.

44. Neil Patrick Harris mentions Whedon e-mailed him saying only that they broke the Internet, but Whedon mentions this in various interviews. Maureen Ryan, "'Dr. Horrible' Speaks: Talking to Neil Patrick Harris about Joss Whedon's Smash-Hit Interweb Thingie," *Chicago Tribune*, July 19, 2008, http://featuresblogs.chicagotribune.com/entertainment_tv/2008/07/dr-horrible-spe.html.

45. Fred Topei, "Tribeca 2014: Zoe Kazan and Michael Stahl David on *In Your Eyes*," *Craveonline*, April 22, 2014, http://www.craveonline.com/film/interviews/678895-tribeca-2014-zoe-kazan-and-michael-stahl-david-on-in-your-eyes.

46. Eric Brown, "Joss Whedon's 5$ *In Your Eyes* Vimeo Distribution Is a Vanity Project, Not a Revolution," *International Business Times*, April, 21, 2014, http://www.ibtimes.com/joss-whedons-5-your-eyes-vimeo-distribution-vanity-project-not-revolution-1574484.

47. Ibid.

48. "In Your Eyes (2014)," *IMDb*, http://www.imdb.com/title/tt2101569/.

49. "The 2009 Hugo Award Winners," *Hugo Awards*, August 9, 2009, http://www.thehugoawards.org/2009/08/2009-hugo-award-winners/; "Emmy Press Release," *61st Primetime Emmy Awards*, September 12, 2009, http://www.emmys.com/sites/default/files/d6tv/CRTV09winners_pressrel.pdf; "1st Annual Nominees & Winners," *Streamy.org*, 2009, http://www.streamys.org/nominees-winners/2009-nominees/.

50. "The Top 10 Everything of 2008," *Time*, November 3, 2008, http://content.time.com/time/specials/packages/completelist/0,29569,1855948,00.html.

51. David Nary, "PGA Honors Joss Whedon," *Variety*, November 23, 2009, http://variety.com/2009/film/news/pga-honors-joss-whedon-1118011746/.

52. Lewis Ward, "Introduction to Joss Whedon in Joss Whedon Cultural Humanism Award," *YouTube*, February 26, 2013, http://www.youtube.com/watch?v=o6_DICN7AKY.

53. "Joss Whedon Cultural Humanist," *Humanist*, 2009, http://www.thenewhumanism.org/authors/video/articles/joss-whedon-cultural-humanist.

54. Ibid.

55. Pascale, *Joss Whedon*, 292–93.

56. Joss Whedon. "More Joss Strike Talk," *Whedonesque*, November 7, 2007, http://whedonesque.com/comments/14650.

57. Ibid.

58. Pascale, *Joss Whedon*, 293.

59. Whedon, "Joss Whedon Accepts Equality Now Award," *EqualityNow.org*, May 15, 2006, http://www.equalitynow.org/media/joss_whedon_accepts_equality_now_award.

60. Ibid.

61. Joss Whedon, "Joss Whedon at Make Equality Reality," *YouTube*, November 6, 2013, https://www.youtube.com/watch?v=pDmzlKHuuoI.

62. Noah Berlatsky, "What Joss Whedon Gets Wrong about the Word *Feminist*," *Atlantic*, November 8, 2013, http://www.theatlantic.com/entertainment/archive/2013/11/what-joss-whedon-gets-wrong-about-the-word-feminist/281305/.

63. Melissa McGlensey, "Dear Joss Whedon, et Al.: Leave *Feminist* Alone," *Ms.*, November 12, 2013, http://msmagazine.com/blog/2013/11/12/dear-joss-whedon-et-al-leave-feminist-alone/.

64. Katie McDonough, "No, Joss Whedon, *Feminist* Is Not a Dirty Word," *Salon.com*, November 11, 2013.http://www.salon.com/2013/11/11/.

65. Simon Parkin, "Zoe Quinn's Depression Quest," *New Yorker*, September 9, 2014, http://www.newyorker.com/tech/elements/zoe-quinns-depression-quest.

66. Kara Warner, "Joss Whedon on Feminism, *Avengers* Leaks and Marvel's Big Slate," *Vulture*, November 14, 2014, http://www.vulture.com/2014/11/joss-whedon-on-feminism-and-the-avengers-leaks.html.

67. Ibid.

68. Joss Whedon, "Whedon on Romney," *YouTube*, October 12, 2012, https://www.youtube.com/watch?v=6TiXUF9xbTo.

69. Sarah Parnass, "Joss Whedon: Mitt Romney Right for 'Zombie Apocalypse,'" *ABC News*, October 29, 2012, http://abcnews.go.com/blogs/politics/2012/10/joss-whedon-mitt-romney-right-for-zombie-apocalypse/.

70. Angela Watercutter, "Joss Whedon's Viral Video Calls Romney Perfect Leader for Zombie Apocalypse," *Wired*, October 29, 2012, http://www.wired.com/2012/10/joss-whedon-romney-zombie-endorsement/.

71. Whedon, "Whedon on Romney."

72. "Your 2008 Eisner Award Winners," *Comics Reporter*, July 26, 2008, http://www.comicsreporter.com/index.php/your_2008_eisner_award_winners/.

73. "Comic Con 07's Fantastic FilmMakers: Joss Whedon Goes into Sugar Shock," *Hollywood.com*, 2007, http://www.hollywood.com/static/comic-con-07s-fantatsic-filmmakers-joss-whedon-goes-into-sugar-shock.

74. Dave Itzkoff, "New Team Retrofits the Old Starship," *New York Times*, April 23, 2009, http://www.nytimes.com/2009/04/26/movies/26itzk.html?_r=3andpagewanted=all.

75. H. Shaw Williams, "J.J. Abrams Compares His *Superman: Flyby* Script to *Man of Steel*," *Screen Rant*, February 15, 2014, http://screenrant.com/jj-abrams-superman-flyby-man-steel/.

76. Claudia Eller and Meg James, "Abrams Lands TV, Film Deals," *L.A. Times*, July 15, 2006, http://articles.latimes.com/2006/jul/15/business/fi-jj15.

77. Ibid.

78. Ibid.

79. Nellie Andreeva, "Bad Robot, ABC Notarize Deal," *Hollywood Reporter*, October 4, 2007, http://www.hollywoodreporter.com/news/bad-robot-abc-notarize-deal-151644.

80. Brian Ford Sullivan, "Interview: *Fringe* Co-Creator JJ Abrams," *Futon Critic*, February 4, 2010, http://www.thefutoncritic.com/interviews.aspx?id=20100204_fringe.

81. Christina Radish, "J.J. Abrams Talks *Star Trek 2*, the *Super 8* Trailer, Fox's *Alcatraz*, *Odd Jobs*, *Person of Interest*, *Undercovers* and *Fringe*," *Collider*, January 12, 2011, http://collider.com/j-j-abrams-interview-star-trek-2-super-8/69744/.

82. Nellie Andreeva, "Critics Choice Awards Honors 8 New Shows," *Deadline.com*, June 9, 2011, http://deadline.com/2011/06/critics-choice-awards-honors-8-new-shows-138754/.

83. Jenny Stevens, "On Location in Chilling Alcatraz," *News.com.au*, February 16, 2012, http://www.news.com.au/travel/world-travel/on-location-in-chilling-alcatraz/story-e6frfqc9-1226268599439.

84. *Alcatraz* premiered with 9.96 million viewers in January but had fallen to 4.7 million by March 27, 2012. Bill Gorman, "Updated TV Ratings Monday: *Alcatraz* Premiere Tops *Terra Nova,* Betty White Has a Nice Birthday, But CBS

Rules the Night," *TV by the Numbers*, January 17, 2012, http://tvbythenumbers. zap2it.com/2012/01/17/tv-ratings-monday-alcatraz-premiere-tops-terra-nova/ 116692/, and "Monday Final Ratings: *Alcatraz*, *DWTS* and *Voice* Adjust Up; *Castle* and *Smash* Adjust Down," *TV by the Numbers*, March 27, 2012, http:// tvbythenumbers. zap2it.com/2012/03/27/monday-final-ratings-alcatraz-dwts-voice-adjust-up-castle-smash-adjust-down/126132/.

85. Christina Radish, "J.J. Abrams Talks *Super 8*, *Star Trek 2* and TV Shows *Alcatraz* and *Person of Interest*," *Collider*, June 10, 2011, http://collider.com/jj-abrams-super-8-star-trek-2-alcatraz-person-of-interest/.

86. Ibid.

87. Tavis Smiley, "Writer-Director-Producer J.J. Abrams," *Pbs.org*, September 24, 2014, http://www.pbs.org/wnet/tavissmiley/interviews/j-j-abrams/.

88. "The International Emmy Awards," International Academy of Television Arts and Sciences, http://www.iemmys.tv/awards_previous.aspx.

89. Ibid.

90. Archie Rice, "Get Lost! JJ Abrams Latest TV Show *Almost Human* Cancelled after Just One Season," *Daily Mail*, April 30, 2014, http://www.dailymail. co.uk/tvshowbiz/article-2616518/JJ-Abrams-latest-TV-Almost-Human-cancelled-just-one-season.html.

91. Kaysi L., "*Revolution* Season 3," *Thepetitionsite.com*, February 11, 2015, http://www.thepetitionsite.com/553/454/200/revolution-season-3/.

92. "Ratings Guy," *Family Guy*, 11.2, 2012.

93. The Lonely Island, "Cool Guys Don't Look at Explosions," *YouTube*, June 5, 2009, https://www.youtube.com/watch?v=Sqz5dbs5zmo.

94. Luke Plunkett, "If You Expect the J.J. Abrams Half-Life Movie to Actually Get Made, You're Gonna Have a Bad Time," *Kotaku.com*, February 6, 2013, http://kotaku.com/5982322/if-you-expect-the-jj-abrams-half-life-movie-to-come-out-youre-gonna-have-a-bad-time.

95. Ibid.

96. Joshua Rothman, "The Story of *S.*: Talking with J.J. Abrams and Doug Dorst," *New Yorker*, November 23, 2013, http://www.newyorker.com/books/page-turner/the-story-of-s-talking-with-j-j-abrams-and-doug-dorst.

97. Ibid.

98. Ashley Lee, "J.J. Abrams, Doug Dorst Talk *S.* Novel, Online Hoaxes," *Hollywood Reporter*, November 30, 2013, http://www.hollywoodreporter.com/news/jj-abrams-doug-dorst-talk-660757.

99. Ibid.

100. Tavis Smiley, "Producer-Director J.J. Abrams," *Pbs.org*, October 30, 2013, http://www.pbs.org/wnet/tavissmiley/interviews/j-j-abrams-3/.

101. For a great, easy-to-understand explanation see S. Marc Cohen, "Identity, Persistence and the Ship of Theseus," University of Washington, 2004, http://faculty.washington.edu/smcohen/320/theseus.html.

102. Doug Dorst and J. J. Abrams, *S.* (New York: Mulholland Books, 2013), 396.

103. Ibid., 396.

104. Ibid., 451.

105. Ibid.

106. Rothman, "The Story of *S.*"

107. Smiley, "Producer-Director J.J. Abrams."

108. Ibid.

109. Abrams credits Dorst with the "heavy lifting" in his interview with Tavis Smiley. Smiley, "Producer-Director J.J. Abrams."

110. "Stranger," *YouTube*, https://www.youtube.com/watch?v=FWaAZCaQXdo.

111. Ben Child, "JJ Abrams Gets Stranger with Teaser for Unnamed Project," *Guardian*, August 20, 2013, http://www.theguardian.com/film/2013/aug/20/jj-abrams-stranger-teaser-star-Wars. Twitter feeds for the response to the trailer are here:https://twitter.com/search?q=stranger%20teaser%20abrams&src=typd&lang=en.

112. Robert Brian Taylor, "What Exactly Is Joss Whedon's Wastelanders?," *Cult Spark*, April 26, 2006, http://cultspark.com/2012/04/26/what-exactly-is-joss-whedons-wastelanders/.

113. Penelope Green, "Mystery on Fifth Avenue," *New York Times*, June 12, 2008, http://www.nytimes.com/2008/06/12/garden/12puzzle.html?pagewanted=alland_r=0.

114. Child, "JJ Abrams Gets Stranger with Teaser."

115. Topei, "J.J. Abrams on the End of *Fringe, Revolution* and *Star Trek: Into Darkness*," *Crave*, January 12, 2009, http://www.craveonline.com/culture/202929-jj-abrams-on-the-end-of-fringe-revolution-a-star-trek-into-darkness.

116. Rosen, "New Media Guru: Meet Joss Whedon the Web Slayer."

6. OH, THE HORROR

1. "Document 01.18.08: The Making of *Cloverfield*," *Cloverfield*, written by Drew Goddard, directed by Matt Reeves, Bad Robot/Paramount Pictures, 2008.

2. Vivian Sobchack, *Screening Space: The American Science Fiction Film* (Trenton, NJ: Rutgers University Press, 1997), 63.

3. For a very good, detailed analysis, see Sobchack, *Screening Space*.

4. J. J. Abrams, "The Mystery Box," *Ted*, March 2007, http://www.ted.com/talks/j_j_abrams_mystery_box?language=en.

5. Michael Leader, "Joss Whedon Interview: *The Cabin in the Woods, The Avengers*, Shakespeare and More," *DenofGeek*, March 29, 2012, http://www.denofgeek.us/movies/1896 8/joss-whedon-interview-the-cabin-in-the-woods-the-avengers-shakespeare-and-more.

6. "Document 01.18.08: The Making of *Cloverfield*."

7. Whedon, "Joss Whedon on *The Cabin in the Woods*: 'It's a classic horror until it explodes in your face'—video," *Guardian*, April 6, 2012, http://www.theguardian.com/film/video/2012/apr/06/joss-whedon-cabin-in-the-woods-buffy-video.

8. Ibid.

9. "Document 01.18.08: The Making of *Cloverfield*."

10. Abrams, "The Mystery Box."

11. Christopher Lloyd, "Reeling Backward: *Close Encounters of the Third Kind* (1977)," *Film Yap*, August 22, 2011, http://www.thefilmyap.com/2011/08/22/close-encounters-of-the-third-kind-1977/.

12. Scott Henderson, "The Illusionist: J.J. Abrams on Film, Television and Rebooting a Franchise," *Screen Education* 55 (2009): 50–54.

13. François Truffaut and Helen G. Scott, *Hitchcock* (New York: Simon and Schuster, 1985), 138.

14. J. J. Abrams, "J.J. Abrams on the Magic of Mystery," *Wired*, April 20, 2009, http://archive.wired.com/techbiz/people/magazine/17-05/mf_jjessay?currentPage=all.

15. Ibid.

16. Daniel North, "Evidence of Things Not Quite Seen: *Cloverfield*'s Obstructed Spectacle," *Film and History* 40, no. 1 (Spring 2009): 75–91.

17. Harry Knowles, "JJ Abrams Drops Harry a Line on all this 1-18-08 Stuff," *Aint It Cool News*, July 9, 2007, http://www.aintitcool.com/node/33261.

18. North, "Evidence of Things Not Quite Seen," 79.

19. Silas Lesnick, "*Cloverfield*," *Dreamindemon.com*, December 14, 2007, http://www.dreamindemon.com/community/threads/cloverfield.521/page-3.

20. "*Cloverfield*-monster?*Spoiler*-Off-Topic Discussion," *Gamespot*, December 2007, http://www.gamespot.com/forums/offtopic-discussion-314159273/cloverfield-monster-spoiler-26112028/.

21. Henderson, "The Illusionist," 51.

22. Abrams, "J.J. Abrams on the Magic of Mystery."

23. Richard Corliss, "*Super 8*: Just as Great as You Hoped It Would Be," *Time Entertainment*, June 2, 2011, http://entertainment.time.com/2011/06/02/super-8-movie-review/2/2.

24. Ibid.

25. J. J. Abrams, commentary, *Super 8* (2011).

26. Ibid.

27. Ibid.

28. Lloyd, "Reeling Backward."

29. Ethan Aames, "Interview: Tom Cruise and Steven Spielberg on *War of the Worlds*," *Internet Archive Wayback Machine*, June 28, 2005, http://web.archive.org/web/ 2008 0206185633/http://www.cinecon.com/news.php?id= 0506281.

30. Corliss, "*Super 8*: Just as Great as You Hoped It Would Be."

31. Sigmund Freud, "The Development of the Libido and the Sexual Organization," in *The Standard Edition of the Complete Psychological Works of Sigmund Freud*, edited by James Strachey (London: Hogarth, 1975), 330–32.

32. "Joss Whedon Explains Why We Fear and Need Horror Films, and How He Knew *Cabin in the Woods* Had a Star in Chris Hemsworth," *Huffington Post UK*, September 25, 2012, http://www.huffingtonpost.co.uk/2012/09/25/joss-whedon-avengers-cabin-in-the-woods_n_1912148.html.

33. Joss Whedon and Drew Goddard, The Cabin in the Woods: *The Official Visual Companion* (London: Titan Books, 2012), 11.

34. Leader, "Joss Whedon Interview."

35. Oliver Franklin-Wallis, "GQ&A: Joss Whedon," *GQ*, March 27, 2012, http://www.gq-magazine.co.uk/entertainment/articles/2012-03/27/joss-whedon-interview-cabin-in-the-woods-avengers-assemble.

36. Whedon and Goddard, The Cabin in the Woods: *The Official Visual Companion*, 12.

37. Drew Taylor, "SXSW '12 Interview: Drew Goddard Talks His Inspiration," *Indiewire*, March 9, 2012, http://blogs.indiewire.com/theplaylist/sxsw-12-interview-cabin-in-the-woods-director-drew-goddard-talks-horror-movies-famous-collaborators-and-superheroes.

38. Eric Kohn, "SXSW Review: Joss Whedon–Scripted *Cabin in the Woods* Turns B-Movie Meta into Scary Pop Art," *Indiewire*, March 10, 2012, http://www.indiewire.com/article/joss-whedon-scripted-cabin-in-the-woods-is-a-highly-amusing-blend-of-pop-art-and-meta-storytelling.

39. Whedon and Goddard, The Cabin in the Woods: *The Official Visual Companion*, 19.

40. Taylor, "SXSW '12 Interview: Drew Goddard."

41. Ibid.

42. Alyse Wax, "Exclusive: Drew Goddard Talks Secrets and Sequels for *Cabin in the Woods*," *Fearnet*, September 14, 2012, http://www.fearnet.com/news/interview/exclusive-drew-goddard-talks-secrets-and-sequels-cabin-woods.

43. As a side note, we don't even know if the director has told the truth about the old gods. The film's monsters have come from us, not from the gods, created

by the scientists out of our nightmares, and we have no proof that the Japanese solution to transfer Kiko's spirit into a happy frog is a failure as described by the scientists. As a matter of fact, we hear Japan has "a hundred percent clearance rate" and has never failed before. We don't really know what will happen next, but it probably cannot be much worse than the system that has just been destroyed.

44. Leader, "Joss Whedon Interview."

45. J. J. Abrams, commentary, *Super 8* (2008).

46. All citations come from *Rottentomatoes.com.*

7. HIT AND MYTH!

1. Tavis Smiley, "Producer-Director J.J. Abrams," *Pbs.org*, October 30, 2013, http://www.pbs.org/wnet/tavissmiley/interviews/j-j-abrams-3/.

2. Sarah Hall, "Scarlett Aborts Mission," *Eonline*, May 9, 2005, http://www.eonline.com/news/49821/scarlett-aborts-mission.

3. J. J. Abrams and Tom Cruise, commentary, *M:I-3* (2006).

4. Hall, "Scarlett Aborts Mission."

5. "*Mission: Impossible-III*," Box Office Mojo, http://www.boxofficemojo.com/movies/?id=mi3.htm.

6. "*Mission: Impossible-III*: Video," Box Office Mojo, http://www.boxofficemojo.com/movies/?page=homevideo&id=mi3.htm.

7. "*Mission Impossible-iii*." *RottenTomatoes*, http://www.rottentomatoes.com/m/mission_impossible_3/, and "Mission Impossible-iii," *Metacritic*, http://www.metacritic.com/movie/mission-impossible-iii.

8. David Edelstein, "Mission: Control; The Tom Cruise Hero-Industrial Complex Cranks out Part 3. Should You Choose to Accept It?" *New York Magazine*, http://nymag.com/movies/reviews/16931/.

9. "Paramount: Cruise Is Risky Business," *CNN Money*, August 23, 2006, http://money.cnn.com/2006/08/22/news/newsmakers/cruise_paramount/index.htm?cnn=yes.

10. I could find no credible source that suggests Cruise actually asked them to pull the episode. The rumor was cited as coming from "industry insiders" and CNN News speculations. Mark Ebner, "Scientologist Tom Cruise Blackmails Viacom into Pulling the 'Trapped in the Closet' Episode of South Park," *Hollywood Interrupted*, March 16, 2006, http://www.hollywoodinterrupted.com/2006/03/23/scientologist-tom-cruise-blackmails-viacom/, and Wolf Blitzer's *Situation Room* in which there is much speculation along with the disclaimer that "there's no evidence that the church itself had anything to do with that episode getting pulled." Blitzer, "Fourth Year of War in Iraq Begins; Could Democrats Launch

Impeachment Campaign against Bush?" *The Situation Room, CNN.com*, March 20, 2006, http://transcripts.cnn.com/TRANSCRIPTS/0603/20/sitroom.03.html.

11. For more on the split between Paramount and Cruise, see David Halbfinger. "Fired or Quit, Tom Cruise Parts Ways with Studio," *New York Times*, August 23, 2008, http://www.nytimes.com/2006/08/23/business/media/23cruise. html?_r=0. Also "Paramount: Cruise is Risky Business."

12. "Unscripted with Tom Cruise and JJ Abrams," *Moviefone*, September 16, 2012, https://www.youtube.com/watch?v=aNdlCdyJ-0A.

13. Dave Itzkoff, "New Team Retrofits the Old Star Ship," *New York Times*, April 23, 2009, http://www.nytimes.com/2009/04/26/movies/26itzk.html?_r= 3andpagewanted=all.

14. Eric Goldman, "Abrams Talks *Trek, Cloverfield 2*," *IGN*, May 16, 2008, http://www.ign.com/articles/2008/05/16/abrams-talks-trek-cloverfield-2.

15. Anthony Pascale, "Grand Slam XVI: Highlights from Orci Q&A," *Trekmovie.com*, April 13, 2008, http://trekmovie.com/2008/04/13/grand-slam-xvi-highlights-from-orci-qa/.

16. "Movie Reviews: *Adoration, Julia, Little Ashes, Revanche*," *LAWeekly.com*, May 6, 2009, http://www.laweekly.com/film/movie-reviews-adoration-julia-little-ashes-revanche-2159664.

17. Roger Ebert, "*Star Trek*," *Reviews*, May 6, 2009, http://www.rogerebert. com/reviews/star-trek-2009.

18. Ibid.

19. Mahnola Dargis, "*Star Trek* (2009): A Franchise Goes Boldy Backwards," *New York Times*, May 7, 2009, http://www.nytimes.com/2009/05/08/movies/08trek.html.

20. "Work in Progress, Review: *Star Trek*," *Amazon.com*, December 6, 2013, http://www.amazon.com/Star-Trek-Chris-Pine/productreviews/B002WV5A9G/ ref=cm_cr_pr_hist_1?ie=UTF8&filterBy=addFiveStar&showViewpoints=0& sortBy=helpful&reviewerType=all_reviews&formatType=all_formats& filterByStar=one_star&pageNumber=1.

21. There are more entries than *Star Trek* films because the nonfranchise (and non–*Star Trek*) film *Galaxy Quest* (1999) came in at number 7. Devin Faraci, "The *Star Trek* Movies as Ranked by *Star Trek* Con-Goers," *BadassDigest.com*, August 11, 2013, http://badassdigest.com/2013/08/11/the-star-trek-movies-as-ranked-by-star-trek-con-goers/.

22. "*Star Trek*," *RottenTomatoes.com*, http://www.rottentomatoes.com/m/ star_trek_11.

23. Based on totals from April 28, 2015, http://www.amazon.com/Star-Trek-Chris-Pine/dp/B002WV5A9G/ref=cm_cr_pr_product_top?ie=UTF8.

24. "Rate J.J. Abrams's *Star Trek*," *Trekweb.com*. May 7, 2009, http:// trekweb.com/polls/vote.php?andpid=4a03a9f9aef8eandresults=1.

25. "Franchises: *Star Trek*," *Box Office Mojo*, http://www.boxofficemojo. com/franchises/chart/?id=startrek.htm.

26. Sheila Roberts, "JJ Abrams Interview, *Star Trek*," *Moviesonline*, May 2009, http://www.moviesonline.ca/movienews_16696.html.

27. Anthony Pascale, "Wondercon 09: *Star Trek* Panel Detailed Report and Pictures," *Trekmovie.com*, February 28, 2009, http://trekmovie.com/2009/02/28/wondercon-09-star-trek-panel-detailed-report-pictures/.

28. Ibid.

29. Roberts, "J.J. Abrams Interview, *Star Trek*."

30. This is something Spock has done previously in *Star Trek II: The Wrath of Khan* (1982) by sending an untrue uncoded message over an open channel.

31. Kirk disobeyed orders many times in the original series and broke the prime directive to do something he deemed ethically more important, as, for example, in "The Apple" (2.5, 1967) in which the Enterprise neutralizes a computer that has provided for the planetary inhabitants in exchange for fuel, thus completely changing the societal structure of the community.

32. Roberts, "J.J. Abrams Interview, *Star Trek*."

33. "Is *Into Darkness* Better than *Star Trek* (2009)?" *Trekweb.com*, May 8 2013, http://trekweb.com/polls/vote.php?&pi32d=518a4f6d6a668&results=1.

34. Harve Bennett, Jack B. Sowards, and Samuel A. Peeples, "*Star Trek II: The Wrath of Khan*," *Internet Movie Script Database*, http://www.imsdb.com/scripts/Star-Trek-II-The-Wrath-of-Khan.html,236.

35. Ibid. Note that the script says "will be," but Nimoy says "shall be" in the film.

36. Bennett, Sowards, and Peeples. *Star Trek II: The Wrath of Khan*, DVD. Roberto Orci, Alex Kurtzman, and Damon Lindelof, "*Star Trek: Into Darkness*, (2013) Movie Script," *Springfield! Springfield!* http://www.springfieldspringfield. co.uk/movie_script.php?movie=star-trek-into-darkness.

37. This number is cited by *Scripted* as the MPAA target audience for recent films up to about 2009 (with the target age rising to twenty-five to thirty-nine afterward). April K., "The Ideal Audiences for Summer Blockbusters," *Scripted/ Industries Cinema and Film*, Summer 2013, https://scripted.com/cpt_experts/ideal-target-audience-for-summer-blockbusters/.

38. This is admittedly in keeping with Kirk's behavior. Kirk's libidinal activities in the original series include Drusilla in "Bread and Circuses," *Star Trek*, 2.25, 1968, and Deela in "Wink of an Eye," *Star Trek*, 3.11, 1968.

39. Extrapolated from data that shows that for every 2.57 male characters, there is on average one female in current films. Stacey L. Smith, Katherine M. Pieper, Amy D. Granados, and Marc Cho, "Assessing Gender-Related Portrayals in Top-Grossing G-Rated Films," in *Conference Papers—International Commu-*

nication Association, International Communication Association annual meeting, January 1, 2008.

40. See http://www.imdb.com/title/tt1408101/fullcredits?ref_=tt_cl_sm#cast and http://www.imdb.com/title/tt0796366/fullcredits?ref_=tt_cl_sm#cast.

41. Rebecca Keegan, "Women Are Underrepresented in Key Movie Positions, USC Study Finds," *L.A. Times*, July 24, 2014, http://www.latimes.com/entertainment/movies/la-et-mn-women-hollywood-usc-study-20140724-story.html.

42. "Is *Into Darkness* Better Than *Star Trek* (2009)?" *Trekweb.com.*

43. See http://trekweb.com/polls/vote.php?&pid=518a4f6d6a668&results=1.

44. Faraci, "The *Star Trek* Movies as Ranked By Star Trek Con-Goers."

45. "Star Trek," *Box Office Mojo*, 2009, http://www.boxofficemojo.com/movies/?id=startrek11.htm, and "*Star Trek: Into Darkness*," *Box Office Mojo*, 2013, http://www.boxofficemojo.com/movies/?id=star trek12.htm.

46. This is true for both adjusted and unadjusted gross as well as the gross adjusted for inflation, http://www.boxofficemojo.com/franchises/chart/?id=startrek.htm.

47. See http://www.boxofficemojo.com/franchises/chart/?id=startrek.htm.

48. Caroline Giardina, "J.J. Abrams to Receive Visual Effects Society Visionary Award," *Hollywood Reporter*, September 23, 2014, http://www.hollywoodreporter.com/behind-screen/jj-abrams-receive-visual-effects-735205.

49. Ibid.

50. David Bloom, "J.J. Abrams at VES Awards: *Star Wars* Sojourn 'a Dream Come True,'" *Deadline Presents Awardsline*, February 4, 2015, http://deadline.com/2015/02/j-j-abrams-star-wars-dream-come-true-ves-awards-1201366546/.

51. Ibid.

52. The film won the audience award at the 2013 Belfast Film Festival and the Independent Film Festival of Boston. "Belfast Film Festival Award Winners Revealed," *Northirelandscreen.co*, April 25, 2013, http://www.northernirelandscreen.co.uk/news/3281/belfast-film-festival-award-winners-revealed.aspx, and "IffBoston 2013 Wrap Up," *Lonely Reviewer*, May 1, 2013, http://www.lonelyreviewer.com/2013/05/01/iffboston-2013-wrap-up/.

53. Ben Child, "Micro-budget Film Is Back with Joss Whedon's *Much Ado about Nothing*," *Guardian*, October 28, 2011, http://www.theguardian.com/film/filmblog/2011/oct/28/joss-whedon-much-ado-about-nothing.

54. Dana Ferguson, "Whedon Jokes about 'Micro-budget' for *Much Ado about Nothing*," *Los Angeles Times*, June 6, 2013, http://articles.latimes.com/2013/jun/06/entertainment/la-et-mn-20130606-much-ado.

55. See http://www.boxofficemojo.com/movies/?id=muchado13.htm.

56. Won for having the largest number of people on a Blu-ray DVD commentary: 16."Most People Recording Commentary for a Blu-ray DVD Extra," *Guin-*

ness Book of World Records, 2013, http://www.guinnessworldrecords.com/world-records/60138-most-people-recording-commentary-for-a-blu-ray-dvd-extra.

57. David Fear, "TONY Q&A: *Much Ado about Nothing*'s Joss Whedon: The Man behind *Buffy the Vampire Slayer* Takes on the Bard," *Time Out*, June 2, 2013.

58. Dana Stevens, "Joss Whedon's *Much Ado about Nothing* as Bracingly Effervescent as Picnic Champagne," *Slate.com*, June 6, 2013, http://www.slate.com/articles/arts/movies/2013/06/joss_whedon_s_much_ado_about_nothing_reviewed.html.

59. Joss Whedon, Much Ado about Nothing, *A Film by Joss Whedon, Based on the Play by William Shakespeare* (London: Titan Books, 2013), 16.

60. Whedon knew the reference to women's lack and as Elizabethan slang for vagina but found the play had to be about more than this, particularly in a current context where a woman's sexuality should not be grounds for her disgrace. Whedon, *Much Ado about Nothing*, 17.

61. Whedon underscored, "Nothing was supposed to be a homonym for 'noting,' and it's all about people sort of observing each other." Whedon, *Much Ado about Nothing*, 16.

62. Steven "Frosty" Weintraub, "Director Joss Whedon The AVENGERS Set Interview," *Collider*, April 2, 2012, http://collider.com/joss-whedon-the-avengers-interview/.

63. Ibid.

64. Dave Itzkoff, "Joss Whedon on Assembling *The Avengers*," *New York Times*, April 11, 2012, http://artsbeat.blogs.nytimes.com/2012/04/11/joss-whedon-assembles-the-avengers-for-the-biggest-film-of-his-career/?_r=0.

65. See http://nationalpriorities.org/blog/2013/05/06/how-much-foreign-aid-does-us-give-away/.

66. Josh Wigler, "Joss Whedon's *S.H.I.E.L.D.* Is about 'Powers' 'Spectacle' and 'Little Things' That Matter," *Hot Stuff Interviews*, January11, 2013, http://splashpage.mtv.com/2013/01/11/joss-whedon-shield-details/.

67. Ibid.

68. Joss Whedon, "Joss Whedon—Harvard Q and A," *YouTube*, February 27, 2013, https://www.youtube.com/watch?v=glJCzqE7fxA.

69. Whedon explains, he "read all the scripts, . . . gave notes and tried to make myself useful without being intrusive." Wigler, "Joss Whedon's *S.H.I.E.L.D.*"

70. Ben Kendrick, "Is *Agents of S.H.I.E.L.D.* Getting Better as Ratings Fall?" *Screen Rant*, November 16, 2013, http://screenrant.com/agents-of-shield-improving-bad-ratings-abc/.

71. Amanda Kondolojy, "Tuesday Final Ratings: *Marvel's Agents of S.H.I.E.L.D.*, *The Voice* and *NCIS* Adjusted Up; *The Goldbergs* and *Chicago*

Fire Adjusted Down," *TV by the Numbers*, September 25, 2013, http:// tvbythenumbers.zap2it.com/2013/09/25/tuesday-final-ratingsm arvels-agents-of-s-h-i-e-l-d-the-voice-the-goldbergs-chicago-fire-adjusted-down/204739/, and Dani Dixon, "ABC L + 3 Results: *S.H.I.E.L.D* Emerges as Number 1 Scripted Show for Timeslot in Adults 18–49," *TV by the Numbers*, October 4, 2015, http:/ /tvbythenumbers.zap2it.com/2015/10/04/abc-l-3-results-s-h-i-e-l-d-emerges-as-number-1-scripted-show-for-timeslot-in-adults-18-49/475877/.

72. *"Marvel's Agents of SHIELD*: Season Two Ratings," *TVSeriesFinale.com*, March 25, 2015, http://tvseriesfinale.com/tv-show/marvels-agents-of-shield-season-two-ratings-34016/, and *"Marvel's Agents of SHIELD*: Season Three Ratings," *TVSeriesFinale.com*, December 9, 2015, http://tvseriesfinale. com/tv-show/marvels-agents-of-shield-season-three-ratings-38242/.

73. Whedon, "Joss Whedon—Harvard Q and A."

74. Chris Lough worries, it "feels like we were cheated. . . . Last season we watched as a black male got his life mangled by Hydra. This season, we see another black male lose his life to halt an alien apocalypse. I don't feel like these two instances justifies [*sic*] a claim of racism or ignorance against the show, but I'm also uncomfortable with the idea that the writers and showrunners . . . might not realize how easily its positioning of black men can become an unhealthy pattern." Lough, "A Bicycle Built for You, But Not You. *Agents of S.H.I.E.L.D.*: 'What They Become,'" *Tor.com*, December 10, 2014, http://www.tor.com/blogs/ 2014/12 /agents-of-shield-what-they-become.

75. Lia Haberman, "Fox Squashes *Firefly*," *Eonline*, December 13, 2002, http://www.eonline.com/news/44314/fox-squashes-firefly.

76. Danielle Attali and Barbara Théate, "Spielberg: 'J'aurais aimé débuter aujourd'hui,'" *La Journal du Dimanche*, February 20, 2012, http://www.lejdd.fr/ Culture/Cinema/Actualite/Speilberg-revient-sur-sa-carriere-interview-488138? from=features.

77. Tim Hayne, "Joss Whedon, *Much Ado about Nothing* Director, on Passion Projects, *S.H.I.E.L.D.* Hype and *Guardians of the Galaxy*," *Moviefone*, June 11, 2013, http://news.moviefone.com/2013/06/11/joss-whedon-much-ado-about-nothing/.

78. David Lavery points out that Whedon and Bay were both graduates of Wesleyan and does a fabulous comparison of the two in terms of style, financial success, and productivity. Lavery, *Joss Whedon: A Creative Portrait: From Buffy the Vampire Slayer to Marvel's* The Avengers (London: I.B. Tauris, 2014), 3–16.

79. Kirsten Acuna, *"Avengers: Age of Ultron* Had a Huge $187 Million Weekend—but It Didn't Beat the All-Time Opening Record," *Business Insider*, May 3, 2015, http://www.businessinsider.com/avengers-age-of-ultron-opening-weekend-2015-5.

80. Todd Cunningham, "*Age of Ultron* Outpacing Original *Avengers* with $700 Million at Global Box Office," *The Wrap*, May 7, 2015, http://www.thewrap.com/age-of-ultron-outpacing-original-avengers-with-700-million-at-global-box-office/.

81. "The Changeling," *Star Trek*, 2.3, 1967.

82. I have discussed the relationship of physical experience and identity more thoroughly in "The Corporate and Corporeal," in *The Apocalypse in Film: Dystopias, Disasters, and Other Visions about the End of the World*, edited by Karen Ritzenhoff and Angela Krewani (Lanham, MD: Rowman and Littlefield, 2016), 203–16.

83. "*Avengers* Director Joss Whedon Quits Twitter," *BBC News.com*, May 5, 2015, http://www.bbc.com/news/technology-32591260.

84. See Jos Truitt, "Let's Talk about *Age of Ultron*'s Rape Joke," *Feministing*, May 1, 2015, http://feministing.com/2015/05/01/lets-talk-about-age-of-ultrons-rape-joke/, and Carolyn Cox, "Chris Evans and Jeremy Renner Call Black Widow a 'Slut' and 'Whore'; New *Age of Ultron* Clip Features Rape Joke," *The Mary Sue*, April 23, 2015, http://www.themarysue.com/grossvengers-age-of-dolton/.

85. *RottenTomatoes.com* has more than three hundred mostly positive critic reviews and some 450 pages of mostly positive audience reviews. See http://www.rottentomatoes.com/m/star_wars_ episode_vii_the_force_awakens/reviews/. Nonetheless it should be noted that *Star Wars*, while it employs more people of color, has an even worse gender imbalance than was found in *Star Trek* and *The Avengers* in terms of casting. The film improves on primary female stars by offering four lead roles to women (Rey, Leia, Maz Kanata, and General Phasma), but there are only 19 female cast members out of 75 listed above the "other cast members" line in IMDb. This is approximately 25 percent (as compared to 29 percent in *Star Trek*). Additionally, there are only 24 women in the "other cast members" section out of 119 listed—about 20 percent (as compared to Star Trek's 25 percent totals) (http://www.imdb.com/title/tt2488496/fullcredits?ref_=tt_cl_sm#cast).

86. Devan Coggan, "Box Office Report: *The Force Awakens* Crosses $1 Billion Globally in Record Time," *EW*, December 27, 2015, http://www.ew.com/article/2015/12/27/box-office-report-star-wars-force-awakens-crosses-1-billion-globally.

87. Anthony Lane, "*Star Wars: The Force Awakens* Review," *New Yorker*, December 18, 2015, http://www.newyorker.com/culture/cultural-comment/star-wars-the-force-awakens-reviewed.

88. Stephanie Zacharek, "*The Force Awakens* Is Everything You Could Hope for in a Star Wars Movie—And Less," *Time*, December 14, 2015, http://time.com/4150168/review-star-wars-the-force-awakens/.

89. Justin Chang, "Film Review: *Star Wars: The Force Awakens*," *Variety*, December 16, 2015, http://variety.com/2015/film/reviews/star-wars-review-the-force-awakens-1201661978/.

90. Al Alexander, "Movie Review: The Empire Strikes Out," *Patriot Ledger*, December 16, 2015, http://www.patriotledger.com/article/20151216/ENTER-TAINMENT/151217353.

91. John Saavedra, "*Star Wars: The Force Awakens* Easter Eggs and Reference Guide," *Den of Geek*, December 29, 2015, http://www.denofgeek.us/movies/star-wars/251420/star-wars-the-force-awakens-easter-eggs-and-reference-guide.

92. Frances Sharpe, "*Star Wars* Character Based on Late Pali High English Teacher, Abrams Tells *Palisadian-Post*," *Palisadian-Post*, December 24, 2015, https://www.palipost.com/star-wars-character-based-on-late-pali-high-english-teacher-abrams-tells-palisadian-post/.

93. Bill Whitaker, "The New Force behind *Star Wars*," *60 Minutes*, CBS, aired December 13, 2015.

8. THE NEXT SPIELBERG?

1. These statistics would no doubt be more stunning if only speeches given after Spielberg had made a name for himself were counted. Ashley Lee, "Oscars: Steven Spielberg is the Most Thanked in History, More than God," *Hollywood Reporter*, February 20, 2015, http://awards.yahoo.com/post/111595418587/oscars-steven-spielberg-is-the-most-thanked-in.

2. Geoff Boucher, "Seven Films That Shaped *Super 8*," *L.A. Times*, April 22, 2011, http://herocomplex.latimes.com/movies/j-j-abrams-seven-films-that-shaped-super-8/.

3. Ibid.

4. Gemma Kappala-Ramsamy, "Joss Whedon: The Film That Changed My Life: How Steven Spielberg's *Close Encounters of the Third Kind* Made an Existentialist of Screenwriter and Director Joss Whedon," *Guardian*, April 14, 2012, http://www.theguardian.com/film/2012/apr/15/joss-whedon-film-changed-spielberg. After reading Sartre at the same time, Whedon says, "I realised, 'Oh! Other people have gone through this!' Basically, the film had made me an existentialist."

5. Joss Whedon, "Joss Whedon—Cultural Humanism Award—Speech (2009)," *YouTube*, February 26, 2013, https://www.youtube.com/watch?v=o6_DICN7AKY.

6. Joss Whedon, "Joss Whedon—Harvard Q and A," *YouTube*, February 27, 2013, https://www.youtube.com/watch?v=glJCzqE7fxA.

7. Ibid.

8. Sara Wayland, "J.J. Abrams on the *Star Trek* Sequel, *Lost*, *Fringe* and ABC's *Undercovers*," *Collider*, January 12, 2010, http://collider.com/jj-abrams-on-the-star-trek-sequel-lost-fringe-and-nbcs-undercovers/.

9. David Hochman, "*Playboy* Interview: J.J. Abrams," *Playboy.com*, April 30, 2013, http://www.playboy.com/articles/playboy-interview-j-j-abrams-on-star-trek-star-wars.

10. John Donovan, "Abrams and Nolan Nab 'A Person of Interest,'" *NPR*, November 14, 2011, http://www.npr.org/2011/11/14/142309102/abrams-and-nolan-nab-a-person-of-interest.

11. This is so in *Much Ado about Nothing*, *In Your Eyes*, and *The Avengers*. *Agents of S.H.I.E.L.D.* has numerous such disappointments and one must simply resign oneself to this, although *Ultron* splits the difference and gives us both a tragic and a happy couple.

12. Hochman, "*Playboy* Interview: J.J. Abrams."

13. Abrams told reporters that "Jack Bender has really been the guy on that show as the directing producer, so it would be wrong for me to come in and be like, 'Oh, move over, I'm going to direct.'" Wayland, "J.J. Abrams on the *Star Trek* Sequel."

14. Whedon, "Whedon—Cultural Humanism Award—Speech."

15. "Things We Love: We Love a New Look at Scarlet Witch and Quicksilver in *Avengers: Age of Ultron*," *The Tracking Board: Hollywood Insider Information*, March 27, 2015, http://www.tracking-board.com/things-we-love-a-new-look-at-scarlet-witch-and-quicksilver-in-avengers-age-of-ultron/. Also Brandon Russell, "New Age of Ultron Footage Focuses on Scarlet Witch and Quicksilver," *TechnoBuffalo*, March 27, 2015, http://www.technobuffalo.com/2015/ 03/ 27/new-age-of-ultron-footage-focuses-on-scarlet-witch-and-quicksilver/.

16. His second *Avengers* film is a bit less successful structurally because there are scenes superfluous to the film itself that Marvel wanted included to set up future films in the franchise.

17. Negative attributes are being ignored or else one might have to add a category of causing controversy given complaints of misogynistic portrayals of women in films from *Jaws* to *Tintin* or of trivializing the Holocaust in *Schindler's List*. See Imres Kertész, "Who Owns Auschwitz?" translated by John Mackay, *Yale Journal of Criticism* 14, no. 1 (2001): 267–72, http://www.english.illinois.edu/maps/holocaust/reflections.htm.

18. Joseph McBride, *Steven Spielberg: A Biography*, 2nd ed. (Jackson: University Press of Mississippi, 1997), 102–5.

19. These numbers come from the *IMDb* website, but determining what counts is difficult since each auteur has done a variety of work from games to

blog videos. I excluded game direction and atypical media to focus on TV and film, thus others' numbers may vary.

20. Abrams seems typically to have done things about six to seven years earlier in his life than Spielberg when it comes to producing.

21. Although interviews indicate that Whedon admires Scorsese, I say this knowing he would probably not be too pleased with the comparison and most likely would not see the resemblance. Whedon is adamant about the fact that he makes *all* of his films for himself. Kevin P. Sullivan, "Joss Whedon Confirms Cutting Marvel Ties with a Supremely Thoughtful Explanation," *EW.com*, January 4, 2016, http://www.ew.com/article/2016/01/04/joss-whedon-marvel-future.

BIBLIOGRAPHY

"10 Questions for Joss Whedon." *New York Times*. May 16, 2003. http://www.nytimes.com/ 2003/05/16/readersopinions/16WHED.html?pagewanted=2.2.

"1st Annual Nominees and Winners." *Streamy.org*. 2009. http://www.streamys.org/nominees-winners/2009-nominees/.

"2006 Will Eisner Comic Industry Awards." *Hahnlibrary.net*. http://www.hahnlibrary.net/comics/awards/eisner06.php.

"The 2009 Hugo Award Winners." *The Hugo Awards*. August 9, 2009. http://www.thehugoawards.org/2009/08/2009-hugo-award-winners/.

Aames, Ethan. "Interview: Tom Cruise and Steven Spielberg on *War of the Worlds*." *Internet Archive Wayback Machine*. June 28, 2005. http://web.archive.org/web/ 2008 0206185633/http://www.cinecon.com/news.php?id=0506281.

Abbott, Jim. "Jim Belushi Keeps the Laughs Coming on Film." *Orlando Sentinel*. August 17, 1990. http://articles.orlandosentinel.com/1990-0817/entertainment/9008160096_1_james-belushi-arthur-hiller-cubs.

Abbott, Stacey. Angel, *T.V. Milestones Series*. Detroit, MI: Wayne State University Press, 2009.

Abrams, J. J. DVD Commentary. *Super 8* (2011).

———. "J.J. Abrams on the Magic of Mystery." *Wired*. April 20, 2009. http://archive.wired.com/techbiz/people/magazine/17-05/mf_jjessay?currentPage=all.

———. "The Mystery Box." *Ted*. March 2007. http://www.ted.com/talks/j_j_abrams_mystery_box?language=en.

———. "Pilot." DVD Commentary. *Lost*, Season 1.

Abrams, J. J., and Tom Cruise. DVD Commentary. *M:I-3* (2006).

Abrams, J. J., and Jonathon Hensleigh. "*Armageddon*." *Internet Movie Script Database*. http://www.imsdb.com/scripts /Armageddon.html.

Abrams, J. J., and Matt Reeves. "Felicity Was Here." DVD Commentary. *Felicity*, Season 4.

Abrams, J. J., and Clay Tarver. DVD commentary. *Joy Ride* (2001).

Acuna, Kirsten. "*Avengers: Age of Ultron* Had a Huge $187 Million Weekend—but It Didn't Beat the All-Time Opening Record." *Business Insider*. May 3, 2015. http://www.businessinsider.com/avengers-age-of-ultron-opening-weekend-2015-5.

"The Agony of Being a Cubs Fan." *BBC.co*. 2002. http://news.bbc.co.uk/dna/ptop/plain/A145441.

Alexander, Al. "Movie Review: The Empire Strikes Out." *Patriot Ledger*. December 16, 2015. http://www.patriotledger.com/article/20151216/ENTERTAINMENT/151217353.

"*Alien Resurrection* Reviews." *Rottentomatoes.com*. http://www.rottentomatoes.com/m/alien_resurrection/reviews/?page=3andsort.

"Amazon Review: *Astonishing X-Men*." 2014. http://www.amazon.com/Astonishing-X-Men-Vol-1-Gifted/productreviews/0785115315/ref=cm_cr_pr_hist_5?ie=UTF8andfilterBy=addFiveStarandshowViewpoints=0andsortBy=bySubmissionDateDescending.

Andreeva, Nellie. "Bad Robot, ABC Notarize Deal." *Hollywood Reporter*. October 4, 2007. http://www.hollywoodreporter.com/news/bad-robot-abc-notarize-deal-151644.

———. "Critics Choice Awards Honors 8 New Shows." *Deadline.com*. June 9, 2011. http://deadline.com/2011/06/critics-choice-awards-honors-8-new-shows-138754/.

"*Angel* Season 5 Episode Guide." *BBC.co*. http://www.bbc.co.uk/cult/buffy/angel/episodes/five/page14.shtml.

"*Armageddon* (1998)." *This Distracted Globe*. June 28, 2007. http://thisdistractedglobe.com/2007/06/28/armageddon-1998/.

Attali, Danielle, and Barbara Théate. "Spielberg: 'J'aurais aimé débuter aujourd'hui.'" *La Journal du Dimanche*. February 20, 2012. http://www.lejdd.fr/Culture/Cinema/Actualite/Speilberg-revient-sur-sa-carriere-interview-488138?from=features.

"*Avengers* Director Joss Whedon Quits Twitter." *BBC News.com*. May 5, 2015. http://www.bbc.com/news/technology-32591260.

BAFTA. "J.J. Abrams: On Filmmaking." *YouTube*. May 8, 2013. https://www.youtube.com/watch?v=bN-On2CusDM.

Balfour, Roger. "Afterlife." *Scriptshadow: Reviewing the Latest Scripts in Hollywood*. October 4, 2009. http://scriptshadow.blogspot.com/2009/10/afterlife.html.

Baltake, Joe. "*Alien Resurrection*." *Rotten Tomatoes*. January 1, 2000. http://www.rottentomatoes.com/m/alien_resurrection/reviews/?page=3andsort.

Batchelor, David Allen. "The Science of *Star Trek*." *NASA*. http://www.nasa.gov/topics/technology/features/star_trek.html.

"Belfast Film Festival Award Winners Revealed." *Northirelandscreen.co*. April 25, 2013. http://www.northernirelandscreen.co.uk/news/3281/belfast-film-festival-award-winners-revealed.aspx.

Benedictus, Luke. "The Ladies' Man." *The Age.com.au*. September 25, 2005. http://www.theage.com.au/articles/2005/09/22/1126982178268.html.

Bennett, Harve, Jack B. Sowards, and Samuel A. Peeples. "*Star Trek II: The Wrath of Khan*." *Internet Movie Script Database*. http://www.imsdb.com/scripts/Star-Trek-II-The-Wrath-of-Khan.html.

Bercovici, Jeff. "*Avengers* Director Joss Whedon on Trying to Be More Like Buffy." *Forbes*. May 3, 2012. http://www.forbes.com/sites/jeffbercovici/2012/05/03/avengers-director-joss-whedon-on-trying-to-be-more-like-buffy/.

Berlatsky, Noah. "What Joss Whedon Gets Wrong about the Word *Feminist*." *Atlantic*. November 8, 2013. http://www.theatlantic.com/entertainment/archive/2013/11/what-joss-whedon-gets-wrong-about-the-word-feminist/281305/.

Bianculli, David. "*Fresh Air* Interview with Joss Whedon." In *Joss Whedon: Conversations*, edited by David Lavery and Cynthia Burkhead, 3–22. Jackson: University Press of Mississippi, 2011.

Biring, Amarpal. "15 Blunders That Ruined J.J. Abrams' *Star Trek* and Destroyed the Franchise." *Whatculture.com*. September 19, 2012. http://whatculture.com/film/15-blunders-that-ruined-j-j-abrams-star-trek-and-destroyed-the-franchise.php.

Blitzer, Wolf. "Fourth Year of War in Iraq Begins; Could Democrats Launch Impeachment Campaign against Bush? " *The Situation Room*, *CNN.com*. March 20, 2006. http://transcripts.cnn.com/TRANSCRIPTS/0603/20/sitroom.03.html.

Bloom, David. "J.J. Abrams at VES Awards: *Star Wars* Sojourn 'a Dream Come True.'" *Deadline Presents Awardsline*. February 4, 2015. http://deadline.com/2015/02/j-j-abrams-star-wars-dream-come-true-ves-awards-1201366546/.

Boucher, Geoff. "*Fringe* Looks to Solve the Trickiest Mystery—Its Own Identity." *Herocomplex: Pop Culture Unmasked*. September 17, 2009. http://herocomplex.latimes.com/uncategorized/fringe-looks-to-solve-the-trickest-mystery-its-own-identity-as-a-show/.

———. "Seven Films That Shaped *Super 8*." *L.A. Times*. April 22, 2011. http://herocomplex.latimes.com/movies/j-j-abrams-seven-films-that-shaped-super-8/.

Bowman, Donna, and Noel Murray. *"Firefly*: 'Objects in Space.'" *A.V. Club*. October 5, 2012. http://www.avclub.com/tvclub/firefly-objects-in-space-85966.

Bronson, Zak. "We Were Trying to Make You More Than You Were." In *The Multiple Worlds of* Fringe: *Essays on the J.J. Abrams Science Fiction Series*, edited by Tanya R. Cochran, Sherry Ginn, and Paul Zinder, 60–76. Jefferson, NC: McFarland and Company, Inc., 2014.

Brown, Eric. "Joss Whedon's 5$ 'In Your Eyes' Vimeo Distribution Is a Vanity Project, Not a Revolution." *International Business Times*. April, 21, 2014. http://www.ibtimes.com/joss-whedons-5-your-eyes-vimeo-distribution-vanity-project-not-revolution-1574484.

Bruni, Frank. "Filmmaker J.J. Abrams Is a Crowd Teaser." *New York Times*. May 26, 2011. http://www.nytimes.com/2011/05/29/magazine/filmmaker-j-j-abrams-is-a-crowd-teaser.html?pagewanted=alland_r=0.

"Buffy the Vampire Slayer, Cult: In Real Life." *BBC.co*. September 2005. http://www.bbc.co.uk/cult/buffy/reallife/jwhedon.shtml.

Canby, Vincent. "Forever Young (1992) Review/Film: Forever Young; Mel Gibson Vehicle for an Age of Miracles." *New York Times*. December 16, 1992. http://www.nytimes.com/movie/review? res=9E0CE2DD1F3EF935A25751C1A964958260.

Capn Rahn. "The Darker Version of Serenity Crew *Alien Resurrection*?!" *Fireflyfans.net*. October 2, 2004. http://www.fireflyfans.net/mthread.aspx?tid=7350.

Carnevale, Rob. *"Cloverfield*—Matt Reeves Interview." *indieLondon*. http://www.indielondon.co.uk/Film-Review/cloverfield-matt-reeves-interview.

Chang, Justin. "Film Review: *Star Wars: The Force Awakens*." *Variety*. December 16, 2015. http://variety.com/2015/film/reviews/star-wars-review-the-force-awakens-1201661978/.

Chiat, Kevin. "Joss Whedon 101: Runaways." In *Joss Whedon, the Complete Companion: The TV Series, the Movies, the Comic Books and More*, edited by Mary Alice Mosley, 320–23. London: Titan Books, 2012.

Child, Ben. "JJ Abrams Gets Stranger with Teaser for Unnamed Project." *Guardian*. August 20, 2013. http://www.theguardian.com/film/2013/aug/20/jj-abrams-stranger-teaser-star-Wars.

———. "Micro-budget Film Is Back with Joss Whedon's *Much Ado about Nothing*." *Guardian*. October 28, 2011. http://www.theguardian.com/film/filmblog/2011/oct/28/joss-whedon-much-ado-about-nothing.

Chu, Brian. "Geek Wars: JJ Abrams vs. Joss Whedon." *Nerd Reactor*. January 16, 2014. http://nerdreactor.com/2014/01/16/geek-wars-jj-abrams-vs-joss-whedon/#ARK8dbuy6e8c7UKk. 99.

"Cloverfield-monster?*Spoiler*-Off-Topic Discussion." *Gamespot*. December 2007. http://www.gamespot.com/forums/offtopic-discussion-314159273/cloverfield-monster-spoiler-26112028/.

Coggan, Devan. "Box Office Report: *The Force Awakens* Crosses $1 Billion Globally in Record Time." *EW*. December 27, 2015. http://www.ew.com/article/2015/12/27/box-office-report star wars-force-awakens-crosses-1-billion-globally.

Cohen, S. Marc. "Identity, Persistence and the Ship of Theseus." University of Washington. 2004. http://faculty.washington.edu/smcohen/320/theseus.html.

"Comic Con 07's Fantastic FilmMakers: Joss Whedon Goes into Sugar Shock." *Hollywood.com*. 2007. http://www.hollywood.com/static/comic-con-07s-fantatsic-filmmakers-joss-whedon-goes-into-sugar-shock.

Corliss, Richard. *"Super 8*: Just as Great as You Hoped It Would Be." *Time Entertainment*. June 2, 2011. http://entertainment.time.com/2011/06/02/super-8-movie-review/2/2.

Covel, Bonnie. "J.J.s Shows." *about entertainment*. October 2006. http://lost.about.com/od/creationoflost/a/Jjabramslost.htm.

Cox, Carolyn. "Chris Evans and Jeremy Renner Call Black Widow a 'Slut' and 'Whore'; New *Age of Ultron* Clip Features Rape Joke." *The Mary Sue*. April 23, 2015. http://www.themarysue.com/grossvengers-age-of-dolton/.

Cunningham, Todd. *"Age of Ultron* Outpacing Original *Avengers* with $700 Million at Global Box Office." *The Wrap*. May 7, 2015. http://www.thewrap.com/age-of-ultron-outpacing-original-avengers-with-700-million-at-global-box-office/.

Dargis, Mahnola. "*Star Trek* (2009): A Franchise Goes Boldly Backwards." *New York Times*. May 7, 2009. http://www.nytimes.com/2009/05/08/movies/08trek.html.

Dixon, Dani. "ABC L + 3 Results: *S.H.I.E.L.D* Emerges as Number 1 Scripted Show for Timeslot in Adults 18-49." *TV by the Numbers*. October 4, 2015. http://tvbythenumbers. zap2it.com/2015/10/04/abc-l-3-results-s-h-i-e-l-d-emerges-as-number-1-scripted-show-for-timeslot-in-adults-18-49/475877/.

"Document 01.18.08: The Making of *Cloverfield*." *Cloverfield*. Written by Drew Goddard. Directed by Matt Reeves. Bad Robot/Paramount Pictures. 2008.

Donovan, John. "Abrams and Nolan Nab 'A Person of Interest.'" *NPR*. November 14, 2011. http://www.npr.org/2011/11/14/142309102/abrams-and-nolan-nab-a-person-of-interest.

Döring, Lütz. *Erweckung zum Tod: Eine kritische Untersuchung zu Funktionsweise Ideologie und Metaphysik der Horror und Science-Fiction Filme* Alien *1–4*. Würzburg, Germany: Königshausen und Neumann, 2005.

Dorst, Doug, and J. J. Abrams. *S.* New York: Mulholland Books, 2013.

Ebert, Roger. "*Armageddon*." *Reviews*. July 1, 1998. http://www.rogerebert.com/reviews/ armageddon-1998.

———. "*The Pallbearer*." *Reviews*. May 3, 1996. http://www.rogerebert.com/reviews/the-pallbearer-1996.

———. "*Regarding Henry*." *Reviews*. July 10, 1991. http://www.rogerebert.com/reviews/ regarding-henry-1991.

———. "*Star Trek*." *Reviews*. May 6, 2009. http://www.rogerebert.com/reviews/star-trek-2009.

Ebner, Mark. "Scientologist Tom Cruise Blackmails Viacom into Pulling the "Trapped in the Closet" Episode of *South Park*." *Hollywood Interrupted*. March 16, 2006. http://www. hollywoodinterrupted.com/2006/03/23/scientologist-tom-cruise-blackmails-viacom/.

Edelstein, David. "Mission: Control; The Tom Cruise Hero-Industrial Complex Cranks out Part 3. Should You Choose to Accept It?" *New York Magazine*. http://nymag.com/movies/ reviews/16931/.

Eller, Claudia, and Meg James. "Abrams Lands TV, Film Deals." *L.A. Times*. July 15, 2006. http://articles.latimes.com/2006/jul/15/business/fi-jj15.

"Emmy Press Release." *61st Primetime Emmy Awards*. September 12, 2009. http://www. emmys.com/sites/default/files/d6tv/CRTV09winners_pressrel.pdf.

Epstein, Daniel Robert. "Interview with Joss Whedon." In *Joss Whedon: Conversations*, edited by David Lavery and Cynthia Burkhead, 129–42. Jackson: University Press of Mississippi, 2011.

Ervin-Gore, Shawna. "Joss Whedon Interview." *Darkhorse.com*. May 2001. http://www. oocities.org/little_wolvie/interviews/Joss-Whedon-interview02.htm.

"Every X-man Ever." *IGN*. January 16, 2015. https://www.youtube.com/watch?x-yt-cl= 84359240andx-yt-ts=1421782837andv=wqT4hXxnjYE.

Faraci, Devin. "The *Star Trek* Movies as Ranked by *Star Trek* Con-Goers." *BadassDigest.com*. August 11, 2013. http://badassdigest.com/2013/08/11/the-star-trek-movies-as-ranked-by-star-trek-con-goers/.

Fear, David. "TONY QandA: *Much Ado about Nothing*'s Joss Whedon: The Man behind *Buffy the Vampire Slayer* Takes on the Bard." *Time Out*. June 2, 2013. http://www.timeout.com/ newyork/film/tony-q-a-much-ado-about-nothings-joss-whedon.

Ferguson, Dana. "Whedon Jokes about 'Micro-budget' for *Much Ado about Nothing*." *Los Angeles Times*. June 6, 2013. http://articles.latimes.com/2013/jun/06/entertainment/la-et-mn-20130606-much-ado.

Fienberg, Daniel. "J.J. Abrams Briefly Discusses the End of *Fringe*." *Hitfix*, January 9, 2013. http://www.hitfix.com/the-fien-print/j-j-abrams-briefly-discusses-the-end-of-fringe.

Flynn, Gillian. "*Fringe*." *Entertainment Weekly*. September 17, 2008. http://www.ew.com/ew/ article /0,,20226409,00.html.

"Franchises: *Star Trek*." *Box Office Mojo*. http://www.boxofficemojo.com/franchises/chart/? id=startrek.htm.

Frankel, Valerie Estelle. *Buffy and the Heroine's Journey: Vampire Slayer as Feminine Chosen One*. Jefferson, NC: McFarland, 2012.

Franklin-Wallis, Oliver. "GQandA: Joss Whedon." *GQ*. March 27, 2012. http://www.gq-magazine.co.uk/entertainment/articles/2012-03/27/joss-whedon-interview-cabin-in-the-woods-avengers-assemble.

Freud, Sigmund. "The Development of the Libido and the Sexual Organization." In *The Standard Edition of the Complete Psychological Works of Sigmund Freud*, edited by James Strachey, 320–38. London: Hogarth, 1975.

Fury, David. "Malice in Wonderland, Wolfram and Hart Extra." *Angel*, Season 4 DVD, disc 6 (2002–2003).

Giardina, Caroline. "J.J. Abrams to Receive Visual Effects Society Visionary Award." *Hollywood Reporter*. September 23, 2014. http://www.hollywoodreporter.com/behind-screen/jj-abrams-receive-visual-effects-735205.

Goldman, Eric. "Abrams Talks *Trek, Cloverfield 2*." *IGN*. May 16, 2008. http://www.ign.com/articles/2008/05/16/abrams-talks-trek-cloverfield-2.

Golick, Jill. "Joss and Four Acts." *Running with My Eyes Closed*. April 22, 2008. http://www.jillgolick.com/2008/04/joss-and-four-acts/.

———. "Joss Whedon Strikes Again." *Running with My Eyes Closed*. April 21, 2008. http://www.jillgolick.com/2008/04/joss-whedon-strikes-again/.

"Gone Fishin' (1997)." *Rotten Tomatoes.com*. http://www.rottentomatoes.com/m/gone_fishin/.

Gorman, Bill. "Updated TV Ratings Monday: *Alcatraz* Premiere Tops *Terra Nova*, Betty White Has a Nice Birthday, But CBS Rules the Night." *TV by the Numbers*. January 17, 2012. http://tvbythenumbers.zap2it.com/2012/01/17/tv-ratings-monday-alcatraz-premiere-tops-terra-nova/116692/.

———. "Where Did the Prime Time TV Audience Go?" *TV by the Numbers*. April 12, 2010. http://tvbythenumbers.zap2it.com/2010/04/12/where-did-the-primetime-broadcast-TV-audience-go/47976/.

Green, Penelope. "Mystery on Fifth Avenue." *New York Times*. June 12, 2008. http://www.nytimes.com/2008/06/12/garden/12puzzle.html?pagewanted=alland_r=0.

Greenberg, Raz. "*Alien Resurrection*, The Unproduced Script That Shaped Joss Whedon's Career." In *Joss Whedon: The Complete Companion*, edited by PopMatters. London: Titan Books, 2012.

Haberman, Lia. "Fox Squashes *Firefly*." *Eonline*. December 13, 2002. http://www.eonline.com/news/44314/fox-squashes-firefly.

Halbfinger, David M. "Fired or Quit, Tom Cruise Parts Ways with Studio." *New York Times*. August 23, 2008. http://www.nytimes.com/2006/08/23/business/media/23cruise.html?_r=0.

Hall, Sarah. "Scarlett Aborts Mission." *Eonline*. May 9, 2005. http://www.eonline.com/news/49821/scarlett-aborts-mission.

Harris, Will. "Joss Whedon—About *Serenity, Buffy, Angel* and *Wonder Woman*." *Bullzeye.com*. December 17 2005. http://www.whedon.info/Joss-Whedon-About-Serenity-Buffy.html.

Havens, Candace. *Joss Whedon, the Genius behind* Buffy. Dallas: Benbella Books, 2003.

Hayne. Tim. "Joss Whedon, *Much Ado about Nothing* Director, on Passion Projects, *S.H.I.E.L.D.* Hype and *Guardians of the Galaxy*." *Moviefone*. June 11, 2013. http://news.moviefone.com/2013/06/11/joss-whedon-much-ado-about-nothing/.

Henderson, Scott. "The Illusionist: J.J. Abrams on Film, Television and Rebooting a Franchise." *Screen Education* 55 (2009): 50–54.

Hensleigh, Jonathon. "The Dialogue: An Interview with Screenwriter Jonathon Hensleigh." *Youtube*. June 2, 2014. https://www.youtube.com/watch?v=F2NShtfNns0.

Hill, Kyle. "A Fan Attempts to Resurrect Character with NASA Data." *Wired*. January 14, 2013. http://www.wired.co.uk/news/archive/2013-01/14/firefly-rant.

Hochman, David. "*Playboy* Interview: J.J. Abrams." *Playboy.com*. April 30, 2013. http://www.playboy.com/articles/playboy-interview-j-j-abrams-on-star-trek-star-wars.

Hogue, Adam. "Joss Whedon vs. JJ Abrams: Comparing the Genius of Sci-Fi's Greats." *Mic.com*. September 16, 2013. http://mic.com/articles/63555/joss-whedon-vs-jj-abrams-comparing-the-genius-of-sci-fi-s-greats.

Hunter, Stephen. "*Alien Resurrection*: Birth of the Ooze." *Washington Post*. November 28, 1997. http://www.washingtonpost.com/wpsrv/style/longterm/movies/videos /alienresurrectionhunter.htm.

"IffBoston 2013 Wrap Up." *Lonely Reviewer*. May 1, 2013. http://www.lonelyreviewer.com/2013/05/01/iffboston-2013-wrap-up/.

"The International Emmy Awards." International Academy of Television Arts and Sciences. http://www.iemmys.tv/awards_previous.aspx.

"In Your Eyes (2014)." *IMDb*. http://www.imdb.com/title/tt2101569/.

"Is *Into Darkness* Better Than *Star Trek* (2009)?" *Trekweb.com*. May 8, 2013. http://trekweb.com/polls/vote.php?andpid=518a4f6d6a668andresults=1.

Itzkoff, Dave. "Joss Whedon on Assembling *The Avengers*." *New York Times*. April 11, 2012. http://artsbeat.blogs.nytimes.com/2012/04/11/joss-whedon-assembles-the-avengers-for-the-biggest-film-of-his-career/?_r=0.

————. "New Team Retrofits the Old Starship." *New York Times*. April 23, 2009. http://www.nytimes.com/2009/04/26/movies/26itzk.html?_r=3andpagewanted=all.

Jacob, Benjamin. "Los Angeles: The City of Angel." In *Reading Angel*, edited by Stacey Abbott, 75–88. London: I.B. Tauris, 2005.

"JJ Abrams Talks Lost and How the End Keeps Changing." Showbiz, ODE, ITN. May 9, 2009. https://www.youtube.com/watch?v=gy84xLfkkAs.

Joel, Bryan. "*Angel: After the Fall*, Review." *IGN*. November 22, 2007. http://www.ign.com/articles/2007/11/23/angel-after-the-fall-1-review.

John, Emma. "Joss Whedon: 'I kept telling my mum reading comics would pay off.'" *Guardian*. June 2, 2013. http://www.theguardian.com/culture/2013/jun/02/joss-whedon-reading-comics-pay-off.

Joseph, Ben. "A Look Back at Joss Whedon's *Roseanne* Episodes." *Splitsider*. May 29, 2012. http://splitsider.com/2012/05/a-look-back-at-joss-whedons-roseanne-episodes/.

"Joss' Input into the End of Marvel's Civil War." *Whedonesque*. February 24, 2007. http://whedonesque.com/comments/12541.

"Joss Whedon Cultural Humanist." *Humanist*. 2009. http://www.thenewhumanism.org/authors/video/articles/joss-whedon-cultural-humanist.

"Joss Whedon Explains Why We Fear and Need Horror Films, and How He Knew *Cabin in the Woods* Had a Star in Chris Hemsworth." *Huffington Post UK*. September 25, 2012. http://www.huffingtonpost.co.uk/2012/09/25/joss-whedon-avengers-cabin-in-the-woods_n_1912148.html.

"Joss Whedon—*Runaways* Comic Book, Newsarama.com Interview." *Whedon.Info*. September 13, 2006. http://www.whedon.info/Joss-Whedon-Runaways-Comic-Book,17943.html.

K., April. "The Ideal Audiences for Summer Blockbusters." *Scripted/Industries Cinema and Film*. Summer 2013. https://scripted.com/cpt_experts/ideal-target-audience-for-summer-blockbusters/.

Kappala-Ramsamy, Gemma. "Joss Whedon: The Film That Changed My Life: How Steven Spielberg's *Close Encounters of the Third* Kind Made an Existentialist of Screenwriter and Director Joss Whedon." *Guardian*. April 14, 2012. http://www.theguardian.com/film/2012/apr/15/joss-whedon-film-changed-spielberg.

Keegan, Rebecca. "Women Are Underrepresented in Key Movie Positions, USC Study Finds." *L.A. Times*. July 24, 2014. http://www.latimes.com/entertainment/movies/la-et-mn-women-hollywood-usc-study-20140724-story.html.

Kendrick, Ben. "Is *Agents of S.H.I.E.L.D.* Getting Better as Ratings Fall?" *Screen Rant*. November16, 2013. http://screenrant.com/agents-of-shield-improving-bad-ratings-abc/.

Kertész, Imres. "Who Owns Auschwitz?" Translated by John Mackay. *Yale Journal of Criticism* 14, no. 1 (2001): 267–72. http://www.english.illinois.edu/maps/holocaust/reflections.htm.

Kinsey, Tammy A. "Transition and Time: The Cinematic Language of *Angel*." In *Reading Angel*, edited by Stacey Abbott, 44–56. London: I.B. Tauris, 2005.

Knowles, Harry. "JJ Abrams Drops Harry a Line on All This 1-18-08 Stuff." *Aint It Cool News*. July 9, 2007. http://www.aintitcool.com/node/33261.

Kohn, Eric. "SXSW Review: Joss Whedon-Scripted *Cabin in the Woods* Turns B-Movie Meta into Scary Pop Art." *Indiewire*. March 10, 2012. http://www.indiewire.com/article/joss-whedon-scripted-cabin-in-the-woods-is-a-highly-amusing-blend-of-pop-art-and-meta-storytelling.

Kondolojy, Amanda. "Tuesday Final Ratings: *Marvel's Agents of S.H.I.E.L.D., The Voice* and *NCIS* Adjusted Up; *The Goldbergs* and *Chicago Fire* Adjusted Down." *TV by the Numbers*. September 25, 2013. http://tvbythenumbers.zap2it.com/2013/09/25/tuesday-final-ratingsm arvels-agents-of-s-h-i-e-l-d-the-voice-the-goldbergs-chicago-fire-adjusted-down/204739/.

Kosinus. "Reviews and Ratings for *Alias*." *IMDb*. March 30, 2006. http://www.imdb.com/title / tt0285333/reviews.

Kozak, Jim. "Serenity Now." In *Joss Whedon Conversations*, edited by David Lavery and Cynthia Burkhead. 85–106. Jackson: University Press of Mississippi, 2011.

Kuhn, Thor. "The History: Help Nathan Buy *Firefly*." *Unstoppable Signals*. April 2011. http://unstoppablesignals.com/hnbf/.

Kushner, David. "Revolt of a T.V. Genius." *Rolling Stone*. February 19, 2009.

L., Kaysi. "*Revolution* Season 3." *Thepetitionsite.com*. February 11, 2015. http://www.thepetitionsite.com/553/454/200/revolution-season-3/.

Lachonis, Jon "DocArzt," and Amy "hijinx" Johnston. *Lost Ate My Life: The Inside Story of a Fandom Like No Other*. Toronto: ECW Press, 2008.

Lane, Anthony. "*Star Wars: The Force Awakens* Review." *New Yorker*. December 18, 2015. http://www.newyorker.com/culture/cultural-comment/star-wars-the-force-awakens-reviewed.

Lavery, David. "*Dollhouse*, An Introduction." In *Reading Joss Whedon*, edited by Rhonda V. Wilcox, Tanya R. Cochran, Cynthia Masson, and David Lavery, 201–4. Syracuse, NY: Syracuse University Press, 2014.

———. *Joss Whedon: A Creative Portrait: From* Buffy the Vampire Slayer *to Marvel's* The Avengers. London: I.B. Tauris, 2014.

Leader, Michael. "Joss Whedon Interview: *The Cabin in the Woods, The Avengers*, Shakespeare and More." *DenofGeek*. March 29, 2012. http://www.denofgeek.us/movies/1896 8/joss-whedon-interview-the-cabin-in-the-woods-the-avengers-shakespeare-and-more.

Lee, Ashley. "J.J. Abrams, Doug Dorst Talk *S.* Novel, Online Hoaxes." *Hollywood Reporter*. November 30, 2013. http://www.hollywoodreporter.com/news/jj-abrams-doug-dorst-talk-660757.

———. "Oscars: Steven Spielberg Is the Most Thanked in History, More than God." *Hollywood Reporter*. February 20, 2015. http://awards.yahoo.com/post/111595418587/oscars-steven-spielberg-is-the-most-thanked-in.

Lee, Patrick. "Joss Whedon Gets Big, Bad and Grown-Up in *Angel*." In *Joss Whedon: Conversations*, edited by David Lavery and Cynthia Burkhead, 14–17. Jackson: University Press of Mississippi, 2011.

Lennix, Harry. "A Private Engagement." DVD featurette. *Dollhouse*, Season 1 (2009).

Lesnick, Silas. "Cloverfield." *Dreamindemon.com*. December 14, 2007. http://www.dreamindemon.com/community/threads/cloverfield.521/page-3.

Lethea. "Loaded 20: Whedon/Abrams Feud Erupts over Social Networking." *DM Fiat*. January 31, 2013. http://www.dmfiat.com/loaded-20/loaded-20-whedonabrams-feud-erupts-over-social-networking.

Lindelof, Damon. "A Tale of Two Cities." DVD Commentary. *Lost*, Season 3 (2006).

Lloyd, Christopher. "Reeling Backward: *Close Encounters of the Third Kind* (1977)." *The Film Yap*. August 22, 2011. http://www.thefilmyap.com/2011/08/22/close-encounters-of-the-third-kind-1977/.

Loeb, Jeph. "Citizen Joss." *Fray*. Milwaukie, OR: Dark Horse Comics, 2003.

The Lonely Island. "Cool Guys Don't Look at Explosions." *YouTube*. June 5, 2009. https://www.youtube.com/watch?v=Sqz5dbs5zmo.

Longworth, James. "Joss Whedon, Feminist." In *Joss Whedon: Conversations*, edited by David Lavery and Cynthia Burkhead, 42–63. Jackson: University Press of Mississippi, 2011.

Lough, Chris. "A Bicycle Built for You: But Not You. *Agents of S.H.I.E.L.D.*: 'What They Become.'" *Tor.com*. December 10, 2014. http://www.tor.com/blogs/2014/12 /agents-of-shield-what-they-become.

Maloney, Devon. "Wired Binge-Watching Guide: *Fringe*." *Wired*. October 29, 2014. http://www.wired.com/2014/10/binge-guide-fringe/.

"Marvel's *Agents of SHIELD*: Season Two Ratings." *TVSeriesFinale.com*. March 25, 2015. http://tvseriesfinale.com/tv-show/marvels-agents-of-shield-season-two-ratings-34016/.

"Marvel's *Agents of SHIELD*: Season Three Ratings." *TVSeriesFinale.com*. December 9, 2015. http://tvseriesfinale.com/tv-show/marvels-agents-of-shield-season-three-ratings-38242/.

Maslin, Janet. "*Buffy the Vampire Slayer* (1992) Review/Film; She's Hunting Vampires, and on a School Night." *New York Times*. July 31, 1992. http://www.nytimes.com/movie/review?res=9E0CE6DC163DF932A05754C0A964958260.

McBride, Joseph. *Steven Spielberg: A Biography*. 2nd ed. Jackson: University Press of Mississippi, 1997.

McCown, Alex. "J.J. Abrams' Stephen King Miniseries 11/22/63 Has a Director or So They Say." *A.V. Club*. April 7, 2015. http://www.avclub.com/article/jj-abrams-stephen-king-miniseries-112263-has-direc-217635.

McDonald, Neil. "Buffy Prime Time Passion Play." *Quadrant* 44, no. 4 (April 1, 2000): 63–67.

McDonald, William. "Film; Sigourney Weaver Eludes the Image Police." *New York Times*. December 7, 1997. http://www.nytimes.com/1997/12/07/movies/film-sigourney-weaver-eludes-the-image-police.html?pagewanted=2.

McDonough, Katie. "No, Joss Whedon, *Feminist* Is Not a Dirty Word." *Salon.com*. November 11, 2013. http://www.salon.com/2013/11/11/.

McGlensey, Melissa. "Dear Joss Whedon et Al.: Leave *Feminist* Alone." *Ms Magazine*. November 12, 2013. http://msmagazine.com/blog/2013/11/12/dear-joss-whedon-et-al-leave-feminist-alone/.

Meek, Tom. "*Alien Resurrection*." *Filmthreat*. November 24, 1997. http://www.filmthreat.com/reviews/1156/#ixzz3OXRujtPp.

Miller, Laura. "The Man Behind the Slayer." *Salon.com*. May 20, 2003. http://www.salon.com/2003/05/20/whedon/.

"*Mission: Impossible-III*." *Box Office Mojo.com*. http://www.boxofficemojo.com/movies/?id=mi3.htm.

"*Mission Impossible-iii*." *Metacritic.com*. http://www.metacritic.com/movie/mission-impossible-iii.

"*Mission Impossible-iii*." *Rottentomatoes.com*. http://www.rottentomatoes.com/m/mission_impossible_3/.

Molloy, Tim. "How Much Does J.J. Abrams Do on a J.J. Abrams Show?" *The Wrap*. November 14, 2013. http://www.thewrap.com/j-j-abrams-tv-shows-almost-human-how-involved-star-wars/.

"Monday Final Ratings: *Alcatraz*, *DWTS* and *Voice* Adjust Up; *Castle* and *Smash* Adjust Down." *TV by the Numbers*. March 27, 2012. http://tvbythenumbers. zap2it.com/2012/03/27/monday-final-ratings-alcatraz-dwts-voice-adjust-up-castle-smash-adjust-down/126132/.

"Movie Reviews: *Adoration*, *Julia*, *Little Ashes*, *Revanche*." *LAWeekly.com*. May 6, 2009. http://www.laweekly.com/film/movie-reviews-adoration-julia-little-ashes-revanche-2159664.

Murphy, Brian. "10 Burning Questions for Jim Belushi." *Page 2, ESPN*. http://espn.go.com/page2/s/questions/belushi.html.

Murray, Noel. "J.J. Abrams." *A.V. Club*. September 2, 2008. http://www.avclub.com/article/jj-abrams-14297.

Nary, David. "PGA Honors Joss Whedon." *Variety*. November 23, 2009. http://variety.com/2009/film/news/pga-honors-joss-whedon-1118011746/.

Nazarro, Joe. Writing Science Fiction and Fantasy Television. London: Titan Books, 2002.

North, Daniel. "Evidence of Things Not Quite Seen: *Cloverfield*'s Obstructed Spectacle." *Film and History* 40, no. 1 (Spring 2009): 75–91.

Nussbaum, Emily. "Must See Metaphysics." In *Joss Whedon: Conversations*, edited by David Lavery and Cynthia Burkhead, 64–70. Jackson: University Press of Mississippi, 2011.

"The Office Nielsen Ratings, Seasons 1–4." *Office Tally*. October 10, 2008. http://www.officetally.com/the-office-nielsen-ratings/2.

Orci, Roberto, Alex Kurtzman, and Damon Lindelof. *"Star Trek: Into Darkness*, (2013) Movie Script." *Springfield! Springfield!* http://www.springfieldspringfield.co.uk/movie_script.php?movie=star-trek-into-darkness.

Orth, Cameron. "Joss Whedon as Cult Auteur: A Case Study in Convergent Production." *Academia.edu*. http://www.academia.edu/3464642/Joss_Whedon_as_Cult_Auteur.

O'Shea, Tim. "David A. Price on the Pixar Touch." *Talking with Tim*. February 11, 2009. http://talkingwithtim.com/wordpress/2009/02/11/david-a-price-on-the-pixar-touch/.

Pandora's Manuscript Box. "Movie 29: *Atlantis: The Lost Empire*." *Pandorasmsbox*. May 4, 2013. http://pandoramsbox.tumblr.com/post/49622036952/movie-29-atlantis-the-lost-empire.

"Paramount: Cruise Is Risky Business." *CNN Money*. August 23, 2006. http://money.cnn.com/2006/08/22/news/newsmakers/cruise_paramount/index.htm?cnn=yes.

Parkin, Simon. "Zoe Quinn's Depression Quest." *New Yorker*. September 9, 2014. http://www.newyorker.com/tech/elements/zoe-quinns-depression-quest.

Parnass, Sarah. "Joss Whedon: Mitt Romney Right for 'Zombie Apocalypse.'" *ABC News*. October 29, 2012. http://abcnews.go.com/blogs/politics/2012/10/joss-whedon-mitt-romney-right-for-zombie-apocalypse/.

Pascale, Amy. "Joss and *Roseanne*: The Early Career of Joss Whedon." *Newsweek*. August 19, 2014. http://www.newsweek.com/joss-whedon-265403.

———. *Joss Whedon, The Biography*. Chicago: Chicago Review Press, 2014.

Pascale, Anthony. "Grand Slam XVI: Highlights from Orci QandA." *Trekmovie.com*. April 13, 2008. http://trekmovie.com/2008/04/13/grand-slam-xvi-highlights-from-orci-qa/.

———. "Wondercon 09: *Star Trek* Panel Detailed Report and Pictures." *Trekmovie.com*. February 28, 2009. http://trekmovie.com/2009/02/28/wondercon-09-star-trek-panel-detailed-report-pictures/.

Petrikin, Chet. "Nine Scribes Worked on Script, Five Get Credit." *Variety*. June 8, 1998. http://variety.com/1998/film/news/armageddon-credits-set-1117471616/.

Phipps, Keith. *"Regarding Henry." A.V. Club*. June 16, 2010. http://www.avclub.com/article/ircgarding-henryi-42151.

Plume, Ken. "Joss Whedon–Ken Plume Interview." *A Site Called Fred*. June 2003. http://asitecalledfred.com/2013/06/29/joss-whedon-ken-plume-interview/.

Plunkett, Luke. "If You Expect the J.J. Abrams Half-Life Movie to Actually Get Made, You're Gonna Have a Bad Time." *Kotaku.com*. February 6, 2013. http://kotaku.com/5982322/if-you-expect-the-jj-abrams-half-life-movie-to-come-out-youre-gonna-have-a-bad-time.

Preece, Caroline. "Looking Back at *Firefly* Episode 14: 'Objects in Space.'" *DenofGeek*. December 1, 2011. http://www.denofgeek.us/tv/21020/looking-back-at-firefly-episode-14-objects-in-space.

Prigge, Steven. "J.J. Abrams." *Interviews*. 2015. http://www.stevenprigge.com/interviews/j-j-abrams/http://www.stevenprigge.com/interviews/j-j-abrams/.

Prindle, Sarah. "The P. Word, Postfeminism and Joss Whedon," *Academia.edu*. December 11, 2009. http://www.academia.edu/2053845/The_P_Word_Postfeminism_and_Joss_Whedons_Dollhouse_.

Radish, Christina. "J.J. Abrams Talks *Star Trek 2*, the *Super 8* Trailer, Fox's *Alcatraz*, *Odd Jobs*, *Person of Interest*, *Undercovers* and *Fringe*." *Collider*. January 12, 2011. http://collider.com/j-j-abrams-interview-star-trek-2-super-8/69744/.

———. "J.J. Abrams Talks *Super 8*, *Star Trek 2* and TV Shows *Alcatraz* and *Person of Interest*." *Collider*. June 10, 2011. http://collider.com/jj-abrams-super-8-star-trek-2-alcatraz-person-of-interest/.

"Rate J.J. Abrams's *Star Trek*." *Trekweb.com*. May 7, 2009. http://trekweb.com/polls/vote.php?andpid=4a03a9f9aef8eandresults=1.

Resnick, Laura. "That Angel Doesn't Live Here Anymore." In *Five Seasons of Angel*, edited by Glenn Yeffeth, 15–22. Dallas: BenBella Books, 2004.

Rice, Archie. "Get Lost! JJ Abrams Latest TV Show Almost Human Cancelled after Just One Season." *Daily Mail*. April 30, 2014. http://www.dailymail.co.uk/tvshowbiz/article-2616518/JJ-Abrams-latest-TV-Almost-Human-cancelled-just-one-season.html.

Ridley, John. "Three Writers Are Drawn by the Allure of Comics." *Morning Edition*. NPR. March 25, 2008. http://www.npr.org/templates/story/story.php?storyId=87867518 andfrom=mobile.

Roberts, Sheila. "JJ Abrams Interview, *Star Trek*." *Moviesonline*. May 2009. http://www.moviesonline.ca/movienews_16696.html.

Robertson, Adi. "J.J. Abrams' Bad Robot Reportedly Producing *The Twilight Zone* Creator's Final Script." *The Verge*. June 15, 2013. http://www.theverge.com/201 3/6/5/4399850/j-j-abrams-bad-robot-reportedly-producing-rod-serling-final-script.

Robinson, Tasha. "Joss Whedon." *A.V. Club*. August 8, 2007. http://www.avclub.com/article/joss-whedon-14136.

———. "Joss Whedon." *A.V. Club*. September 5, 2001. http://www.avclub.com/article/joss-whedon-13730.

Roco. "J.J. Abrams Reveals How *Felicity* Gave Birth to *Alias*, Talks *Lost*." *Seriable.com*. January 3, 2012. http://seriable.com/jj-abrams-reveals-how-felicity-gave-birth-to-alias-talks-lost/.

Rose, Lacey. "Emmys 2012: J.J. Abrams Misses *Felicity* More Than *Lost*." *Hollywood Reporter*. September 12, 2012. http://www.hollywoodreporter.com/news/emmys-2012-jj-abrams-felicity-lost-369667.

Rosen, Lisa. "New Media Guru: Meet Joss Whedon the Web Slayer." *Written By*. January 2009. http://www.wga.org/writtenby/writtenbysub.aspx?id=3438.

Rothman, Joshua. "The Story of *S.*: Talking with J.J. Abrams and Doug Dorst." *New Yorker*. November 23, 2013. http://www.newyorker.com/books/page-turner/the-story-of-s-talking-with-j-j-abrams-and-doug-dorst.

Russell, Brandon. "New *Age of Ultron* Footage Focuses on Scarlet Witch and Quicksilver." *TechnoBuffalo*. March 27, 2015. http://www.technobuffalo.com/2015/ 03/27/new-age-of-ultron-footage-focuses-on-scarlet-witch-and-quicksilver/.

Russell, Mike. "The CulturePulp QandA: Joss Whedon." In *Joss Whedon: Conversations*, edited by David Lavery and Cynthia Burkhead, 107–28. Jackson: University Press of Mississippi, 2011.

Ryan, Maureen. "'Dr. Horrible' Speaks: Talking to Neil Patrick Harris about Joss Whedon's Smash-Hit Interweb Thingie." *Chicago Tribune*. July 19, 2008. http://featuresblogs.chicagotribune.com/entertainment_tv/2008/07/dr-horrible-spe.html.

Saavedra, John. "*Star Wars: The Force Awakens* Easter Eggs and Reference Guide." *Den of Geek*. December 29, 2015. http://www.denofgeek.us/movies/star-wars/251420/star-wars-the-force-awakens-easter-eggs-and-reference-guide.

Said, S. F. "Joss Whedon—About *Buffy*, *Alien* and *Firefly*. Shebyches.com Interview." *Whedon.info*. May 24, 2006. http://www.whedon.info/Joss-Whedon-About-Buffy-Alien.html.

Sciretta, Peter. "Comic-Con: J.J. Abrams and Joss Whedon." *Film Blogging the Real World*. July 26, 2010. http://www.slashfilm.com/comic-con-jj-abrams-and-joss-whedon-part-2/.

Sepinwall, Alan. *The Revolution Was Televised: The Cops, Crooks, Slingers, and Slayers Who Changed TV Drama Forever*. New York: Simon and Schuster, 2012.

———. "Sepinwall on TV: *Dollhouse* Review." *Star-Ledger*. February 11, 2009. http://www.nj.com/entertainment/tv/index.ssf/2009/02/sepinwall_on_tv_dollhouse_revi.html.

Sharpe, Frances. "*Star Wars* Character Based on Late Pali High English Teacher, Abrams Tells *Palisadian-Post*." *Palisadian-Post*. December 24, 2015. https://www.palipost.com/star-wars-character-based-on-late-pali-high-english-teacher-abrams-tells-palisadian-post/.

Smiley, Tavis. "Producer-Director J.J. Abrams." *Pbs.org*. October 30, 2013. http://www.pbs.org/wnet/tavissmiley/interviews/j-j-abrams-3/.

——— "Writer-Director-Producer J.J. Abrams." *Pbs.org*. September 24, 2014. http://www.pbs.org/wnet/tavissmiley/interviews/j-j-abrams/.

Smith, Stacey L., Katherine M. Pieper, Amy D. Granados, and Marc Cho. "Assessing Gender-Related Portrayals in Top-Grossing G-Rated Films." In *Conference Papers—International*

Communication Association, 1–36. International Communication Association annual meeting. January 1, 2008.

Smith, John W. "NYCC Day 1: 'Civil War Fallout: The Initiative' Full Panel Report." *Comic Book Resources*. http://www.comicbookresources.com/?page=articleandold=1andid=9775.

Sobchack, Vivian. *Screening Space: The American Science Fiction Film*. Trenton, NJ: Rutgers University Press, 1997.

Spielberg, Steven. "Steven Spielberg Inspirational Speech." *Youtube*. September 7, 2013. https://www.youtube.com/watch?v=ULwhcNgf3jA.

"*Star Trek* (2009): Customer Reviews." *Amazon.com*. http://www.amazon.com/Star-Trek-Chris-Pine/productreviews/B002WV5A9G/ref=cm_cr_dp_see_all_summary?ie=UTF8andshowiewpoints=1andsortBy=byRankDescending.

"Star Trek." *Box Office Mojo*. 2009. http://www.boxofficemojo.com/movies/?id=startrek11.htm.

"Star Trek." *RottenTomatoes.com*. http://www.rottentomatoes.com/m/star_trek_11.

"*Star Trek: Into Darkness*." *Box Office Mojo*. 2013. http://www.boxofficemojo.com/movies/?id=star trek12.htm.

"*Star Trek* User Reviews." *Metacritic.com*. February 14, 2014. http://www.metacritic.com/movie/star-trek/user-reviews?dist=negative.

Steinmetz, Johanna. "Taking Care: Just a Juvenile Fantasy World." *Chicago Tribune*. August 17, 1990. http://articles.chicagotribune.com/1990-08-17/entertainment/9003090092_1_belushi-cubs-fan-charles-grodin.

Sterba, Wendy. "The Corporate and Corporeal." In *The Apocalypse in Film: Dystopias, Disasters, and Other Visions about the End of the World*, edited by Karen Ritzenhoff and Angela Krewani, 203–15. Lanham, MD: Rowman and Littlefield, 2016.

Stevens, Dana. "Joss Whedon's *Much Ado about Nothing* as Bracingly Effervescent as Picnic Champagne." *Slate.com*. June 6, 2013. http://www.slate.com/articles/arts/movies/2013/06/joss_whedon_s_much_ado_about_nothing_reviewed.html.

Stevens, Jenny. "On Location in Chilling Alcatraz." *News.com.au*. February 16, 2012. http://www.news.com.au/travel/world-travel/on-location-in-chilling-alcatraz/story-e6frfqc9-1226268599439.

"Stranger." *YouTube*. https://www.youtube.com/watch?v=FWaAZCaQXdo.

Sullivan, Brian Ford. "Interview: *Dollhouse* Creator Joss Whedon." *Futon Critic*. January 6, 2009. http://www.thefutoncritic.com/interviews.aspx?id=20090106_dollhouse#27Sc4k304JtJ6fOO.99.

———. "Interview: *Fringe* Co-Creator JJ Abrams." *Futon Critic*. February 4, 2010. http://www.thefutoncritic.com/interviews.aspx?id=20100204_fringe.

———. "Interview: *Fringe* Co-Creators JJ Abrams, Roberto Orci and Alex Kurtzman." *Futon Critic*. September 8, 2008. http://www.thefutoncritic.com/interviews.aspx?id=20080908_fringe.

Sullivan, Kevin P., "Joss Whedon Confirms Cutting Marvel Ties with a Supremely Thoughtful Explanation." *EW.com*. January 4, 2016. http://www.ew.com/article/2016/01/04/joss-whedon-marvel-future.

Sullivan, Michael Patrick. "Joss Whedon—UnderGroundOnline.com Interview." *Whedon.info*. December 10, 2003. http://www.whedon.info/Joss-Whedon-UnderGroundOnline-com.html.

Symonds, Gwen. "Solving Problems with Sharp Objects: Female Empowerment, Sex and Violence in *Buffy the Vampire Slayer*." *Slayage*. April 2004. http://slayageonline.com/essays/slayage11_12/Symonds.htm.

Taylor, Drew. "From *Avengers* to Shakespeare: If Joss Whedon Can Do It All, 5 Film Projects We'd Love to See Him Tackle." *Playlist*. June 4, 2013. http://blogs.indiewire.com/theplaylist/from-avengers-to-shakespeare-if-joss-whedon-can-do-it-all-5-film-projects-wed-love-to-see-him-tackle-20130604.

———. "SXSW '12 Interview: Drew Goddard Talks His Inspiration." *Indiewire*. March 9, 2012. http://blogs.indiewire.com/theplaylist/sxsw-12-interview-cabin-in-the-woods-director-drew-goddard-talks-horror-movies-famous-collaborators-and-superheroes.

Taylor, Robert Brian. "What Exactly Is Joss Whedon's Wastelanders?" *Cult Spark*. April 26, 2006. http://cultspark.com/2012/04/26/what-exactly-is-joss-whedons-wastelanders/.

"Things We Love: We Love a New Look at Scarlet Witch and Quicksilver in *Avengers: Age of Ultron*." *The Tracking Board: Hollywood Insider Information*. March 27, 2015. http://www.tracking-board.com/things-we-love-a-new-look-at-scarlet-witch-and-quicksilver-in-avengers-age-of-ultron/.

Thomson, David. *The Alien Quartet: A Bloomsbury Movie Guide*. London: Bloomsbury, 1999.

"The Top 10 Everything of 2008." *Time*. November 3, 2008. http://content.time.com/time/specials/packages/completelist/0,29569,1855948,00.html.

Topei, Fred. "J.J. Abrams on the End of *Fringe, Revolution* and *Star Trek: Into Darkness*." *Crave*. January 12, 2009. http://www.craveonline.com/culture/202929-jj-abrams-on-the-end-of-fringe-revolution-a-star-trek-into-darkness.

———. "Tribeca 2014: Zoe Kazan and Michael Stahl David on *In Your Eyes*." *Craveonline*. April 22, 2014. http://www.craveonline.com/film/interviews/678895-tribeca-2014-zoe-kazan-and-michael-stahl-david-on-in-your-eyes.

"Total Film Exclusive: JJ Abrams Directing US Office." *Total Film*. September 15, 2006. http://www.gamercaptain.com/total-film-exclusive-jj-abrams-directing-the-us-office/.

Tracy, Kathleen. *The Girl's Got Bite: The Original Unauthorized Guide to Buffy's World*. New York: St. Martin's Griffin, 2003.

Truffaut, François, and Helen G. Scott. *Hitchcock*. New York: Simon and Schuster, 1985.

Truitt, Brian. "Innovators and Icons: Joss Whedon Genre Slayer." *USA Today*. June 13, 2013. http://www.usatoday.com/story/life/movies/2013/06/12/joss-whedon-innovators-icons/2368059/.

Truitt, Jos. "Let's Talk about *Age of Ultron*'s Rape Joke." *Feministing*. May 1, 2015. http://feministing.com/2015/05/01/lets-talk-about-age-of-ultrons-rape-joke/.

"Unscripted with Tom Cruise and JJ Abrams." *Moviefone*. September 16, 2012. https://www.youtube.com/watch?v=aNdlCdyJ-0A.

U.S. Department of Justice. "Bureau of Justice Statistics, Special Reports." *Bjs.gov*. August 1995. http://www.bjs.gov/content/pub/pdf/FEMVIED.PDF.

Vint, Sheryl. "Who Would Win in a Fight between Bad Robot and Mutant Enemy?" *Los Angeles Review of Books*. December 15, 2013. http://blog.lareviewofbooks.org/tag/whedon/.

Walters, Mikey. "Joss Whedon Spills the Beans on *Toy Story*." The Disney Blog. August 4, 2005. http://thedisneyblog.com/2005/08/04/joss_whedon_spi/.

Ward, Lewis. "Introduction to Joss Whedon in Joss Whedon Cultural Humanism Award." *YouTube*. February 26, 2013. http://www.youtube.com/watch?v=o6_DICN7AKY.

Warner, Kara. "Joss Whedon on Feminism, *Avengers* Leaks and Marvel's Big Slate." *Vulture*. November 14, 2014. http://www.vulture.com/2014/11/joss-whedon-on-feminism-and-the-avengers-leaks.html.

Watercutter, Angela. "Joss Whedon's Viral Video Calls Romney Perfect Leader for Zombie Apocalypse." *Wired*. October 29, 2012. http://www.wired.com/2012/10/joss-whedon-romney-zombie-endorsement/.

Wax, Alyse. "Exclusive: Drew Goddard Talks Secrets and Sequels for *Cabin in the Woods*." *Fearnet*. September 14, 2012. http://www.fearnet.com/news/interview/exclusive-drew-goddard-talks-secrets-and-sequels-cabin-woods.

Wayland, Sara. "J.J. Abrams on the *Star Trek* Sequel, *Lost, Fringe* and ABC's *Undercovers*." *Collider*. January 12, 2010. http://collider.com/jj-abrams-on-the-star-trek-sequel-lost-fringe-and-nbcs-undercovers/.

Weintraub, Bernard. "Roseanne's Witching Hour, the Goddess of the Working Class Calls It Quits Tonight after Nine Years of Blurring the Line between Life and Art." *New York Times*. May 20, 1997. http://articles.sun-sentinel.com/1997-05-20/lifestyle/9705160368_1_she-devil-roseanne-s-witching-hour-wicked-witch.

Weintraub, Steven "Frosty." "Interview: Director Joss Whedon—*Dollhouse*." *Collider*. February 6, 2009. http://collider.com/interview-joss-whedon-dollhouse/.

———. "Director Joss Whedon *The Avengers* Set Interview." *Collider*. April 2, 2012. http://collider.com/joss-whedon-the-avengers-interview/.

Whedon, Joss. *Alien Resurrection* Script. *Horrorlair.com*. http://www.horrorlair.com/scripts/alienresurrection_early.html.

———. *Buffy the Vampire Slayer* (film)/Original Script. *Buffy.wikia.com*. http://buffy.wikia.com/wiki/Buffy_the_Vampire_Slayer_%28film%29/Original_Script.

———. "Joss Whedon Accepts Equality Now Award." *EqualityNow.org*. May 15, 2006. http://www.equalitynow.org/media/joss_whedon_accepts_equality_now_award.

———. "Joss Whedon: Atheist and Absurdist." *YouTube*. March 28, 2010. https://www.youtube.com/watch?v=EReyF2ZzXGA.

———. "Joss Whedon at Make Equality Reality." *YouTube*. November 6, 2013. https://www.youtube.com/watch?v=pDmzlKHuuoI.

———. "Joss Whedon—Cultural Humanism Award—Speech (2009)." *YouTube*. February 26, 2013. https://www.youtube.com/watch?v=o6_DICN7AKY.

———. "Joss Whedon Explains *Angel*." *YouTube*. April 21, 2011. https://www.youtube.com/watch?v=G8UqUdz6vHo.

———. "Joss Whedon—Harvard Q and A." *YouTube*. February 27, 2013. https://www.youtube.com/watch?v=glJCzqE7fxA.

———. "Joss Whedon on *The Cabin in the Woods*: 'It's a classic horror until it explodes in your face'—video." *Guardian*. April 6, 2012. http://www.theguardian.com/film/video/2012/apr/06/joss-whedon-cabin-in-the-woods-buffy-video.

———. "More Joss Strike Talk." *Whedonesque*. November 7, 2007. http://whedonesque.com/comments/14650.

———. Much Ado about Nothing, *A Film by Joss Whedon, Based on the Play by William Shakespeare*. London: Titan Books, 2013.

———. "Not Fade Away." DVD Commentary. *Angel*, Season 5 (2004).

———. "Objects in Space." DVD Commentary. *Firefly*, Season 1 (2002).

———. "Whedon on Romney." *YouTube*. October 12, 2012. https://www.youtube.com/watch?v=6TiXUF9xbTo.

Whedon, Joss, Abbie Bernstein, Bryan Cairns, Karl Derrick, and Tara Di Lullo. Firefly: *The Official Companion*. Vol. 1. London: Titan Books, 2006.

Whedon, Joss, Brett Matthews, and Will Conrad. *Serenity Better Days*. Milwaukie, OR: Dark Horse Comics, 2008.

———. *Serenity: Those Left Behind*. Milwaukie, OR: Dark Horse Comics, 2006.

Whedon, Joss, Brian K. Vaughn, Georges Jeanty, Cliff Richards, and Jo Chen. Buffy the Vampire Slayer: *No Future for You*. Milwaukie, OR: Dark Horse Comics, 2008.

Whedon, Joss, Brian Lynch, and Franco Urru. Angel: *After the Fall*. San Diego, CA: IDW Publishing, 2007.

Whedon, Joss, and Drew Goddard. The Cabin in the Woods: *The Official Visual Companion*. London: Titan Books, 2012.

Whedon, Joss, Drew Goddard, and Georges Jeanty. Buffy the Vampire Slayer: *Wolves at the Gate*. Milwaukie, OR: Dark Horse Comics, 2008.

Whedon, Joss, and Fabio Moon. *Sugarshock!*. Milwaukie, OR: Dark Horse Comics, 2009.

Whedon, Joss, and Georges Jeanty. Buffy the Vampire Slayer: *The Long Way Home*. Milwaukie, OR: Dark Horse Comics, 2007.

Whedon, Joss, and John Cassaday. *Astonishing X-Men*. Vols. 1 and 2. New York: Marvel Entertainment, 2013.

Whedon, Joss, Karl Moline, and Andy Owens. *Buffy the Vampire Slayer: Time of Your Life*. Milwaukie, OR: Dark Horse Comics, 2009.

———. *Fray*. Milwaukie, OR: Dark Horse Comics, 2003.

Whedon, Joss, and Michael Ryan. *Runaways*. Vol. 8: Dead End Kids. New York: Marvel, 2009.

Whedon, Joss, and Stan Lee. *Stan Lee Meets The Amazing Spider-Man*. New York: Marvel Worldwide, 2006.

Whedon, Joss, Zach Whedon, and Chris Samnee. *Serenity: The Shepherd's Tale*. Milwaukie, OR: Dark Horse Comics, 2010.

Whitaker, Bill. "The New Force behind *Star Wars*." *60 Minutes*. CBS. Aired December 13, 2015.

Wigler, Josh. "Joss Whedon's *S.H.I.E.L.D.* Is about 'Powers' 'Spectacle' and 'Little Things' That Matter." *Hot Stuff Interviews*. January 11, 2013. http://splashpage.mtv.com/2013/01/11/joss-whedon-shield-details/.

Williams, H. Shaw. "J.J. Abrams Compares His *Superman: Flyby* Script to *Man of Steel*." *Screen Rant*. February 15, 2014. http://screenrant.com/jj-abrams-superman-flyby-man-steel/ .

"Work In Progress, Review: *Star Trek*," *Amazon.com*. December 6, 2013,http://www.amazon.com/Star-Trek-Chris-Pine/productreviews/B002WV5A9G/ref=cm_cr_pr_hist_1?ie=UTF8&filterBy=addFiveStar&showViewpoints=0&sortBy=helpful&reviewerType=all_reviews&formatType=all_formats&filterByStar=one_star&pageNumber=1.

"Your 2008 Eisner Award Winners." *The Comics Reporter*. July 26, 2008. http://www.comicsreporter.com/index.php/your_2008_eisner_award_winners/.

Zacharek, Stephanie. "Review: *The Force Awakens* Is Everything You Could Hope for in a *Star Wars* Movie—And Less." *Time*. December 14, 2015. http://time.com/4150168/review-star-wars-the-force-awakens/.

INDEX

ABOUT THE AUTHOR

Wendy Sterba is a professor of German and film at the College of St. Benedict/St. John's University in Minnesota, where she teaches film history and theory, as well as German modernist literature. She received her PhD from Rice University in 1988, working on the cross-disciplinary topic of the prostitute in German- and English-language film. Sterba's current work concerns contemporary applications of feminist theory and the Frankfurt School to image in popular culture and film. She has published variously on dystopian film, the body and the apocalypse, and the photograph and gender in the contemporary detective film. Sterba has one published book: *Reel Photos: Balancing Art and Truth in Contemporary Film* (Rowman & Littlefield, 2015). She is devoted to her husband, her work, and her very spoiled English bulldog.